ORIGINAL COPY

A VOLUME IN THE SERIES

Becoming Modern: Studies in the Long Nineteenth Century

EDITED BY
Elizabeth A. Fay

ORIGINAL COPY

Ekphrasis, Gender,
and the National Imagination
in Nineteenth-Century American Literature

CHRISTA HOLM VOGELIUS

University of Massachusetts Press
AMHERST AND BOSTON

Copyright © 2025 by University of Massachusetts Press
All rights reserved
Printed in the United States of America

ISBN 978-1-62534-844-9 (paper); 845-6 (hardcover)

Designed by Jen Jackowitz
Set in Minion Pro by Jen Jackowitz
Printed and bound by Books International, Inc.

Cover design by adam b. bohannon
Cover photo by Derrick, *Art within Art*, Adobe Stock 754013588.

Library of Congress Cataloging-in-Publication Data
A catalog record for this book is available from the Library of Congress.

British Library Cataloguing-in-Publication Data
A catalog record for this book is available from the British Library.

To my parents, true originals

Contents

List of Illustrations ix

Acknowledgments xi

INTRODUCTION
First Things, Third Things
1

CHAPTER ONE
Phillis Wheatley Peters's Antebellum Remediation
29

CHAPTER TWO
"The Fusion of the Races Among Us"
Summer on the Lakes and Margaret Fuller's Aesthetic Nationalism
66

CHAPTER THREE
"Folded up in a Veil"
Sophia Peabody Hawthorne's Familial Ekphrasis
and the Antebellum Travelogue
101

CHAPTER FOUR
Longfellow, *Michael Angelo*, and the "Middle-Class" Curator
131

CODA
Ekphrastic Citizenship
Claudia Rankine's American Lyrics
176

Notes 185

Index 217

List of Illustrations

Figure 1. "Portrait of Beatrice Cenci," by Guido Reni [?], circa 1600. Courtesy, Palazzo Barberini, Rome.   2

Figure 2. "Joining Copies No. 1," small copybook, Phillis Wheatley Papers, Stuart A. Rose Manuscript, Archives, and Rare Book Library at Emory University. Courtesy, Emory University Library. 36

Figure 3. "The Voice of Freedom," large copybook, Phillis Wheatley Papers, Stuart A. Rose Manuscript, Archives, and Rare Book Library at Emory University. Courtesy, Emory University Library.   38

Figure 4. "Frontispiece," *Memoir and Poems of Phillis Wheatley, a Native African and a Slave. Dedicated to the Friends of the Africans* (Boston: Geo. W. Light, 1834). Courtesy, Emory University Library.   62

Figure 5. Title Page, "Being Notes of a Journey to the West, by S. M. Fuller, June 1843," Margaret Fuller Papers, Massachusetts Historical Society. Courtesy, MHS.   81

Figure 6. "Ganymede with Jupiter's Eagle," by Bertel Thorvaldsen, 1817, A44, photographer Jakob Faurvig. Courtesy, Thorvaldsen's Museum, Copenhagen, DK.   87

Figure 7. January 26, 1859, Diary, Sophia Peabody Hawthorne Papers, Berg Collection, New York Public Library. Courtesy, NYPL. 124

Figure 8. "Rose in Rome," Henry W. and Albert A. Berg Collection of English and American Literature, The New York Public Library. Journal. Rome, beginning March 17, 1858. (Mar.–Oct. 1858: v. 1). Courtesy, NYPL.   128

Figure 9. "Dedication" in *Michael Angelo: a Dramatic Poem*, by Henry Wadsworth Longfellow Papers, (Boston: Houghton, Mifflin, 1884). Courtesy, Making of America.   160

Figure 10. *Michael Angelo.* A.MS. Henry Wadsworth Longfellow papers, Houghton Library. Author's photograph. Courtesy, Harvard University.   164

Acknowledgments

My first debt is to my editors at the University of Massachusetts Press, especially Brian Halley and series editor Elizabeth Fay, for believing in this project, and to the anonymous reviewers for their insightful feedback. But any project that stretches over many years, and in this case also over two continents, incurs many debts, and many more than can properly be acknowledged. At Michigan, my advisors Kerry Larson, Sara Blair, Julie Ellison, and Yopie Prins were models of scholarship and generosity. My deepest thanks to Kerry, who encouraged this project from its earliest stages. Rackham Graduate School at the English Department at the University of Michigan provided essential funding and support; Rackham, the American Antiquarian Society, and the University of Nottingham provided generous grants for travel and study. Eliza Richards's work and person inspired and inspires. Mary Lou Kete offered valuable insights on her brief visit to Ann Arbor. The Visual Culture Workshop at the University of Michigan provided helpful comments on an early version of the project. Gigi Barnhill and the staff at American Antiquarian Society and Anita Israel of the Longfellow Historical Site were generous with their time, expertise, and resources. Thanks also to the assistance of the staff at the University of Michigan Libraries, the Berg Collection at the New York Public Library, and the Houghton Library at Harvard University. The members of my departmental cohort in the English Department were almost unnaturally kind and talented; in Ann Arbor, thanks especially to Nasia Anam, Navaneetha Mokkil, Anna Kroth, Julia Hansen, Sara Schaff, Ben Landry, Christopher Becker, and Tyra Johnson. Nan Z. Da, Britt Sonnenberg, and Sara Blair brought some of Ann Arbor back on their brief visits to Copenhagen; Josefin Ekström made the move easy by making it first. And thanks most of all to Korey Jackson, who read and was everything.

I owe Tuscaloosa, Alabama a deepened appreciation for archives, the internal workings of libraries, and especially librarians; a nostalgia for ranch houses; and the wise counsel of Alexa Tullett. Thanks also to Jason Battles and the Council on Libraries and Information Resources who made the fellowship possible.

In Copenhagen, first at the University of Copenhagen and now at the University of Southern Denmark, I am grateful for a range of institutional and personal support. At Engerom, thanks to the community of Katy Halvorsen, Martyn Bone, Dave Struthers, Elizabeth Rodriguez Fielder, Martina Koegler-Abdi, Maria Damkjaer, Tina Lupton, Cian Duffy, and Alex Knopf. At the Department for Arts and Cultural Studies, I was given the gift of imagining a project beyond this one. In that process, thanks to Mette Sandbye and the photo research group as well as Stefanie Heine and the environmental humanities group. At the University to Southern Denmark, I've been lucky to join an American studies community once again, and in that process, thanks especially to Flemming Just of the Jacob Riis Museum Jørn Brøndal of the Center for American Studies. I am also grateful for funding from the Novo Nordisk Foundation and the New Carlsberg Foundation that has made so much possible over the last several years, and archive grants from the American Antiquarian Society, the Maine Women Writers Collection, the British Library, and the Rose Library at Emory University. The AAS came with the added perk of the expert guidance of Molly O'Hagan Hardy and Paul Erikson. Many friends and colleagues near and far have commented on later versions of the project. For invaluable writing exchanges thanks especially to Elissa Zellinger, Maria Damkjær, Julia Hansen, Steve Zultanski, Nina Cramer, and Tais Terletskaja. Thanks to Lucia Hodgson for brainstorming and to Michelle Neely for the constancy of Americanist conferences.

Dehlia Hannah says that cohabitation is the essence of friendship, and I have been lucky in both of those respects. Thanks to Kristina Nya Glaffey, Anders Haarh Rasmussen, Johanne Mygind and Alma Taospern for welcoming me into their homes, and to Sarah Davies, Raffael Himmelsbach, Dehlia Hannah, Jeuno Kim, Henriette Sennenvaldt, Maja Lee Langvad, Lucia Odoom, Camilla Reyman, Lone Nikolajsen, Nan Gerdes, Mie Mortensen, Sarah El-Taki, Steve Zultanski, Ronah Sadan, Stefan Pedersen, and Josefin Ekström for doing so more indirectly. Thanks to Anaïs Rassat for thirty years, and to Tais Terletskaja for being the person that I needed and never could have imagined. And to my family, especially my parents to whom this book is dedicated, for everything.

ORIGINAL COPY

INTRODUCTION
First Things, Third Things

> In Rome, people with fine sympathetic natures stand up and weep in front of the celebrated "Beatrice Cenci the Day before her Execution." It shows what a label can do. If they did not know the picture, they would inspect it unmoved, and say, "Young girl with hay fever, young girl with her head in a bag."
>
> −Mark Twain, *Life on the Mississippi*, 1883[1]

The oil portrait at the Palazzo Barberini in Rome is a shadowed image of an adolescent girl looking back at the viewer over her shoulder, historically attributed to Guido Reni, and said to depict Beatrice Cenci, a young woman condemned to death in 1599 for the murder of her father after years of incestual abuse. The simple portrait and its dark backstory was one of the nineteenth century's recurrent subjects for ekphrasis, the literary description of a visual work of art, and it recirculated in print not only through the visual copies that, as Sophia Hawthorne wrote in 1859, could be found "in every picture dealer's shop, of every size," but also in textual reiterations in the form of poems, plays, novels, and European travelogues.[2] In this sense, Mark Twain's critique of the sentimental labeling of the work in this epigraph speaks directly to these ekphrastic representations, which by the 1880s had become cultural touchstones. Twain, in suggesting that the unmediated Cenci portrait is only improperly legible to the casual viewer, hits on the apprehension surrounding the growing presence of mute and ambiguous images in the earlier part of the nineteenth century, an apprehension to which ekphrasis as a genre was a partial response. The first part of the nineteenth century was, as Henry James writes, "the age in which an image had, before anything else, to tell a story"—but the image alone sometimes failed.[3] Textual labels in the form of ekphrasis as well as other art writing could correct, or at least gesture toward correcting, this interpretive instability.[4]

FIGURE 1. "Portrait of Beatrice Cenci," by Guido Reni [?], circa 1600. Courtesy, Palazzo Barberini, Rome.

First Things, Third Things   3

In the long nineteenth century, then, text and image are apparently allied even as they are in many ways fundamentally disconnected. Many textual works assume a reader's familiarity with prominently reprinted artworks, but few are illustrated with the images that they describe. Other texts have unclear visual referents, either because they fail to name their subjects, or because the literary and visual responses to a particular artwork are widespread enough that the ekphrasis could be based on a secondary source. If ekphrasis is a verbal "reproduction" of a visual work, as one critic describes it, then ekphrasis in the age of print is a copy continuously dislodged from its point of origin, a copy in a hall of mirrors.[5] Textual mimesis could describe an original artwork in a museum, an (accurate or inaccurate) print of an original work in a periodical, or another writer's (possibly secondhand) response to an artwork.[6] This disjunction between the singular text and the plurality of its (possible) sources argues for critical readings that pay attention to the historical contexts in which ekphrastic writing takes place and is disseminated. Nineteenth-century ekphrastic responses, in aiming in a general sense to domesticate and verbalize images, render individual "originals"—when they are retrievable at all—somewhat beside the point.[7]

Original Copy takes its starting-point in the ekphrastic art object, real or imagined, that was at the center of so many poems, travelogues, personal essays, and plays in nineteenth-century American literary culture, and argues that the use of ekphrasis was then, as it is often today, inherently political, centered on the active participation of the American spectator-citizen in the creation of a national artistic canon. Poems, stories, and essays addressed to particular works of art were a conventional form in nineteenth-century collections and periodicals. This convention is compelling for the very fact of its existence in a historical period of burgeoning print and image reproduction. Why did this form, which in earlier periods had functioned at least in part to stand in for the irreproducible visual object, thrive during decades when its practical function as imitation was challenged by cheaper means of visual reproduction, and when the insistence on American "originality" was the mantra in nationalist literary circles? And what might this paradox tell us about the genre's popularity among female and feminized writers, who have traditionally been associated with the imitative function that nationalism positioned itself against?

Original Copy argues for the significance of mediation, imitation, and intimate author–reader relations to the development of an American literature.

The authors in this study—Phillis Wheatley Peters, Margaret Fuller, Sophia Hawthorne, and Henry Wadsworth Longfellow—worked within conventionally feminized traditions such as artistic copying, pedagogical recitation, and literary imitation, at the same time as American critical circles increasingly invested in the project of literary consolidation and nationalist imagination. But precisely because editors and critics framed women—and much more broadly femininity—as derivative, their works often obliquely or directly function as meditations on the meaning of this status. These meditations frequently crystallize in ekphrasis, a fundamentally replicative mode that was in the nineteenth century somewhat paradoxically both an entrenched literary convention, and a conventional mode for investigating artistic creativity. Claudia Stokes has argued that the conventional forms of literary "unoriginality" offered access and "necessary credentials" to "marginalized writers, such as white women, writers of color, and working-class aspirants."[8] This argument applies equally to ekphrasis, especially when this convention was integrated into popular forms such as the travelogue and the gift book.

Original Copy offers tells the story of a feminine nineteenth-century literary culture equally invested in cultural nationality and convention, in which the explicitly feminized forms of copying or translating between and within media became a productive means by which writers across a variety of genres interrogated the ill-defined but ubiquitous idea of an "original" American literature. This book, rather than staking itself as a study of imitation or innovation, centers on the slippages between conventional forms and investments in originality, drawing out a literary culture in which the two were closely enmeshed. And although it centers predominantly on women writers, who have been understudied both in relation to ekphrasis and nationalism, it is not a study of women writers but rather of femininity as floating signifier, a term that critics and readers in the nineteenth century apply to a range of writers who fall outside of constructions of individual genius and originality.

EKPHRASTIC THEORY AND ITS OTHERS

Ekphrasis is, in the words of one of its central theorists, W. J. T. Mitchell, "a minor and rather obscure literary genre," a subgenre or mode whose English pronunciation and spelling is up for debate.[9] But at the same time, as Mitchell argues, it is also a genre that stands in for much broader social and artistic encounters. Its staging of a meeting between writer, reader, and art object, and its status as a translator between the often-contested and traditionally gendered spaces of verbal and visual media also means that it represents, according to Mitchell, encounters with otherness in many forms. The literary work functions as the writer's attempt to make sense of this encounter, and to translate it, however haltingly, to a third party.

Mitchell sees the complete ekphrastic translation as an impossibility whose attempt is nonetheless also a basic literary aim. Most theorists of ekphrasis, Mitchell included, have examined this encounter almost exclusively through white male writers—typically British Romantics and modernists—and have followed the early modern tradition considering the text as masculine, the image as feminine. Through this model, the translation of image to text is necessarily contentious, a competition around the abilities and limitations of the different media in the tradition of aesthetic treatises from Leonardo da Vinci's *Treatise on Painting* to G. E. Lessing's *Laocoon; Or, On the Limits of Painting and Poetry* (1766), or what has become known as the "paragone" in interarts writing.[10]

But both the paragonal model and the ekphrastic canon are products of a particular critical moment, as James Edward Ford III writes in "Notes on Black Ekphrasis": "despite the term's age, the terminological history for Western Ekphrasis is based on a mid-twentieth-century consensus." As Ford notes, it was only in 1955 that Leo Spitzer claimed Keat's "Ode on a Grecian Urn," now often treated a prototype of the genre, as an example "of the *ekphrasis*, the poetic description of a pictorial or sculptural work of art."[11] So, although later theorists of ekphrasis such as Mitchell and James Heffernan have updated the framework for their readings, the canon of writing itself is to a large extent the relic of earlier criticism, and has certain inbuilt limitations, with Mitchell for instance writing in 1994, "All this would look quite different, of course, if my emphasis had been on ekphrastic poetry by women."[12] To that, Ford and other critics working on Black Ekphrasis would add writers of color.

Writers in the last ten years have focused their attention in particular to this latter category. As Elizabeth Loizeaux writes in her study of twentieth-century ekphrasis, "If Anglo-American ekphrasis looks at first especially male, it also looks especially white." In 2015, Carl Plasa's essay "Ekphrastic Poetry and the Middle Passage" launched a series of critical investigations into what has become known as Black Ekphrasis through its readings of "ekphrasis as a vehicle for reflecting on the slave trade and its legacies" through the work of contemporary poets Elizabeth Alexander, Olive Senior, and Honorée Fanonne Jeffers, with the aim of "directing attention to texts in which the author's gaze is not white but black." Much of this critical work has centered on contemporary writing, but critics such as James Ford have also investigated the roots of African American ekphrasis through, for instance, Phillis Wheatley Peters. And the focus on "correcting the biases intrinsic to much of the existing criticism on ekphrasis" in Plasa's essay also extends into related fields such as postcolonial ekphrasis.[13]

Similarly, a number of critics in recent years have responded to Mitchell's challenge to expand the model of these media encounters, with studies of ekphrasis by women writers, both historical and contemporary. These studies, in composing an alternative ekphrastic canon that significantly expands the limited selection of male Romantic and modernist poets that have been the primary case studies for ekphrastic theory in the past, have at the same time moved away from the framework of ekphrasis as media competition. Instead, they stress works that frame text and image as analogous, working within a "sister arts" tradition that emphasizes the overlap between the verbal and the visual; as Loizeaux frames it in her study (which grants roughly equal space to male and female writers), ekphrasis has an inherently "self-reflexive nature": "writing on a work of art becomes a way of looking sideways at poetry."[14] Another collection of twentieth-century women's writing understands the mode as a writer's means of reflecting on "the resources of her own artistic medium," while Susan Williams argues that her canon of antebellum prose ekphrasis expresses "less a desire to overcome a feminized 'other' than a nostalgic attempt to combine form and content, sign and referent," a means of stabilizing widely reproduced portraiture.[15] More recently, in her critique of Franco Moretti's *Distant Reading* (2013), Lisa Rhody understands this digital humanities approach as falling prey to precisely the fallacious opposition of text and image that writers like Lessing depended on in their treatises, and offers examples of twentieth and twenty-first-century ekphrasis as an alternative synergistic mode of considering different media.[16]

There is a strong historical basis for reading ekphrastic writing of the long nineteenth century in these synergistic terms, as sister arts rather than medial competitors. In the first half of the nineteenth century, for instance, ekphrastic practices were generally more at home in the popular periodical press than in the context of early modern aesthetic treatises. The most widely circulated of these periodicals owed much of their readership to their illustrations, and editors competed in boasting about the quantity, quality, and general renown of the images that they obtained.[17] Most Americans came into contact with artworks, not through the still-rare public collection, but in "the art gallery of the world" as a contemporary historian called these illustrated periodicals.[18] And with the burgeoning visual culture of these publications—prominent periodicals like *Graham's* and *Harper's* printed several engravings in each issue—came a demand for writers to interpret this work. This "literary illustration," as Nathaniel Hawthorne derisively called it, often became the commissioned labor of women writers, who were tasked with drawing a line—often a moralizing one—between text and image, and explicating an increasingly expansive visual culture to nineteenth-century viewers largely untrained in spectatorship.[19]

The historical and theoretical argument for focusing on women's ekphrasis as a discrete category is on much shakier ground. Much popular ekphrasis was published anonymously or pseudonymously, making definitive gender attribution difficult. From the beginning of the print revolution, women were associated with the luxury of illustration, but this association reflected misogyny more than actual use; some contemporary writers referred to all "illustrated magazines," even those with clearly mixed-gender audiences, as "feminine" or "lady-literature."[20] And as critics have been arguing nearly since the early days of recovery work, there are historical and ideological problems inherent in isolating women's writing as an object of study, including the reality that neither writerly nor readerly networks were segregated by gender, the danger of reproducing traditional value judgments around gender, and the threat of overly simplistic binaries like the association of men with public life and women with the private sphere. Movements contain their own counter-movements, and though *American Literature* published its provocative special issue arguing for the end of separate spheres in literary study a full twenty-five years ago, women's literature continues to exist as a scholarly and literary field in ways that can sometimes feel quite separate.[21]

My bibliography is clearly indebted both to works that ground themselves in women's literary studies, and to the development of this field over the last many decades. But my project likewise leans into queer theory's understanding of masculinity and femininity as characteristics that can be split from bodies coded male or female, and to queer nineteenth-century thinkers such as Margaret Fuller, who explicitly argued against the gender binary.[22] In my study, this understanding of sex and gender merges with a historical landscape in which these categories were often equally fluid; as Travis Foster asks, "What isn't queer about nineteenth-century American literature?"[23] In this era before the scientific or pseudo-scientific categorizations of sexology took hold, many works evidence what one critic, referencing Melville, calls a "comically anarchic sensuality," a kind of queerness that in its fluidities might speak more clearly to our own era than to the modern era that directly succeeded it.[24] Rather than focusing on women's writing as such, this project takes its starting point in the idea of femininity as a floating term that applied to both male- and female-identified writers and that was used by critics and editors to signify a cluster of traits that included derivation, mimicry, and domesticity.[25] If, as Jack Halberstam writes of female masculinity, "far from being an imitation of maleness, [it] actually affords us a glimpse of how masculinity is constructed as masculinity," male femininity might afford some of the same insight.[26] The recent flourishing of transgender studies in historical contexts, including the US nineteenth century, pushes this point.[27]

There are some ways in which ekphrasis might be particularly suited to investigating these questions of gender and sexuality. On the one hand, the imitative failures of ekphrasis echo both the failures of gender, and the reclamations of this failure within queer theory. W. J. T. Mitchell, in his theorization of ekphrasis as a genre, outlines its three stages as: ekphrastic hope (the anticipation that the medial differences between text and image might be overcome), ekphrastic fear (the worry that these differences need to be policed and maintained), and ekphrastic indifference (the realization of ekphrasis's impossibility). Reflecting on this breakdown, Brian Glavey in his book *The Wallflower Avant-Garde: Modernism, Sexuality, and Queer Ekphrasis* (2015) writes, "we might say that ekphrasis has been a queer art of failure for centuries" in Halberstam's sense that "under certain circumstances failing . . . may in fact offer more creative, more cooperative, more surprising ways of being in the world."[28] If ekphrasis is, at least in Mitchell's formulation, about policing difference, and particularly gender difference, its inevitable failure also opens up a space for potentiality. With a foundation in Judith Butler's famous assertion that gender "is a kind of imitation for which there is no original," Glavey asserts, "One of the primary and inaugural insights of queer theory, we might say, is that gender and sexuality are themselves ekphrastic illusions. To see this is not to throw them away."[29]

In some cases, the writers in this project were grouped and anthologized by contemporaries under the rubric of women's writing, in others not, but for all, gender and its associations helped to define the way that they and their contemporaries understood their work in relation to issues like nation and originality. In Longfellow's case, for instance, Margaret Fuller questioned his "full sympathy" for "what is large and manly" in the same review that she deemed him "artificial and imitative," while Walt Whitman's judgment that Longfellow was an "adopter and adapter" coincided with his categorization as the "universal poet of women and young people."[30] Fuller herself, meanwhile, was routinely masculinized in critical language, an assessment that was not generally intended as complementary, but that did coincide with an evaluation of her work both as innovative and nationally significant.

In a similar vein, popular ekphrasis did not take aesthetic sides, and often relied centrally both on media competition and synergy. Lydia Sigourney, one of nineteenth-century America's most popular poets and most prolific writers of ekphrasis, is a case in point. As a woman from a working-class background who would become one of America's first professional writers, she is a good illustration of Claudia Stokes's idea of convention as a "necessary credential" for marginalized figures.[31] Her ekphrastics fell into several categories, each of which performed slightly different functions: in addition to commonly reprinted freestanding ekphrastics such as "Lady Jane Grey" and "The Last Supper," she also produced an illustrated ekphrastic volume of her European travels, as well as commissioned works to accompany periodical illustrations.[32] The first of these forms had a didactic function, and were sometimes reproduced in volumes designed for students, guiding spectatorship and modeling the process of finding a concise moral lesson in an often ambiguous visual object. This pedagogical function was present in the other forms of ekphrasis as well, but was complicated by the practical reality of the differing economic value of text and image. In the case of her travelogue, for instance, Sigourney argued with publishers about the importance of including (expensive) illustrations in the volume, eventually switching publishing houses to secure her vision for the book.[33] Sigourney's commissioned periodical illustrations also reveal an imbalance in a culture where reproduced images, though increasingly affordable, still cost more to engrave and reproduce than the texts of well-known writers. Of one commissioned story, Sigourney writes to her friend George Griffin, "It was written for a Religious Souvenir, & I was obliged to adapt it to a picture. . . . I never liked the dialogue with which, for the sake of explaining the picture, it was made to commence."[34] In the landscape of text and image, image in many ways still came first, while text performed a secondary explicative function. Popular ekphrasis in this sense vied explicitly with media competition and the uneven value of text and image, even as print culture brought the two media into proximity.[35]

With examples like Sigourney in mind, I approach ekphrasis through both its synergistic and competitive models, as well as both male and female writers. The sister-arts understanding of the visual art object as an analogy for the literary work, a meta-reflection on the creative act more generally, is key not only to feminist reconsiderations of the genre, but to the predominantly male works in Mitchell's ekphrastic canon. And Mitchell's understanding of ekphrasis as a "triangular relationship" typically expressing a "desire for a visual object" and "an offering of this expression as a gift to the reader"[36] represents confoundingly well the type of popular print that he specifically does not address. This period's ekphrasis does not generally reproduce the precise imagistic details of the object, and much of it falls under the category of what John Hollander calls "notional ekphrasis," or works that do not refer clearly to any known image.[37] The writers in this study, working in an environment of increasing image reproduction and availability, approach ekphrasis without any pretensions toward mimesis, but rather to model the act and experience of spectatorship. The works in this project are united by a meta-reflection on the act of artistic creation, a concern with the translation of physical forms, and an intimate relation to the reader, the ultimate reinterpreter of the artistic offering.

This socially engaged element of ekphrasis is one of the ways in which it could be considered political. In *Specters of Democracy* (2011), Ivy Wilson considers the ways that "African Americans manipulated aurality and visuality in art that depicted images of national belonging not only as a mode of critique but as an iteration of democratic representation itself."[38] The visual arts, in other words, become a means of engaging in and interrogating a national sphere for subjects who have been denied full participation or citizenship. In fact, as Wilson argues, the relatively accessible cultural sphere can function as a stand-in for the more resistant realm of democratic representation: "antebellum African Americans conceived of representation in art as a proxy for their desired representation in politics."[39] While my intention here is not to conflate the political impasses of white feminized subjects with those of African Americans, for women as for racialized subjects, the cultural sphere offered a means of engaging in national dialogues in spite of the absence of direct political representation. And for all such subjects, what Homi Bhabha calls colonial mimicry (which resists political power in an act of iteration that must "produce its slippage, its excess, its difference") or what Wilson calls "the remix" (a "repetition [that] is always transformative and always solicits retransformation") are elements of their politicized aesthetic production.[40] It is in this sense that ekphrasis, a form whose (always impossible) repetitions and reiterations are inbuilt, has a particular pull for subjects barred from formal political representation. Or as Dana Seitler writes about "representations of art within art," in *Reading Sideways: The Queer Politics of Art in Modern American Fiction* (2019), "what we might find is not just an aesthetic recursion but a political one in which the reflective moment is bound up in an unruly set of questions about personhood, sociality, desire, and forms of intimacy and communication."[41]

In this period in American literary culture, when the arts were increasingly tied to the nationalist project, ekphrasis, formally attuned to questions of copying and originality, became a central means of considering what forms the literature of the new nation could, and sometimes more prescriptively, should, take. Art description took on this function, even for writers who, like most of the writers in this project, have not typically been framed as taking part in nationalist and canon-building conversations any more than they have been theorized as writers of ekphrasis. And as I suggest in the coda, the dialogue between ekphrasis and nation that developed in the early national period continues into the present day, when writers like Claudia Rankine lean on the mode to discuss representation and belonging.

LITERARY NATIONALISM(S)

In her investigation of the place of violence in art, *The Art of Cruelty* (2011), Maggie Nelson writes of her methodology: "Mostly I want to point to third things—unruly, inscrutable, multivalent, un-ownable third things—without knowing exactly what they have to say or teach."[42] Like Nelson's framework— and Jacques Rancière's investigations of spectatorship as an active agent in art-making, from which she borrows the term—this project centers on the art object as an intermediary between a writer and their audience. The main function of art description, according to Nelson, is not to "imitate or represent a reality from which spectators are barred" but to mediate, to bring speaker and audience into a shared imaginative space that is both individualized and collective, distanced and associated.[43] Rancière's conceptualization of spectatorship is similarly centered around a "third thing that is owned by no one, whose meaning is owned by no one, but which subsists between them," an imaginary that holds creative and utopian possibility.[44] Ekphrastic theory formulates the relationship in strikingly similar terms, as W. J. T. Mitchell writes that ekphrasis "is more like a triangular relationship than a binary one [that] must be pictured as a *menage à trois* in which the relations of self and other, text and image, are triply inscribed. If ekphrasis typically expresses a desire for a visual object (whether to possess or praise), it is also typically an offering of this expression as a gift to the reader."[45] While Mitchell's sexual metaphor for the dynamics of ekphrasis betrays this model's gendered (and heteronormative) assumptions, his understanding of the mode also as a "gift to the reader" overlaps with Rancière and Nelson in emphasizing social, collective space. My argument in this book is precisely that the use of ekphrasis in nineteenth-century America was, as in these twenty-first-century models, inherently political and social, centered on the active participation of the American spectator-citizen in the creation of a national artistic canon.

If what ekphrasis offers is an imagined space that is individual and collective, shared but never fully, scholars have theorized the nation in much the same terms. Benedict Anderson's famous formulation of the nation as imagined community takes print culture, and especially the daily newspaper, as a key example for how this "deep, horizontal comradeship" is built in the late eighteenth to nineteenth centuries.[46] Through collective but individual acts, like reading the same text on the same day, an imagination of a nation could take shape, in which shared language, ideals, and concerns bound groups too far-flung to form more direct communities. It is perhaps not that surprising, then, that part of what the collective but individual space of ekphrasis in this national literary period imagines is the shared space of the nation, as it was and as it could be.

Literary nationalism is either a small affair or an all-encompassing representative mode, depending on how you look at it. Its conventional outline in the US begins in the Revolutionary and post-Revolutionary periods, when cultural leaders began calling for work on distinctively American scenes and themes, spurring a first wave of literary nationalists like Philip Freneau, Noah Webster, and Washington Irving, who sketched the mythologies of the new nation through frontier scenes or other American landscapes. In the 1840s and 1850s, writers and editors associated with and championed by New York's Young America circle constituted a second wave of cultural nationalism, one that was intermeshed with the Democratic Party and the political push for westward expansion. This wave is more fully entrenched in the cultural canon today through figures like Emerson, Whitman, Hawthorne, and Melville. Leaders of the literary movement, like editor Evert Duyckinck, who published the American books that English wits questioned whether anyone would read, and advocated for the international copyright that would give American writers a viable chance at a profession, were instrumental to this second wave. And while it grew out of the nationalism of the previous decades, it was also often at odds with it, deriding this earlier wave's reliance on convention and European models.[47]

Though nationalism was always in equal parts aesthetic and economic, as historians of print culture like Meredith McGill have shown, and advocacy for the American book was staked as much on the printed object and the forces that would profit from it as abstract ideals, twentieth-century canon-building works such as F. O. Matthiessen's *American Renaissance* (1941) have emphasized the latter. Through a material lens, the earliest understanding of what constituted the American book might be exemplified by Evert Duyckinck's father, a New York bookseller of the same name who made a name selling books, both by American and British authors, that were printed, bound, and sold in the US. But far from this early Republican definition, Matthiessen positioned the coterie of Duyckinck the son—mid-century figures like Hawthorne, Whitman, and Melville—as American literature's "first maturity" on the basis primarily of "aesthetic judgments": their "imaginative vitality" and their "devotion to the possibilities of democracy."[48] In many ways, it is through the stylistically-focused writing of Matthiessen and other early twentieth-century critics like Van Wyck Brooks (and later Richard Poirier), that aesthetic originality has entrenched itself so firmly in the definition of literary nationalism. And though American literary studies have long since broadened to include the popular and women writers that Matthiessen understood only as "a fertile field for the sociologist and the historian of our taste," the framework for the nationalist conversation in the nineteenth century has lagged behind, remaining largely moored in the figures and terms of these two early nineteenth-century movements.[49]

That mid-century scholars like Matthiessen have offered the most lasting critical definition for American literary nationalism suggests why a simultaneous reconsideration of nationalism and ekphrasis makes sound literary historical sense. As with nationalism, scholarly studies of ekphrasis first emerged in significant numbers in the mid-twentieth century, and the canons that they worked with were shaped by this period's assumptions about what constituted writing worthy of study. The lines that I draw here between the larger literary movement of nationalism and the smaller sub-genre of ekphrasis are an attempt not to conflate the two, but to suggest that they come out of similar histories of reading, both of which have purposely sidelined femininity as well as aesthetic modes such as derivation, translation, and repetition. More recent critical work by scholars, such as Mitchell and Heffernan, have updated the critical vocabulary for considering ekphrasis as a genre, but by and large relies on the same canon of literary work that mid-century critics laid out. As I outlined in the previous section, this situation has shifted only relatively recently, as seen in part through new studies that take gender, as well as race, into more active consideration.

In this same vein, precisely because literary studies have changed while the idea of literary nationalism has (until recently) not, literary historical treatment of the mode has in the last few decades tended to be dismissive, critiquing it in broad strokes as a vehicle for white imperial power, or sidelining it as a niche historical mode.[50] But nationalism, like ekphrasis, becomes bigger and more variegated the longer you look at it. In recent years, some critics have begun to consider what it might mean to frame the nineteenth century as a literary culture in which the question of nation was unruly and even ubiquitous, not relegated to particular periodicals or cliques of East Coast writers and editors. David Reynold's *Beneath the American Renaissance* (1988) began the push by contextualizing Matthiessen's small canon within a broader and more popular cultural context; more recent work like Robert Levine's *Dislocating Race and Nation* (2008) and J. Gerald Kennedy's *Strange Nation* (2016) have further expanded what American literary nationalism can signify and what forms it can take. Levine strives to complicate the movement by emphasizing its "conflicted, multiracial, and contingent dimensions," discussing both "white writers who undermined hegemonic models and some black writers who found certain aspects of the national ideology inspiring," while Kennedy paints antebellum nationalism as a "noisy, multifaceted campaign," highlighting the incongruities between nationalist mythology and social reality, through which "stories of national life got stranger and stranger."[51] Both emphasize varieties of national engagement over consensus, and understand nationalism in the broader sense of a national consciousness, rather than what Etienne Balibar calls "the imaginary singularity of national formations."[52]

In fact, literary nationalism, like ekphrasis, has always been a plural affair. As Paul Giles has shown in his treatment of authors such as Emerson and Thoreau, this period's nationalism was by necessity deeply transnational, imbued with the global political and geographical concerns that structured the continent, and Giles's argument of Emerson, that he "marks his originality not through mimesis but through intertextuality, through taking icons and ideas from classical European culture and spinning them round in a new way," could be made for all of the writers in my study.[53] As Giles notes, a unified national imaginary only developed in any real sense with the greater geographical unification of the United States after the Civil War, and the "tentative, optative dimension" of antebellum nationalism underlines the basic imaginary dynamics of nationalism in Benedict Andersen's sense.[54] Alex Leslie, in his analysis of Evert Duyckinck's *The Literary World* goes even further in stressing geographic fragmentation, arguing that "nationalist discourse within this contested cultural landscape was often not about the nation at all but rather about one or another of the regions jostling for cultural space."[55] Reading the journal through what he calls "regional nationalism," or the use of nationalist rhetoric to promote a particular regional culture, he frames the New York-based Young Americans not as representative of a broader nationalist movement, but as a regional interest and "one program for national literature among many" in the US.[56] Some of these regional nationalisms, notably that in New England, called for a more international and multilingual approach to a national literature, echoing Giles's transnational argument.[57]

My project builds on this work, while placing feminized writers central to the question of what national forms encompassed. Newer reconsiderations of nationalism(s) often include women writers, but as of yet without any thorough discussion of what this inclusion changes in the way that the mode has been defined. Much as Levine argues that the compilation of a multiracial nationalist canon undermines the wholesale association of nationalism with white imperialism, I find that the close examination of ideals of femininity and nationalism forces to the fore the murky, ill-defined, but almost ubiquitous presence of literary originality in definitions of nationalism around mid-century and thereafter. Because femininity in the nineteenth century was often sweepingly associated with imitative and conventional forms, what Eliza Richards calls the "mimic powers of poetesses," the work of feminized writers would seem anathema to a mode whose explicit focus lies in the creation of new forms.[58] But my argument in this book is that precisely because this question of originality was written into the critical conversation around nationalism, an important aspect of these writers' encounters with the mode lay in thinking through what forms "originality" could take. In this way, they highlight what has always been the case: that nationalist originality has taken varied forms in both its earlier and later stages, many of which have depended centrally on practices of copying, imitative recreation, and convention. Centering on ekphrastic examples written or circulated from the 1830s to the 1880s further allows me to demonstrate that authorial and national self-consciousness, traits that critics have primarily identified as appearing in women's writing near the end of the century, or at earliest in the postbellum period, were present, as with male authors, throughout the century.[59] And insofar as region is an important element in thinking through nationalism, all of the writers in this study are New England–based, associated with many of the same nodes in the nationalist conversation, but at the same time insistently transnational in scope. In this sense, this book offers more selection than survey, and suggests a way into the gendering of other regional nationalisms.

FEMININITY, ORIGINALITY, AND THE NATIONAL(IST) CANON

Literary nationalism in the US is closely associated with publications like *The Democratic Review* and *The Literary World*, but nationalist debates and issues appeared widely in print culture, including in magazines that, while they had a broader audience, were explicitly addressed to female and feminized readers. *Godey's Lady's Book*, for instance, became a site in the debate between literary nationalist factions when it printed Edgar Allen Poe's six-part *The Literati of New York* (1846), a series of profiles of editors, critics, and writers that presented, in typically contentious style, "some honest opinions at random."[60] It provided an overview of the New York's nationalist landscape, satirizing the more traditionalist Knickerbocker camp, valorizing that of Duyckinck and the Young Americans, and producing, as it was intended to, a flurry of responses in the periodical press.[61] In this survey, Poe includes figures like N. P. Willis, Anna Mowatt, Margaret Fuller, Caroline Kirkland, and

Fanny Osgood, to imply not just their centrality to literary circles, but their place in debates around what constituted an American literature.

Female and feminized writers also make their mark in the anthologies that were a central component of nationalist consolidation projects. While it would be a mistake to conflate the early nineteenth century's rage for anthologizing (national and otherwise) with literary nationalism, there is some overlap between the two tendencies. The anthologies of American literature that began appearing in the early decades of the nineteenth century and culminated around mid-century with several ambitious collections, are not by definition canonization projects, as American literary canonization is strongly associated with the college-level textbooks that began appearing in the 1920s, or as John Guillory puts it, "the problem of the canon is the problem of syllabus and curriculum."[62] Nineteenth-century anthologies targeted more general readers, and there was no academic curriculum of American literature in the nineteenth century to speak of. Further, as Alex Socarides writes in her analysis of nineteenth-century women's poetry anthologies, these volumes were capacious rather than carefully selective, and included minimal editorial apparatus for framing the cultural significance or selection of the writers.[63]

Nonetheless, I would argue that these volumes, often compiled by editors with outspoken nationalist positions, eagerly reviewed in nationalist journals, and framing the work through the lens of national authorship, suggest a push at least toward a popular if not academic American canon. These traits are perhaps best evidenced by Evert and George Duyckinck's monumental two volume *Cyclopedia of American Literature* (1855), totaling over 1,400 pages and written in part as a response to the shorter, unambiguously nationalist anthologies of American writers compiled in the 1840s by Rufus Griswold, who championed American authors and advocated for international copyright to even the playing field against the European authors whose works could be reprinted at lower cost.[64] Though the Duyckincks' volumes were critically lampooned for their factual errors (an attack led by Griswold), they clearly attempted to bring to a culmination what shorter anthologies since the 1820s had set into motion: the collection of American literature, from its dispersed and often periodical sources, into a (relatively) comprehensive and more easily accessible form. Griswold's scathing review of the work in the *New York Herald*, reprinted as a forty-page pamphlet, points out in minute detail both scholarly and grammatical errors, and demonstrates not just the pettiness of nationalist factions, but the stakes of these volumes for the literary community of the time.[65] His critical exposé is cloaked in nationalist duty, going on the offensive only, he insists, because the volume "ostentatiously claims recognition as a national work of the highest importance."[66]

Therefore, though the Duyckinck brothers downplayed their own role as gatekeepers, professing in the preface to "welcome all guests who come reasonably well introduced," it is reasonable to assume that contemporary readers would have seen through this apparent modesty.[67] As the editors and publishers most closely associated with the literary side of the Young America movement, the Duyckincks would likely have understood these volumes in the same context as "The Library of American Books," which Evert edited in the mid-1840s, and the *Democratic Review*, which he was literary editor of around the same time: as implicit, and sometimes explicit tools for national definition. In the "massive" *Cyclopedia*, Alex Leslie writes, "Duyckinck came as close as anyone to encompassing the equally unwieldy literary production of the nation."[68] The outcome of this project was the reinvention of "the antebellum literary field as national retroactively," from its regional roots.[69] In this sense, it is significant that the second volume, which picks up from the early national period, includes almost sixty women writers, among them those known today and those less so, just as it is significant that the Library of American Books published Margaret Fuller's work alongside of Hawthorne's and Poe's. Female and critically feminized writers, such as Longfellow, were always a part of this nationalizing project, even when not explicitly addressing national or political themes.

In anthologies of women's writing from this period, the national is likewise a focal point. In Caroline May's *The American Female Poets* (1848) and Rufus Griswold's *Female Poets of America* (1849), both editors frame the volumes, and the act of collecting and reading American women writers more generally, in nationalist terms. May opens her preface by stating that "One of the most striking characteristics of the present age is the number of female writers, especially in the department of belles-lettres. This is even more true of the United States than of the old world."[70] She continues later on the same page in this comparative mode:

> As a rare exotic, costly because of the distance from which it is brought, will often suffer in comparison of beauty and fragrance with the abundance of wild flowers of our meadows and woodland slopes, so the reader of our present volume, if ruled by an honest taste, will discover

First Things, Third Things 19

in the effusions of our gifted countrywomen as much grace of form, and powerful sweetness of thought and feeling, as in the blossoms of woman's genius culled from other lands."[71]

Though May here only explicitly asserts the equality of American women's writing to that of other countries, the metaphor of the exotic flower, less beautiful and more expensive than the local wildflower, pushes the comparative point, positioning the goods of American authors as better deals for the local market in both aesthetic and economic terms.

Griswold echoes many of May's sentiments.[72] In the *Female Poets of America* he emphasizes, as May, that the number of American women writers outnumber those in other countries, and he devotes a full paragraph to refuting the assumptions behind the idea that "the American people have been thought deficient in that warmth and delicacy of taste, without which there can be no genuine poetic sensibility," naming "earlier speculation on the subject," by others, including Alexis de Tocqueville. He presents his anthology as one element in the "weight of cumulative testimony" against "such prejudices," explicitly positioning the volume in the service of literary nation-building, a function that could easily extend to many of the other anthologies of the period, including May's and Thomas Buchanan Read's *The Female Poets of America* (1848).[73] Griswold's accomplishment in his anthologies of American literature, as Perry Miller writes, was to stress the significance of compiling writers from all regions of the nation, a move that "would so reformulate the program of nationalism that Young America would find their occupation gone," relegated to a regionalist movement.[74] Griswold may represent a "conservative nationalism" that emphasizes the "national in spirit, not subject-matter," but is nonetheless representative of one of the many forms of nationalism and nationalist canon-building during this period.[75]

For Griswold, gender mattered to the nationalist question because women and women writers were already deeply enmeshed in the questions of imitation and originality that were foundational to literary nationalism. Griswold opens his preface not with a national comparison, as does May, but a gendered one, musing, "It is less easy to be assured of the genuineness of literary ability in women than in men."[76] He then delves into a stock comparison of masculine intellection and feminine sensibility in writing that culminates in an equally conventional consideration of feminine mimicry, suggesting that "the most exquisite susceptibility of spirit, and the capacity to mirror in dazzling variety the effects which circumstances or surrounding minds work upon it, may be accompanied by no power to originate, nor even, in any proper sense, to reproduce."[77] He admits that he began editorial work on his volume "with something of this antecedent skepticism," but finds himself reading "with frequent admiration and surprise."[78] He overcomes his own earlier prejudices as an editor, then, and goes on to suggest that in part because women are less commonly "devoted to business and politics" they may be the most likely to answer the nationalist cultural challenge: "Those who cherish a belief that the progress of society in this country is destined to develop a school of art, original and special, will perhaps find more decided indications of the infusion of our domestic spirit and temper into literature, in the poetry of our female authors, than that of our men."[79] Within one paragraph of this preface, then, Griswold neatly flips the conventional perception of women's writing as inherently imitative to a nationalist understanding of the work as central to the canon-building of an "original and special" school.

This flip, staged in the US's most popular anthology of women's verse, is indicative of the ways that the period's powerful editors and publishers positioned women writers within narratives of nationalism, but it is equally indicative of some of the ambiguity behind the aesthetic ideals of nationalism, and the underdefined murkiness of central aesthetic terms like "originality." Criticism in recent years has recovered the place of imitation in nineteenth-century women's literature and beyond, an important corrective to a long-standing privileging of formal innovation. The early decades of the nineteenth century saw the traditional "craftsman" model of creative work coming into contact with notions of original and proprietary authorship. But as critics such as Lara Langer Cohen and Eliza Richards remind us, this notion of originality was never as simple as a retrospective glance may suggest. Cohen sees the antebellum period's predilection for critical puffery, literary hoaxes, and rampant accusations of plagiarism as a part of a larger sense that the developing American literature itself could be nothing more than "fraudulence." But, she posits, the culture of mass-produced print, rather than destroying the original, as in the Benjaminian construction, may have created the first sustained idea of it: "It is the conceivability of the derivative that is the prerequisite for imagining, and privileging the authentic." And if originality is, as she writes, a "second-order phenomenon," it is also, as a term, inherently unstable.[80] Richards suggests a similar instability in her study of Poe and the poetesses of his literary circle; she notes that these writers "decline to enforce or accept a clear division between original and copy, genius and mimicry, poet and poetess" and "retain skepticism about the possibility of true mimesis," finding a productive ground in the space between these terms. The functions of "lyric mimicry"—"echo, quotation, paraphrase, repetition"—are, Richards argues, essential to reading the social, cultural, and aesthetic work of the lyric during this time.[81]

What was originality, then, in the early national sense? Scholars such as William Huntting Howell, Ezra Tawil, and Claudia Stokes have convincingly argued that imitation and antiquarianism were dominant forces in nineteenth-century American literature and culture, countering the still-common association of the period with the stylistic innovation of the American Renaissance.[82] But the term "originality" nonetheless unquestionably came up in nationalist discourse across geographical regions and throughout the nineteenth century. As Stokes notes, "Samuel Johnson's 1755 *Dictionary of the English Language* omitted the word 'originality' as well as its cognates, but by 1828 these terms appeared in Noah Webster's Dictionary, a shift that confirms the decisive entrance of novelty and innovation into American public discourse during the intervening seventy-five years."[83] A similar phenomenon is at work in the nationalist discourse of the long nineteenth century. Griswold was far from the only critic to privilege the "original and special"; variations on "originality" come up in any periodical search, and the term is particularly prevalent in book and art reviews. The precise denotation and connotations of the term, though, varied nearly as much as who was using it.

This book begins to investigate this range of meaning. Originality resounds differently for Griswold than for Emerson, and neither use the term in the way that writers have commonly used it in the last century, to connote a radical stylistic or thematic break. By investigating a series of very different writers concerned in different ways with the national and with origination, I argue that the idea of the original, though closely intermingled with what many now understand as convention, was a driving concern for broad swath of American writers, and was closely imbricated in their own understandings of themselves as Americans. As Jess Roberts points out, convention is everywhere that language is, and what readers recognize as "conventional" depends entirely on their own (most often unspoken) norms and expectations.[84] We recognize a convention when it is different from our own, and in this light it is not surprising that much of nineteenth-century popular and women's writing, so entrenched in unfamiliar pieties and forms, is legible to us primarily through its rules. But the relativity of convention does not mean that it does not exist, and recent works by Roberts, Alex Socarides, Dorri Beam, and Jennifer Putzi have undertaken the important task of nuancing and historicizing the understanding of convention in nineteenth-century American women's writing.[85]

As these historicized investigations of convention highlight granularity, individual variation, and even originality, a historicized investigation of originality underlines its conventions, and even its existence as convention. Elissa Zellinger argues that lyric interiority, far from being an invention of twentieth-century criticism, was a trait that nineteenth-century writers, especially those denied the political rights of liberal self-determination, actively claimed for their work.[86] This question of free and independent liberal subjecthood is likewise written into many Romantic and pre-Romantic definitions of originality, which aligned imitation with slavery, and innovation with masculinity, whiteness, and "recognized legal personhood."[87] In this same vein, then, I understand the idea of originality, not (only) as an anachronistic characteristic applied to the nineteenth century by twentieth-century critics, but as a term that, while signifying differently then than now, nineteenth-century writers, including those lacking gendered or racial self-determination, consciously used to think through the aims and values of their work. It is not surprising in this light that Black Ekphrasis has staked a claim as a critical category, a development that I take stock of in my considerations of Phillis Wheatley Peters and Claudia Rankine. If originality in the dominant tradition is strongly associated with both masculinity and whiteness, what emerges in this book are complex and varying definitions of originality more closely tied to imitative practices and set forms, which can help to establish a more thoroughly historicized manner of understanding both originality and convention in the long nineteenth century.

CONVENTION AND THE COLLECTIVE

Part of the historical backdrop to understanding convention in the long nineteenth century, especially through the lens of nationalism, is the philosophy of mind and aesthetics known as associationism, which was influential to the communal thinking of Fourierism, transcendental utopian experiments, and, as Theo Davis has shown, the basic structures and assumptions of American nationalist writing of the 1820s and 1830s. Associationism underlined the dynamic nature of mental processes, understanding thought and imagination as a chain that unfolds through the association of individual images and ideas. As Davis has shown, much of the literary understanding of associationism came to Americans through writings of figures such as Lord Kames and Archibald Alison, who stressed an audience-centered aesthetic, in which "the best art is art which disappears, leaving one to reflect upon trains of responses to the art rather than the art itself."[88] This approach to art valued familiar scenes and topics, which would already be imbued by readers with a rich range of associations, over a novelty that offered no such references. In this light, the particularities of American life and landscape, the focus of much early nationalist work, presented the challenge of unfamiliarity: "recognizably American subjects did not trigger trains of images, as did Europe's enviably affecting 'moss-clad ruins.'"[89] A reliance on types and conventions within new scenes, then, allowed American writers access to the readymade responses that were the aim of an artistic experience; as Kerry Larson writes, "literary nationalism takes it for granted that the building blocks for any literature must be a storehouse of objects, each stamped, as it were, with readily identified and commonly shared emotions."[90]

This aesthetic also offers a lens through which to read the ekphrasis of this period. The associationist understanding of literature centers the readerly experience more than any particular object, stressing not the author's finished work, but an experience or relation that the work can reproduce in the reader. This emphasis on reception resonates with ekphrasis as a convention centered on the act of looking, of narrating this experience, and of creating in the process a shared space between writer and reader. In associationist thought, the divide between the categories of reader and writer breaks down almost entirely, as the writer's initial experience and the reader's later reception are equally "disembodied," equally "abstract experiences," and so "the difference between authors and readers hard to see."[91] If both original experience and reimagination are equally abstract, equally "separated from its object," literary ekphrasis can function as a powerful means for the circulation of aesthetic experience, creating replications of artistic encounters that have no true originals.[92] In an atmosphere where cultural anxieties centered on the lack both of collective imagination and national artistic reference points, the particular appeal of an endlessly replicative ekphrasis resonates.

In the tradition of medial competition, associationist philosophy privileges text over image, and suggests some of the functions of this era's ekphrasis.

Unlike the visual artist, who in Archibald Alison's words, "can give to the objects of his scenery, only the visible and material qualities which are discernable by the eye, and must leave the interpretation of their expression to the imagination of the spectator," the writer can describe the temporal processes behind a scene or visual image.[93] Such description conveys associations and emotions "by bestowing on the inanimate objects of his scenery the characters and affections of the Mind" and so the writer is much more likely than the painter to produce the desired response or experience in his audience.[94] Rather than relying on a single fixed image, the literary description opens a chain of images to the reader, creating a dynamic experience where the act of spectatorship is itself the artwork. Following this understanding of literature, ekphrasis performs a significant function. In narrating the act of visual spectatorship and opening up the scene to the reader's own reimagination, ekphrastics make images emotionally legible. In this era of image proliferation through the means of print culture, ekphrasis was an increasingly valuable act of translation, and one that could bring the image into the national imaginary through the medial advantages of the text.

STRUCTURE

This book in some sense functions as a study of a single convention, ekphrasis, which was both uniquely accessible to even amateur women writers because of its humble position as imitation or "illustration," and at the same time well positioned to encourage meta-reflection on art and nation. Each chapter is centered on a single author, presenting case studies for different historical, ideological, and geographical nationalisms. Phillis Wheatley Peters is the pre-national poet who thought deeply about nation in transnational contexts, and whose recovery by editors in the 1830s and 1840s speaks posthumously to the nationally disunifying conflict over slavery. Margaret Fuller was affiliated with Evert Duyckinck's network as well as the European nationalist movements from which Young America took its name, and used her Western travels as a way of imaginatively binding the American landscape. Sophia Hawthorne, who was imbricated in Young America through her husband's career, was also an artist and visual copyist of paintings whose travel writings meditate on what constitutes artistic originality. Henry Wadsworth Longfellow, through his long career, was both a late nineteenth-century writer, and one associated with the earliest, internationally oriented phase of New England nationalism. All of these writers were affiliated with New England or New York modes for thinking through nation, a narrow geographic margin that can begin to suggest the rich range of regional nationalisms in play through the nineteenth century.

My first chapter, "Phillis Wheatley Peters's Antebellum Remediation," sets the stage for an examination of antebellum nationalism through Peters, who published the first collection of poetry by an African American woman, *Poems on Various Subjects, Religious and Moral* (1773), in the years leading up to the founding of the nation. Criticism of Peters has often focused on her mastery of style, with some scholars dismissing her work as derivative, and others celebrating its subtle subversions. This chapter confronts the charge of derivation through the lens of her antebellum celebration and republication by abolitionist authors and editors. In the early nineteenth century, Peters's work regained prominence as her writing was used, like slave narratives, to evidence the basic inhumanity of the institution. But I argue that Peters's movement between imitative and originary practices likewise spoke to the stylistic challenges that antebellum American writers contended with in the era of literary nationalism. Through close discussion of archival copybooks, which liberally and sometimes ambiguously mix excerpts from popular magazines, copies of anonymous and cited poems, popular sayings, and manuscript versions of Peters's poems, I show her stylistic innovations to be a direct offshoot of her collecting and replicative practices, and uniquely at home in the antebellum era that most unequivocally embraced her writing. With particular attention to poems that respond directly to other authors and artists, I argue that Peters structures her poetry, much like the copybook, as a conversation between artistic allies, positioning herself and other African American artists within a new creative pantheon.

My second chapter, "'The Fusion of the Races Among Us': *Summer on the Lakes* and Margaret Fuller's Aesthetic Nationalism," turns to Margaret Fuller's Midwestern travelogue *Summer on the Lakes, in 1843* (1844), which nationalist editor Evert Duyckinck called, "the only genuine book I can think this season," in the context of Fuller's ideas on women's education and self-expression.[95] Duyckinck's admiration for the text may have had much to do with its project of national consolidation through a mapping of the country's Western reaches and histories, but this was a straightforward project that the fragmentary, digressive, mixed-genre form of the travelogue complicated. In *Summer on the*

Lakes, Fuller imposes descriptions of artworks onto the Midwestern landscape of her travels as a means of arguing for forms of visual and literary creativity that were uniquely suited to the American climate. The composition of an artwork is, according to Fuller, an act ideally undertaken in conversation with a particular natural setting. At the same time, the travel narrative and Fuller's teaching methods—both her Socratic secondary school instruction and the series of conversation classes that she held for women in Boston—also depend centrally on the framework of the conversation, and what she refers to as the reproduction of knowledge. By comparing archival student journals from Fuller's time at the progressive Greene Street School in Providence with manuscript and print editions of the travelogue, I argue that the dynamic conversation between different media, genres, and people was the key means through which Fuller understood American creativity in her literary moment.

In my third chapter, "'Folded up in a Veil': Sophia Peabody Hawthorne's Familial Ekphrasis and the Antebellum Travelogue," I examine the popular mid-century form of the travelogue through Sophia Hawthorne's *Notes in England and Italy* (1869), which reimagines its own well-trodden ground as a space for creativity within convention. Sophia's familial associations with nationalism are well-known—her husband Nathaniel published more stories in the nationalist *Democratic Review* than any other periodical, and his meeting with Melville, engineered by Evert Duyckinck, is sometimes seen as the culmination of the New York branch of nationalism. At the same time, Sophia, as a painter and celebrated copyist preoccupied with the line between original and imitative work, was in her own way equally engaged in this cultural moment, and her travelogue makes surprising claims for the mimicry associated with both women's writing and ekphrasis. These claims depend in large part on the author's acts of translation: in rewriting manuscript descriptions of family life as meditations on painting or sculpture for the print publication of *Notes*, Hawthorne shields her prominent family from exposure, while transforming European ekphrasis into a dynamic record of her own family's American domesticity. The illustrated journals that form the basis for *Notes* reveal loving details of family life that reemerge in the travelogue through descriptions of Madonnas, and more disturbingly, Guido Reni's portrait of Beatrice Cenci, the historical victim of incest and perpetrator of patricide. Throughout the text, in meditations on the nature of originality in painting and the virtues and sins of various copyists, Sophia self-consciously

First Things, Third Things   27

carves out her own space in American literary historiography through the most apparently self-effacing of literary forms.

Henry Wadsworth Longfellow, as one of the nineteenth century's most beloved poets, and a writer who had a contentious relationship with canonization, is the focus of this book's fourth chapter. In "Longfellow, *Michael Angelo*, and the 'Middle-Class' Curator," I argue that Longfellow's eclectic practices of home art collection and arrangement can be seen as a model for his literary methodology, which engaged self-consciously with American literary nationalism. A writer whom contemporary Margaret Fuller called a "middle-class" poet, and who was associated with the more traditionalist Knickerbocker set of writers, Longfellow confronted accusations of plagiarism, effeminacy, and mediocrity throughout his career. But his home in Cambridge, now both museum and archive, brings together extremes of elite and popular, fine art and artisanship, and in so doing imagines the instability associated with "middle-class" artists as productive rather than problematic. In the context of this home museum, I locate Longfellow's posthumously published drama in verse, *Michael Angelo: A Fragment*, which he revised throughout his life but never clearly finished, as a self-reflexive examination of the hierarchies of imitation and originality in American literary culture. I analyze the play's archival scatters, which I argue stage a defense of an aesthetics of borrowing and pastiche, what Fuller called his tendency to present readers "not with a new product in which all the old varieties are melted into a fresh form, but rather with a tastefully arranged Museum."[96] Through the life of Michelangelo, who Longfellow frames as craftsman-artist hybrid, Longfellow looks back at his own career in American letters in the decades where American literature was moving toward canonization, a process that would eventually write him out of serious literary contention.

In my coda, "Ekphrastic Citizenship: Claudia Rankine's American Lyrics," I extend some of these ideas into the interarts writing of our current time, examining movements including the particular versatility of ekphrasis to new media forms, and the continuing relevance of the mode to discussions of nation. Focusing on Claudia Rankine's ekphrastic works *Citizen* and *Don't Let Me Be Lonely*, I argue that far from being a niche or outdated genre, ekphrasis serves the increasingly important function of conceptualizing the consumer-citizen's encounter with visual and verbal media forms. In Rankine's canon, the act of spectatorship is, as for many nineteenth-century authors, a primary means of shaping national citizens, and of creating categories of belonging and exclusion.

Ekphrastics were often occasional, addressing a historical work and demanding to be read in the contexts in which they were written, but they also model broader encounters of collectivity and difference that were central to the nationalist mode. The art object in the works that I examine functions as a mediated space in this flexible dialectic of author and reader, where forms are left intentionally open-ended or unfinished in order to facilitate a collaboration between text and audience. In this sense, ekphrasis is the emblematic form of literature as collective production, a key to the nationalist form during this period. A copy that overwrites the significance of the original, ekphrasis models imitation, adaptation, and reconfiguration as a matter of course, condensing the basic vocabulary for literary origination through the nineteenth century. That this is a process that continues into the present day, with its anxieties about the dominance of imagistic media forms and new possibilities for combining text and image, is, like convention itself, both remarkable and not.

A note on terms: throughout this book, I use the term remediation in its media theory sense, or specifically as Richard Grusin and Jay Bolter define it in *Remediation: Understanding New Media* (2000) as the translation of one medium into another in a manner that reshapes both media. Though the authors use the term primarily to think through the ways that new digital media interact with older media forms, it is relevant, as they note, to other media interactions, including the translation of visual media into text. To frame ekphrasis as remediation is to insist on an interaction that is dynamic and mutually creative.

CHAPTER ONE

Phillis Wheatley Peters's Antebellum Remediation

THE SHIP AND THE NATION

In the first chapter of *The Black Atlantic: Modernity and Double Consciousness* (1993), Paul Gilroy's now-classic call to rethink the boundaries of the nation, the trope of the ship, "a living, micro-cultural, micro-political system in motion" provides a concrete image for, as Gilroy writes, "the middle passage . . . the various projects for redemptive return to an African homeland . . . the circulation of ideas and activists as well as the movement of key cultural artefacts: tracts, books, gramophone records, and choirs."[1] Later, he expands:

> The ship provides a chance to explore the articulations between the discontinuous histories of England's ports, its interfaces with the wider world. Ships also refer us back to the middle passage, to the half remembered micro-politics of the slave trade and its relationship to both industrialisation and modernisation. As it were, getting on board promises a means to reconceptualise the orthodox relationship between modernity and what passes for its prehistory.[2]

In this argument against discrete cultural nationalisms, and in favor of a multinational Black Atlantic culture shaped by both forced and voluntary migrations, the ship for Gilroy images the geographical and temporal transits that make up the modern world.

When Christina Sharpe picks up the image of the slave ship in *In the Wake: On Blackness and Being* (2016), forming each of her four chapters around an element of the transatlantic circuit ("The Wake," "The Ship," "The Hold," "The Weather,") the metaphor has similar, but darker resonances. The ship brings us from past to present, "from the forced movements of the enslaved to the forced movements of the migrant and the refugee, to the regulation of Black people in North American streets and neighborhoods, to those ongoing crossings of and drownings in the Mediterranean Sea."[3] The resonance of past and present migrations, as well as enclosures "in the form of the prison, the camp, and the school" challenge, as with Gilroy, the construction of the discrete nation-state.[4] But Sharpe's vision of nationlessness does not glide on the cultural optimism of Gilroy's multinational Black Atlantic, and does not conclude in the both/and space of modernity, but rather in the neither/nor statelessness of the contemporary refugee. As she writes, "For, if we are lucky, we live in the knowledge that the wake has positioned us as no-citizen. I want *In the Wake* to declare that we are Black peoples in the wake with no state or nation to protect us, with no citizenship bound to be respected, and to position us in the modalities of Black life lived in, as, under, despite Black death: to think and be and act from there."[5] The "re/seeing, re/inhabiting, and re/imagining the world" that *In the Wake* encourages draws not from a surfeit of allegiances, but from an absence.[6]

I take both of these nationless ships, sailing nearly thirty years apart, and their dual challenges to rethink the bases of our current world, as an entry point into Phillis Wheatley Peters's eighteenth-century publication and nineteenth-century re-circulations. Peters was a poet whose life and literary career were defined more than most in the period, and certainly in a broader variety of ways than most, by transatlantic circuits; she was, following Alexis Pauline Gumbs, one of the "undrowned," the survivors of the Middle Passage whose "breathing in unbreathable circumstances" continues today through "the chokehold of racial gendered ableist capitalism."[7] In 1761, Wheatley was shipped as a child of around seven from Western Africa, most likely modern-day Senegal or Gambia, to Boston, where she was named by the family that bought her after the ship that she arrived on, the Phillis. This pragmatic and seemingly unsentimental choice presages a life that would be marked precisely by the transcontinental in-betweenness of the ship's currents. When Phillis, bought to work as a domestic servant for the Wheatley family matriarch, Susanna, showed her linguistic prodigy, the daughter of the family taught her to read and write, and her poetry would soon reach a broader public in Boston. But although Peters secured some fame for her writing in the colonies, and individual poems were published as broadsides, it was only once she traveled to England 1772, accompanying the son of the Wheatley family on a business trip, that she was able to secure the British patronage for the publication of her book, *Poems on Various Subjects, Religious and Moral*. This volume was reprinted in the colonies the following year, but in the years after the Revolutionary War, Peters failed in her attempts to secure patronage or subscription support for her second volume of poems, now lost. The economic hardships of the early national period may have played a part, but some critics have also pointed to the national sympathies of the Wheatley family and friends, many of whom were Royalists and returned to Britain during or after the Revolution. Phillis Wheatley Peters's canon, then, written in the years leading up to American independence and immediately thereafter, is the record of a precarious and shifting transatlantic relationship, a template for the kind of mixed geographical and cultural allegiances that characterized this period and the one immediately following it.[8]

Peters's triangulated experiences, allegiances, and precarious dependencies make their clear mark on her poetry, which was inspired both by Pope and Milton, but recorded the networks between Africa, North America, and Britain. Her most anthologized and controversial poem, "On Being Brought from Africa to America" concerns the Atlantic passage in a brief few lines, opening famously with a Christianized reading of the transit: "'Twas mercy brought me from my *Pagan* land." Allusions to the Middle Passage and to a collective conception of a displaced African culture abound, for instance, in her reflections on this "pagan land"; her references and self-parallels to Terence, the enslaved Roman-African poet who is often considered the first writer of the African diaspora; and in her poem to Scipio Moorhead, an enslaved African American artist and possibly the painter behind the engraved frontispiece in her one published book of poetry. Other forms of transit are likewise common: poems to figures traveling to England for their health, or from Jamaica to America, or Odes to celebrated transatlantic figures like the Methodist preacher George Whitefield, who brought the Evangelical movement to the colonies in the first Great Awakening. In fact, if we consider the elegy in the manner that Peters herself often framed it, as a record of passage from one sphere to another, then nearly every poem in Peters's abbreviated canon could be considered a poem of transit.[9]

Peters's work has often been weighed down by its status as first: first book of poetry by an African American author, first book by an African American woman, and (arguably) the first significant writer in an African American literary lineage. More recently, critics have claimed her as the first in the lineage of Black Ekphrasis.[10] This series of firsts would be a difficult one for any writer to carry; it is one that Peters, whose verse seems conventional and conciliatory as often as it does bold and unapologetic, sometimes folds under. It is with some caution, then, that I introduce her in this first chapter, as another sort of first. The lineage that I am claiming here is that of femininized American writers in the long nineteenth century who wrote, albeit often vexedly, about and to nation and national identity, and who did so at least in part through interarts description. Peters was certainly not the first woman writer to consider the idea of nation, but a short career that neatly bridges the pre- and post-Revolutionary periods, a particularly transcontinental life and work, and a recirculation during the 1830s in publications of the abolitionist movement, all make her canon particularly well-suited as a starting-point. Her status as enslaved child-poet placed her at a double remove from political subjecthood, and with the poetic as her only means of engagement with the public sphere.[11] And this status has made the question of imitation and originality in her canon a vexed one from its first publication to the present day.

Although Peters had never been entirely out of print after her death in 1784, in the 1830s a flurry of new publications appeared, first in William Lord Garrison's abolitionist newspaper, the *Liberator*, and then in editions independently and alongside of the enslaved early nineteenth-century poet George Moses Horton. Peters, as Horton, clearly and very explicitly functioned in her own lifetime and thereafter as an example of, as an early editor wrote, "an unvarnished record of African genius," a potentiality that has both enabled and burdened the way that critics read Peters's poetry into the present day.[12] But as I argue, another way into Peters's verse is through its abolitionist resurgence and republication, which also coincided with a high point in American literary nationalism, the cultural movement that attempted to define an American artistic and literary canon in the early decades of the nineteenth century. Although Peters, whose published verse is decidedly pre-national, is rarely discussed in terms of this nationalist framework, I argue that questions of national allegiance are rife not just in her own poetic canon, but in the paratextual introduction and framing of her work by editors and biographers to readers in the early nineteenth century. In many ways, I show, it was at least as essential for Peters's editors during this period to position her as an American poet, as it was to emphasize her "African genius." Such positioning required a simplification of the networks, racial, cultural, and national, that she was a part of in her lifetime, but also tapped into real questions and considerations in her poetic canon.

Cultural nationalism, as I will be arguing throughout this book, was often centered as much around questions of copying and convention as political and geographic concerns. With this focus in mind, I begin my reading of Wheatley Peters with an examination of two small copybooks kept collectively by the "Scholars in King Street," in which a manuscript poem by Peters appears, possibly in her own hand.[13] The books provide, I argue, a concrete context for Peters's verse outside of the more formal structure of her 1773 *Poems on Various Subjects*, as well as a sense of the alternately loose and reverential attitudes toward convention and citation in her writing and its late eighteenth-century contexts. Skipping directly from this pre-publication to Peters's 1830s republications, first in the *Liberator* and then in independent and collective editions, I pay particular attention to biographical and editorial frameworks that structure this introduction of Peters to new audiences. Here nationalism and aesthetic originality, issues that had a particular charge at the time of Peters's writing, shift in resonance with her recirculation, taking on other meanings in relation to the growing tensions between Northern and Southern states and the aesthetic demands of cultural nationalism. I read both editorial frameworks and these republished poems as attempts to define a national language, an effort that was nearly as tenuous during Peters's recirculation as at the time of her original publication. Peters's poems, I argue, attempt to honor both a broader American and a specifically African American canon, defining a mode of creativity through forms such as ekphrasis and an explicit focus on the act of origination. Throughout this work, Peters's self-conscious play with copying, citation, and origination claims convention as a means to write herself both into and against tradition and nation. If both Romantic and pre-Romantic definitions of originality aligned imitation with slavery, and innovation with masculinity, whiteness, and "recognized legal personhood," part of what emerges in Peters's writing and its nineteenth-century reception is an alternate route to national inclusion.[14]

Because so much of my focus in this chapter is on Peters's reception and canonization, including centrally the 1834 biographical sketch by Margaretta Odell that has shaped critical understandings of Peters into the present day,

I devote more time to reading words about Peters than Peters's own words. This is a liability of reception histories generally, and a necessity when thinking about the republication of a pre-national poet in the antebellum era. The paratextual to a large extent trumps the textual, and has a fascinating life of its own. But the paratextual is also an uncomfortable focus to take in relation to this poet in particular, who has always seemed more written about than read, more considered as a specimen of genius than a speaker. In an effort to counterbalance this focus, and also to show that the national claims that later editors made for Peter's authorship existed not just in her biography but in the verse itself, I end the chapter with a reading of Peter's best-known ekphrastic poem, "To S. M., a Young African Painter, on Seeing his Works," which imagines the creative process as a means both to liberation and nationality.

Peters's names are likewise part of her literary and reception history, and it is with that in mind that I chose the married name that she signed herself and that she used to publish her last poems. If Phillis's first name, taken from a slave ship, attests to her status as "no-citizen" and her transits between Africa, America, and Britain, her last name, or the last name which it is critical convention to use, Wheatley, endows her with a false sense of familial belonging that goes against her own choices as an author. The poet signed her first volume with the surname of her white owners, but in her proposal for her second volume, as well as individual published poems and letters to friends in the later part of her life, she used her married name, Phillis Wheatley Peters, or simply Phillis Peters. Her marriage to a free Black man after her return from England was a subject of controversy among her early biographers, as we will see, and it is one of the most obvious legacies of her nineteenth-century editors and critics that the name they reinstated in their re-publications, Wheatley, is the one that is most commonly used today. In this chapter, it is with an awareness of the particular agendas of her nineteenth-century readers, as well as the with deference for the author's own choice, that I revert back to the eighteenth-century Wheatley Peters or Peters. Recently, in *Before Modernism*, Virginia Jackson reflects on her persuasion by attempts to reinstate the name Wheatley Peters, but muses, "literary history has referred to her as 'Phillis Wheatley,' and since this book is about literary history, I have retained that name here. I recognize that as a bad choice. The name dictated by patriarchy is better than the name dictated by slavery, but adding patriarchy to slavery does not solve the problem."[15] In this chapter on Wheatley's nineteenth-century literary history, Wheatley Peters likewise does not solve any problems, but it does draw attention to the construction of the poet as Wheatley, and takes the path of highlighting the multiple allegiances—or perhaps, an absence of allegiances altogether—that Wheatley Peters's antebellum editors and biographers could not accommodate.[16]

JOINING COPIES

In the Rose Library at Emory University, two small and densely composed copybooks from eighteenth-century Boston—the first titled "Joining Copies No. 1"—collect citations of poems and passages from magazines, and carefully numbered or alphabetized lists of moral epigraphs, all in keeping with copybooks' general function as student journals intended to provide both educational and moral instruction (see figure 2). But the second of these two books holds a striking find: a manuscript version of one of Wheatley Peters's poems, "A Hymn to Humanity," with significant textual differences from the slightly earlier print edition, and a full dedication, "To S. P. Galloway Esq., who corrected some Poetic Essays of the Authoress," that does not appear anywhere else. While critics have commented briefly on the variant in this copybook, none have discussed the broader context of the books themselves.[17] In fact, little concrete information is available on the books beyond the basic facts of their acquisition at the Boston Antiquarian Book Fair in 1996, and their original inclusion in the papers of a New York family that was associated with a Boston family—not the Wheatleys—for whom Peters had worked.[18]

Most essentially, the authorship—or collaborative authorship—of the books is unclear. These books' connection to a family for whom Peters had worked, and the full dedication of Peters's poem implies that the copyist, if not Peters herself, was someone who knew her. But the research trail is unclear: Emory's finding aid lists Wheatley Peters as the books' "creator," but the curator who acquired the books, Randall Burkett, notes that they appear to be written in several different hands, and Vincent Carretta, Peters's most recent biographer and editor, judges that the poem is likely not in Peters's handwriting. (Julian Mason, another editor, states more definitively that the poem "is not her handwriting.") The titling of the first book as "Joining Copies," argues for collective authorship, as does a crossed-out register of six names on its inside cover under the heading "List of Scholars in King Street." If the "Scholars" on this list are the pupils who kept the copybook, Wheatley Peters's name

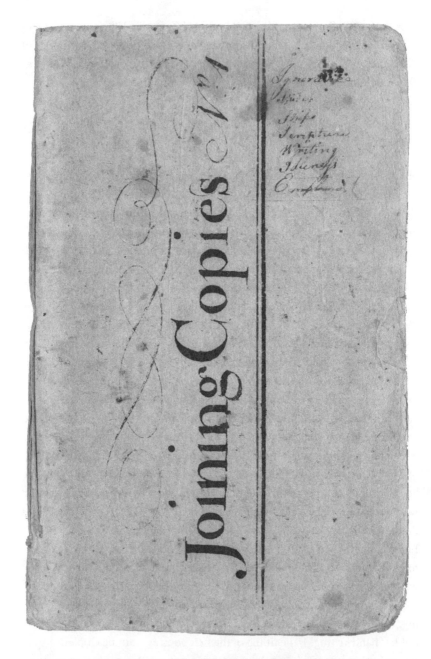

FIGURE 2. "Joining Copies No. 1," small copybook, Phillis Wheatley Papers, Stuart A. Rose Manuscript, Archives, and Rare Book Library at Emory University. Courtesy, Emory University Library.

Phillis Wheatley Peters's Antebellum Remediation 37

is not among them, but Emily Greenwood, in her work on Peters's classicism, considers the books as a "tantalizing clue that Phillis might have had access to more formal education" than homeschooling, because King Street is the same Boston street on which the Wheatleys lived. Randall Burkett suggests that Peters and these "Scholars" may have had the same tutor, the "S. P. Galloway Esq." of her poem's dedication, whose identity is otherwise unknown.[19]

These historical questions aside, the ease with which Peters's work conforms to the conventionalized context of the copybook speaks to the place of the copy and imitation in her canon, while the dedication of "A Hymn to Humanity" to an editor, and the poem's inclusion in these collectively assembled books attests to Peters's participation in pre-national literary networks that guided both the style and the content of her verse. In fact, although Peters's authorship was significant enough in Boston literary circles at the time of the poem's dating that she, alongside of figures such as Shakespeare and Dryden, is one of the books' few signed authors, and its only American, the themes of many of the books' unsigned compositions could be lifted from Peters's other poems. Hymns, elegies, and reflections on letter writing are among the unsigned works in both books, while the first book includes copies from some of Peters's favorite writers, including Pope and Horace, and an ekphrastic poem. Several other passages in this book cite *The Gentleman's Magazine*, where Peters herself published, and in the second book, where Peters's signed poem appears, none of the other works is signed. It's compelling to imagine Peters standing behind the copying or composition of these works, but in the end, the shared cultural context of the copybook also makes any such an imagination feel beside the point.

The shared context of the books is apparent in part through their recurrent common themes. Nationalism is a topic that surfaces in both signed and unattributed poems, and poems in the two copybooks make parallels between political corruption or servitude and slavery, a theme in Peters's own published work.[20] The first poem of the second book, for instance, which appears immediately before Wheatley's "Hymn to Humanity," is titled "The Voice of Freedom," subtitled with the epigraph "By Uniting we stand, by Dividing we fall!" and opens "Americans attend to Freedom's cry! / Who scorns her voice deserves in chains to die" (see figure 3). Vincent Carretta notes that this poem, dated January 1773, is written in the same hand as "Hymn to Humanity," and suggests that if this hand is Peters's, we may have a rare example of an unprinted and previously unattributed poem. This is a compelling possibility, but the difficulty of making this attribution in the collective context of the copybooks, where the repetition of common themes and images dominates over singular authorship, also seems to argue against its ultimate significance.[21]

These networks of composition are an explicit focus of "Hymn to Humanity," the only poem in the two books that we know for certain to be Peters's own. The poem's subject is the descent of Christ to "this dark terrestrial dome," and is not explicitly political, but like "The Voice of Freedom," this poem centers the collective over the individual. In "Hymn to Humanity," the dedication to Galloway is far from merely titular; a direct address to the editor dominates the poem from the fourth stanza, midway through the poem. Galloway's presence supersedes that of Christ in this fourth stanza, which begins with a description of the one figure and ends with an address to the other:

> He wings his Course from Star to Star
> And leaves the bright abode:
> The Virtue did his Charms impart,
> Then *Galloway*! then thy raptur'd Heart,
> Perceiv'd the rushing God!

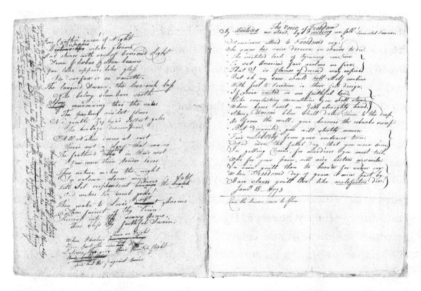

FIGURE 3. "The Voice of Freedom," large copybook, Phillis Wheatley Papers, Stuart A. Rose Manuscript, Archives, and Rare Book Library at Emory University. Courtesy, Emory University Library.

In a poem that ostensibly centers on Christ's sacrifice to humankind, this abrupt shift feels unorthodox, especially given that the last two stanzas devote themselves entirely Galloway's relationship to the speaker. Here, we follow Galloway's "bounteous Hand" commanding the nine muses to "my Song Demand," and prompting the speaker's "grateful Heart." The poem concludes, "Immortal Friendship! Laurel-crown'd, / The smiling Graces all surround / And ev'ry heav'nly Art," making only a weak gesture toward a return to the dominant religious thematic of the first three stanzas. In this context, Randall Burkett's speculation that Galloway was Peters's tutor feels convincing: Galloway stands behind the inspiration of Peters's own "Afric Muse," emphasizing a deeply collaborative form of creation, a "heav'nly Art" that involves terrestrial and divine inspiration as well as the intervention of "Immortal Friendship." And if this editor was also the tutor of the other pupils who had a hand in composing the copybooks, "Hymn to Humanity" functions as a statement of collective gratitude not just for Peters's inspiration, but that of some of the other (anonymous) authors in the manuscript books.

While there are strategic conventions behind Peters, as an enslaved Black woman, positioning her work as not-entirely-her-own, and clear limitations to what forms of authorship she could profess, reading this poem in the context of the copybooks also makes apparent how much her work was part of a broader atmosphere of collective composition. Imitation is a subtext in many of the two copybooks' short passages. A reading of these books reveals what would be true of many such collections of this era: that they often fail to make clear distinction between outright imitation, imitation with adjustment, and new composition. Some copied poems and passages cite their author or place of publication, but most do not; some epigrams are clearly common sayings, while others are more idiosyncratic, the work of particular (uncited) authors. An alphabetized list of epigrams at the end of the first book allows a standard page for each letter, and while many, like, "All is not gold that glitters [sic]" are stock sayings or slight variations on stock sayings, others seem to be individual compositions. Phrases such as, "Be very cautious in all you say and do" bear the mark of a particular author, while epigrams for some of the more obscure letters are obvious constructions made to fit the formal bounds of the book, including tongue-in-cheek phrases for difficult letters such as "X is a letter begins no English word."

Imitation and its merits are also sometimes a more explicit focus in the copybooks' passages. The first book opens with the numbered epigrams

"Rules for Life," the fourteenth of which reads, "Imitate what we see that is amiable in the conduct of others, & shun what is disagreeable. For Mankind judge alike as to good, and bad behavior; in general; & what appears agreeable to us in others, will appear agreeable to others if seen in us." This maxim, which assumes a shared foundation for understanding "good, and bad behavior" that could easily be extended to aesthetics, argues for the imitation of what is "good" with a clear sense that it is the form, rather than authorship or origination that matters. The alphabetized proverbs at the end of the first book likewise echo this philosophy, reading for instance, under "E": "Examples good & great, Labor to imitate"; and then again under "L": "Labor to imitate examples of good and great." Certainly much of the other content of the two copybooks, cited poems and passages from recognized British authors and periodicals, follows these maxims.

Encountering Peters's verse in this context of explicit imitation, and imitation that is purposefully difficult to extricate from idiosyncratic composition, provides a valuable backdrop to reading her work, which has been criticized from the time of its publication to the present day for an imitativeness that was in fact a broader cultural value. In the antebellum period, when abolitionism and literary nationalism converged around Peters's recirculation, this question of imitation became particularly vexed.

NATIONALIST CANONIZATION

In the decade after Wheatley Peters began to be taken up for the abolitionist cause, she appeared in the anthologies that were central to formalizing the place of women writers in a national rubric, and editors' biographical presentations of her work strongly emphasize her Americanness. In Rufus Griswold's *Female Poets of America* (1848), Peters appears famously if obliquely in the general introduction to the volume as a poet who demonstrates that "the muse is no respecter of conditions."[22] In this passage, Griswold taps into the general assumption of American women's middle-class leisure, allowing him to suggest that women poets may be particularly well-positioned "to develop a school of art, original and special" because unlike American men, who "foreign critics" have suggested are "too much devoted to business and politics to feel interest in pursuits which adorn but do not profit," their relative independence from the public and economic sphere grants them more ready access to "genuine poetic sensibility."[23] But exceptions to this gendered rule exist, as he writes: "Several persons are mentioned in this volume whose lives have been no holydays of leisure: those, indeed, who have not in some way been active in practical duties, are exceptions to the common rule. One was a slave—one a domestic servant—one a factory girl: and there are many in the list who had no other time to give to literature but such as was stolen from a frugal and industrious housewifery, from the exhausting cares of teaching, or the fitful repose of sickness."[24] In the kind of neat reversal (or contradiction) that is common in Griswold's writing, Wheatley Peters (and Maria James, and Lucy Larcom) initially stand out as exceptions to the rule of female leisure, but by the end of the passage, come to function more simply as examples of the ways that women writers of all positions compose literature in between their other responsibilities. Rather than an exception, then, the enslaved poet (or the servant, or the factory worker) ultimately provides an image for the fragmentation of female poetic labor. But even this discussion, apparently centered on gender, reflects at least as much on nation, as Griswold writes that the fact that "the muse is no respecter of conditions" is "especially interesting in a country where, though equality is an axiom, it is not a reality."[25]

As throughout his volume, then, nation is paramount to the way that Griswold understands and frames the collected poets, and he closely entwines the particular strengths and weaknesses of the American condition with the advantages and disadvantages of the feminine position to suggest what *The Female Poets of America* can offer to readers. Not surprisingly, then, nation is also an important aspect of the way that he frames Wheatley Peters, through both biographical introduction and poetic selection. Peters, given the anthology's chronological layout, is one of the first poets featured, and although her biography and poetry take up in all only three pages, both elements betray Griswold's focus on nation and on considering the place of even pre-national poetesses in the construction of an American literature. The biography— which takes up two of the pages—begins with the line, "This 'daughter of the murky Senegal,' as she is styled by an admiring contemporary critic, we suppose may be considered as an American, since she was but six years of age when bought to Boston and sold in the slave-market of that city, in 1761."[26]

In this same vein, two of the three poems that Griswold selects for Peters's entry deal explicitly with questions of nation: "On the Death of the Rev. Mr. George Whitefield—1770" and "A Farewell to America." The first of these, an elegy to the Anglican preacher who was an important figure in the first Great

Awakening, celebrates his impact in clearly nationalist terms, noting that "He prayed that grace in every heart might dwell; / He longed to see America excel." The admonition to accept God is similarly geographically loaded: "'Take him, my dear Americans,' he said, / 'Be your complaints on his kind bosom laid: / Take him, ye Africans, he longs for you; Impartial Saviour is his title due;'" reflecting Whitefield's devotion to evangelical revival in America as well as his understanding of African Americans as spiritual equals, who could be converted and saved. Whitefield's later defenses of slavery, and this poem's embrace of America as a site of salvation provide a sense of the particularly conflicted and racialized form of Christian nationalism that runs through many of Peters's other poems, such as for instance "On Being Brought to America."

The other work included in the anthology, "A Farewell to America," is one of Peters's most personal nationalist poems, dedicated to Susanna Wheatley on the occasion of the speaker's travels from New England to London to recover her health. Quietly melancholic, it opens on an image of a New England spring, its "smiling meads" and "flowery plain" distant from both the speaker who finds her "health denied," and Susanna's "tender falling tear, / At sad departure's hour." The movement into "Britannia's distant shore" is celebratory, bringing with it "Health," but also "Temptation," a sentiment that as several critics have noted likely refers not just to London's urban charms, but to the recently passed Mansfield Act, which granted enslaved individuals from the colonies automatic manumission on entry to Britain.[27] Nation matters acutely in these two poems, both as a particularized site of salvation, and as a site that polices the line between slavery and freedom.

The biographical portrait that precedes these two poems is short but draws on several sources, relying for instance both on Peters's contemporary and French translator Abbé Gregoire as well as Margaretta Odell, Peters's antebellum biographer and self-described "collateral descendant" of Susanna Wheatley. Odell's biography of Peters has in more recent criticism been dismissed for its idealization of the Wheatley family, which verges arguably on a patriarchal apology for slavery.[28] Although Odell's biography was the most frequently reproduced text on Peters in the nineteenth century, Griswold anticipates the concerns of current criticism by critiquing Odell's harsh description of Peters's free Black husband as "too proud and too indolent to apply himself to any occupation below his fancied dignity," a stance taken up more recently in Rafia Zafar's statement that "Peters serves as a lightning rod for the prejudices of those who would admire his wife, then and now."[29] Griswold also observes that Odell's account "shows an undue partiality for his [sic] maternal ancestor" and breaks with Odell's convention of using only the Wheatley family surname, which most contemporary critics, even those critical of Odell's account, continue to perpetuate. Griswold instead lists the poet as Phillis Wheatley Peters, the name that she herself used in the letters and publications of her later married life, and that twenty-first century critics such as Zachary Mcleod Hutchins have convincingly argued for adopting as standard practice.[30]

Six years later, the Duyckinck brothers' compendium, *Cyclopedia of American Literature* (1855) expands Peters's profile, including the two nationalist poems in Griswold's anthology, and appending an additional four, all among Wheatley's most patriotic and political works. The tone of the biographical profile is also remarkably nationalist, though staging Peters more clearly as a figure from an older phase of nation-building. Where Griswold refrains from making aesthetic judgments of Peters's work beyond the brief assessment in the first paragraph that "If not so great a poet as the abbé [sic] Gregoire contended, she was certainly a remarkable phenomenon, and her name is entitled to a place in the histories of her race, of her sex, and of our literature," the Duyckincks' aesthetic commentary places Peters firmly within the early nationalist literary framework.[31] After a biographical profile that leans heavily on Odell's (and relies also on Odell's designation of the poet as "Phillis Wheatley") the editors write, "The poems themselves show as marked indications of the feeding-grounds of the readers and imitators of verse in the eighteenth century, as do those of Mistress Anne Bradstreet in the seventeenth."[32] Locating Peters within an American literary context in which "the formal muse of Pope" dominated, she was, they conclude, "a very respectable echo of the Papal strains."[33] She offers, though, something slightly more than a "glowing translation" of neoclassicism, as they suggest in citing two lines from the ekphrastic poem "Niobe in Distress for her Children Slain by Apollo" that "would do honor to any pen" and "are not a translation of anything in Ovid."[34]

The Duyckincks' highlighting of this poem as "not a translation" is remarkable both because it explicitly announces itself as a translation—in fact, a double translation—at the same time as its sources testify to Peters's status as more than a "respectable echo" of Pope's neoclassicism. The poem, subtitled "from Ovid's Metamorphoses, Book VI. and from a view of the Painting of Mr. Richard Wilson," is based both on Ovid's tale and Wilson's early Romantic landscape painting of the myth, which Peters may have seen while in London in the summer of 1773, when she wrote the poem, or more likely, in popular engraved reproductions such as the one by William Wollett.[35] Peters's poem announces itself from the first lines as a third-level reproduction, calling out to the muse "who dids't first th' ideal pencil give, / and taught'st the painter in his works to live." Featuring a dark, windswept landscape, with the relatively small figures of Niobe's children struck down by Apollo's arrows in the foreground, Wilson's painting emphasizes the destructive force of nature before the smaller-scale destruction of the mythical figures becomes legible in the upper lefthand corner. As the Duyckincks emphasize in citing Peters's description of Apollo poised to shoot ("The feather'd vengeance quiv'ring in his hands"), her writing poses the deity in a much more "striking" position than Ovid's telling, emphasizing a dramatic unfolding of events that contrasts with his "business-like" description, in which Apollo "covers the field with the slain in the shortest possible time."[36] Indeed, Peters's narrative poem stresses temporality over its twenty stanzas, documenting the deaths of each of Niobe's fourteen children individually in a manner that contrasts not only with Ovid's myth, but also with Wilson's painting, which instead of a temporal unfolding shows a moment at the height of the myth's action. Further, as Jennifer Thorn notes, Peters's choice of this myth, focused on the punishment of Niobe for gloating about her "large progeny" in relation to the goddess Latona's small family, has a particular resonance in the context of the "anti-reproductivity of the Northern slavery," where, in contrast to Southern slavery, the children of the enslaved held little value for the domestic economy of slaveholders. (Peters's own life was likely shaped by this reality, as she would marry and have children after her manumission).[37]

In this sense, the Duyckincks' choice to highlight this ekphrastic poem, which participates in the paragonal or competitive tradition within ekphrasis by both registering its debt to other sources and proclaiming its ability to surpass them, is part of their effort to frame Peters as an originator, an example of her time but also a suggestion of something more. This positioning of Peters as a little more than just a translator of the classics justifies her inclusion in the anthology of American verse, and her (slight) originality ties implicitly to the Duyckincks' nationalist angle. In this vein, the editors conclude their biography by noting that "the most important" of Wheatley's verses are "the lines to General Washington, in 1775," a judgment that they let stand unjustified, the nationalist theme of the verse and the letter from Washington praising

the "elegant lines" as "striking proof of your poetical talents" strongly suggesting the cause for their significance.[38]

That these antebellum anthologies center on the place of nation in Wheatley Peters's canon is perhaps not surprising, given the focus of the collections overall and Peters's position as a Revolutionary-era poet. But as I will
show in the next section, this framework of nation was equally significant
for the abolitionist editors who recirculated Peters's poems. Specifically, her
self-representation as African American (rather than African, or Afro British), and her exceptionalist claim to American soil as a site of salvation for
enslaved Africans could read in abolitionist contexts as an argument for the
manumission of slaves within the US, at a time when the more popular and
more conservative colonization movement supported the relocation of former slaves to a West African territory. In the context of antebellum abolitionism, then, Peters's proclamation of a strong national allegiance, as well as her
biographical decision to return to America in spite of the lures of a possible
British manumission, could read as a politically progressive argument for
the establishment of a free African American culture in the context of US
national belonging.

ABOLITIONIST REPRINTINGS

It seems Wheatley Peters's fate, a fate that she shares with many African
American and women writers, to always exist on the verge of historical forgetting and continuous historical rediscovery. This is the erasure "in plain sight"
that Alex Socarides has identified as a characteristic of nineteenth-century
American women's verse, and her argument that "because of this poetry's
widespread embrace of certain conventions, it was always-already both
everywhere and nowhere" applies equally well to Peters, who critics began
identifying as a representative of a distant time only a few decades after her
death.[39] The narrative of recovery, in other words, was as much present in the
nineteenth century as in our own time, and was then, as now, misleading. In
her 1834 "memoir" of Peters, Margaretta Odell already frames Peters's cultural
significance as lost, or at least maintained only through an antiquated back-
wards glance: "Here and there, we find a solitary pilgrim, belonging to the
days of the years that are gone, treasuring Phillis's poems as a precious relic."[40]
In the same vein, figures such as abolitionist and women's rights activist Lydia

Maria Child insistently placed Peters in the context of her own time rather than the antebellum cultural milieu, concluding that it would "be absurd to put Phillis Wheatley in competition with . . . modern writers; but her productions certainly appear very respectable in comparison with most of the poetry of the day."[41] Given the common antebellum understanding of most neoclassical and early national verse as stilted and imitative, this assessment is faint praise—but it is also, like Odell's analysis, somewhat misrepresentative.

At the opening of the 1830s, it had been almost fifteen years since the last American edition Peters's poetry, but her verse had never really gone out of circulation, and by the time that both Odell and Child were writing, she had already been picked up for republication by a new generation of progressive abolitionists, who were committed to the integration of former slaves within the American landscape, rather than their emigration to distant settlements such as Liberia. The first nineteenth-century reprinting of Peters's poems appeared in 1801, when they were appended to an English translation of a French abolitionist novel by Joseph Lavallée. In 1814 they were printed at the end of Olaudah Equino's *Interesting Narrative*, in what Max Cavitch notes was perhaps the first material attempt to establish a lineage of Afro British writers, a tradition that critics had argued for since the late eighteenth century.[42] Later in the nineteenth century, the framework for reprinting was more often in the US context, and abolitionist American periodicals took up Peters's work on repeated occasions. In 1827, *Freedom's Journal*, the first African American owned and operated newspaper, published three biographical sketches of Peters and two of her poems. Then in 1832, William Lloyd Garrison and George Knapp printed most of Peters's previously published poems serially in the abolitionist newspaper *The Liberator*, alongside of prominent contemporary writers such as Hannah Gould, Lydia Sigourney, and John Greenleaf Whittier. Within ten months, thirty-seven of Wheatley's poems would appear in the newspaper in support of the incorporationist logic of the new abolitionist movement.[43]

Several republications of Wheatley Peters's poems in book form followed in the course of the 1830s, inspired perhaps by *The Liberator*'s spotlight. George Light's 1834 edition reprinted all of the works from *Poems on Various Subjects* and was the first to include Margaretta Odell's "Memoir" of Peters. Another edition of this work appeared the following year, identical except for the inclusion of Wheatley Peters's correspondence with George Washington and the poem that she dedicated to him, which the Duyckincks would go on to declare her "most important" verse. *The Liberator* promoted both editions as "anti-slavery" publications, and advertised them alongside of works by John Greenleaf Whittier, Child, and Garrison. In 1838, Isaac Knapp, William Garrison's collaborator on *The Liberator*, printed an edition that brought together Peters's work with that of the then-living enslaved poet George Moses Horton. This juxtaposition, and the titling of the work as "Memoir and Poems of Phillis Wheatley, a Native African and a Slave. Also, Poems by a Slave" speaks to the editor's sense of her relevance to antebellum causes, as well as the recognition-value of her name in relation to Horton's.

As with *The Liberator*'s decision to serialize Peters alongside of well-known white abolitionists, the decision to reprint her in tandem with Horton canonizes her retroactively as a nineteenth-century American writer. As Max Cavitch notes, incorporationist abolitionists like Knapp reprinted writers like Peters with white, abolitionist-leaning readers in mind, "who wanted assurances of the potential for social and intellectual elevation among black Americans."[44] In Peters's case, her self-styling, as Vincent Carretta puts it, as "a proto-national American muse" can only have been an advantage.[45] Her willingness to speak to national subjects not only transformed her to a spokesperson for a version of abolition centered on citizenship, but also brought her into a canon of nineteenth-century American writers who understood the anti-slavery movement and patriotism as aligned. At roughly the same time that Rufus Griswold, Caroline May, and the Duyckinck brothers were placing Wheatley Peters near the beginning of their lineages of American women writers, the Black abolitionist author and educator William Allen, in a much more limited 1849 edition, once again paired Peters and Horton, with the more explicit aim of creating a Black American literary lineage; as he writes, "What [the African] is capable of becoming, the past clearly evinces."[46] George Moses Horton, who published his poetry with the stated aim of raising money for his emigration to Liberia, paired in some ways oddly with Peters's insistent nationalism, but not more oddly than Lydia Sigourney or Lucy Larcom. Horton's legacy, like Peters's, is weighted with firsts—first African American to publish a book in the US, first enslaved American to publish a book—and although neither poet benefited from the rights of national belonging, the authority of nation unquestionably defined the circumscriptions of their lives, and the editions of the 1830s and 1840s represent the first attempt to understand both through an African American lineage.

ODELL'S WHEATLEY

The memoir by Margaretta Odell was a central component to framing Peters's national and nationalist credentials, although it is most frequently discussed in recent criticism for its ubiquity and unreliability. It appears in the introductions to most of Peters's recirculations from the 1830s on, or else is heavily cited, acknowledged or not, in the paratextual material. As Jennifer Young writes in her survey of Peters's antebellum reception, "this apocryphal biography would later be accepted as fact by subsequent authors."[47] So much so that it circulated independently of (and more frequently than) Peters's verse itself, as for instance in the profile in the 1846 biographical collection *Intelligent Negros*, and in B. B. Thatcher's 1834 "memoir" of Peters geared toward young readers, both of which lean heavily on Odell's dates and anecdotes, without acknowledging their source.[48] We might say that the publication of Odell's memoir in 1834 marked the beginning of the period in which Peters as a biographical figure overtook (or more fully overtook) Peters as a poet to be read.

If it is with Odell's narrative that Peters became what editors had been trying to make her since the beginning of the nineteenth century, a link in a lineage, it is worth taking the time to consider what this narrative had to say. Griswold was ahead of his time in critiquing Odell's account for its biases and allegiances to the Wheatley family, but for most nineteenth-century editors, this proximity seemed to offer evidence of an emotional, if not a strictly factual truth. Today, Odell's account is difficult to gloss uncritically, and although published in an abolitionist context, its defenses of the Wheatley family often read as a paternalistic apology for slavery in its domestic forms. Additionally, as Vincent Carretta points out, the biography is riddled with factual errors and clear aberrations from even the scant historical record. At the same time, a close reading of Odell's framework can offer insights into the canonization of women writers as a part of social history. Cara Glatt, while acknowledging both the text's factual errors and its biases, has recently uncovered compelling historical context for the privileging of the Wheatley family, in particular its female members, in Odell's writing. Odell never published anything beyond her account of Wheatley Peters, and not much is known about her life, but as Glatt uncovers, she spent her last decades, from 1847 to 1881, in a private asylum specializing in "those complicated nervous affections, in which females are peculiar sufferers." Odell's uncle petitioned for her institutionalization as "mentally incompetent," less than five months after he had made a similar petition for his sixty-two-year-old sister, an aunt to whom Odell was particularly close, and who would also spend the rest of her life in guardianship. In this context, Glatt asserts that "Odell, the evidence leads one to suspect, had fallen victim, not to what we would today consider clinical insanity, but to both a psychiatric regime prone to pathologizing female emotion and a social order with limited space for unattached women."[49] Even though the institutionalizations took place after Odell's writing, they can offer a perspective on the general climate for her work and inspire a reading of the positive portrayal of the Wheatley family women as a matriarchically "reimagined version of the nineteenth-century domestic ideal," rather than an apology for slavery.[50] Odell's version of Peters, bought by Susanna and taught to read by her daughter, is a matrilineal genius, saved, educated, and promoted by women. The biography, in other words, might argue all too insistently for the innocence of white women, without necessarily arguing for the innocence of all slaveholders.

This reevaluation suggests that there are other ways to read Odell than as just a bad biographer, although she undoubtedly also was that. In this spirit I focus on the memoir's entanglement of family and nation as instrumental to the later framing of Peters as an American writer. Odell's nationalist framework, in spite of its abolitionist context, relies on eliding or at least underplaying race, suggesting the conflicted relationship between Blackness and citizenship even within the incorporationist abolitionist community. George Light's short editorial introduction to the 1834 volume in which the memoir first appeared introduces some of these conflicts. Light presents Peters as a fruitful example for the abolitionist cause at least in part because of the way that her publications overlap with the war for American independence, noting that she was "sold and bought like a beast in the market . . . in the same land where, shortly after, the people rose in their indignation against oppression, and asserted . . . that 'All men are born free and equal.'"[51] "How," he asks, "can a free people be a slave-holding people?" and concludes the introduction by anticipating that, thanks to the abolitionist movement, one day "the African shall be as the American, and the black man as the white."[52] That this statement of racial equality is also one of transnational and transcontinental equality is significant, but so, too, is his choice to equate, rather than conflate, both categories. Although Light argues for African equality, he stops short of anticipating an African American identity or national belonging, a hesitation that also makes itself felt in Odell's representation of race, family, and nation.

If African and North American constitute for the editor separate but equal categories, for Odell both race and nation are equally important, but more clearly conflicted categories. Presenting herself as a "collateral," or indirect, descendant of Susanna Wheatley, Odell relies centrally on the trope of family to discuss both race and nation. In her description of Peters's place within the Wheatley home, Odell consistently reiterates the familial nature of the bond: she "was to [Susanna] as a daughter" and "she had a child's place in [the Wheatleys'] house and in their hearts."[53] But this familial status comes at the cost of other kinds of bonds. As Odell explains, when the family becomes aware of Peters's intellectual precocity, "She was not devoted to menial occupations, as was at first intended; nor was she allowed to associate with other domestics of the family, who were of her own color and condition, but was kept constantly about the person of her mistress."[54] While this proximity is framed as a privilege, it is not difficult to imagine how it might have been experienced differently. Odell relates, for instance, an occasion in which Susanna Wheatley, looking out the window to see Peters returning by carriage from a visit, sees the carriage driver, "also an African and a slave" sitting on the same seat as her. Later, this driver "received a reprimand for forgetting the dignity . . . attached to the sable person of 'my Phillis.'"[55] Susanna Wheatley's claim to Peters "as a daughter" comes with a double price: the loss of both Peters's biological family, which Odell writes that "she does not seem to have preserved any remembrance of," and her separation from those "of her color and condition."[56] As Mary Louise Kete puts it, "the Wheatleys considered her a special kind of object: less functional than decorative, almost but not quite family. They had made her that way."[57]

In Odell's account of the years leading up to the Revolutionary War and immediately thereafter, personal familial ties and national ones conflate as Odell frames conflicting allegiances on both sides as the source of Peters's difficulties in the last years of her life. Peters returns, Odell recounts, from England to attend to Susanna Wheatley's deathbed in 1774, and the deaths of Susanna's husband and daughter soon follow, leaving Peters "utterly desolate" and alone, "a strange change to one who had enjoyed . . . the happiness of a fireside where a well regulated family were accustomed to gather."[58] The dissolution of what Odell frames as Peters's domestic family coincides with "the troubles with the mother country," a time during which "every home was darkened, and every heart was sad." This period of dissolution is also one of another type of union, or as Odell puts it, "At this period of destitution, Phillis received an offer of marriage."[59] Odell's overwhelmingly negative

Phillis Wheatley Peters's Antebellum Remediation   51

portrayal of John Peters, Phillis's husband, is a story in and of itself, and one that as Rafia Zafar notes, is part of a long tradition of racist double standards against Black men.[60] (It is also one of the elements of Odell's memoir that has remained unquestioned the longest, and that lives on in the common elision of her married name). Odell describes John Peters as "utterly unworthy of the distinguished woman who honored him by her alliance," in contrast to the remaining relatives of the white Wheatley family, who in the last years of her life, witnessed and attempted to compensate for the failures of her "negligent husband" to provide in the post-Revolutionary period.[61] The conflict between what Odell frames as Peters's true family and its usurper comes to a head in the statement that "we never heard Phillis named, or alluded to, by any other appellation than that of 'Phillis Wheatley,'" a statement which overlooks Peters's own use of her married name in her correspondence and in her efforts to secure the publication of her second volume.[62] But reinscribing Phillis as a Wheatley rather than a Peters has the effect of prioritizing her white lineage, or pseudo-lineage, a seemingly strange move in an abolitionist document.

It is precisely this kind of reinscription and prioritization that critics today justifiably take issue with in Odell's account: its boosterism of the white Wheatley family, its trivialization of slavery through an emphasis on affective ties, and its stress on the difficulties of Peters's later years as neatly coinciding with her freedom from enslavement in the Wheatley home. But much as Cara Glatt's recovery of Odell's institutionalization puts a wrinkle in this critique, I would propose here that we (also) read this clearly biased biography through the lens of nationalism. Odell's focus on American history and literary history is an aspect of the account that critics generally overlook, but it dominates the conclusion of her biography, as the last difficult decade of Peters's life overlaps with the more general hardship of the Revolutionary War. What if we read Odell's memoir, focused on the Revolutionary era and written during a period of general cultural nationalism, as at least in part a tool for framing Peters's place in a national canon? Such a reading does not in any way redeem the biography, but it does shed light on Odell's whitewashing of Peters as logically motivated beyond an apology for slavery.

By the end of her brief text, Odell has presented Peters's place in America, and in American literary history, as aligned with her place in the white Wheatley family. Calling America "that country which was hers by adoption, or rather compulsion," Odell echoes the structure of privileges and obligations that she has outlined in relation to Peters's place within the Wheatley home. And Peters's "adoption" within this country brings with it another privilege, or obligation: that of being a first, not in an African American literary lineage, as she is often hailed, but in an American lineage of knowledge in any form. As Odell writes near the end of her memoir, in Peters's time, "We had no philosophers, no historians, no poets, and our statesmen . . . had not then breathed forth those mighty energies which girded the warrior for battle and nerved the hearts of a whole people as the heart of one man." Only with the Revolution, she continues, did the "spirit of Liberty" breathe "upon our sleeping nation, awakening the genius of the people to appear from time to time in a thousand new and multiplying forms of ever-varying beauty."[63] In conflating the nationalist war and culture, Odell places Peters at the very beginning of a lineage of American knowledge production, an adopted, or coerced, family member whose race ends by signifying much less than her nationality, or perhaps more properly, who becomes white in order to become American.

In this way, Odell avoids the kind of separate-but-equal rhetoric of George Light's introduction, which anticipates a moment in which "the African shall be as the American, and the black man as the white" but she does so by taking Peters's race out of the equation entirely. If races and nations in Odell's telling are both families, it seems that you need to choose your side, or have your side chosen for you. This perspective speaks in part to the conflicts of the abolitionist movement from which Odell was writing, in which incorporationist abolitionists such as the editors reprinting Wheatley's poems argued against both slavery and colonization. In this sense, claiming Wheatley as American had a significant and unspoken political agenda. This nationalist telling goes against the basic outlines of her life, and against Gilroy's more networked understanding of the Black Atlantic, both in modernity and its prehistories. But it is a useful reminder, if we need such a reminder, that the pressures to think nation as one entity also often comes with a similar pressure on the idea of race. Odell claims citizenship for Peters, but it is a form of citizenship not at odds with Christina Sharpe's assertion that "we live in the knowledge that the wake has positioned us as no-citizen."[64]

RACIAL AND NATIONAL MEMORY

If the conflation of family and nation is central to Odell's incorporation of Peters into American literary history, her equally insistent focus on memory, and through it imitation and originality, is key to her presentation of Peters as an African American woman writer. Odell, as I have shown, consistently underplays Peters's race to claim her national identity, and in this same vein the biographer's struggles with the issue of Peters's (faulty) memory is the nexus for a range of unarticulated cultural anxieties about race and gender in artistic production. These preoccupations emerge within the first few pages of the sketch, immediately following Odell's account of Peters's arrival in Boston and purchase into the Wheatley family, when she notes that Peters "does not seem to have preserved any remembrance of the place of her nativity, or of her parents, excepting the simple circumstance that her mother *poured out water before the sun at his rising*—in reference, no doubt to an ancient African custom."[65] Odell does not disguise her concern that this image is Peters's sole memory, musing that most children have many more memories from before the age of seven, and returns to this gap repeatedly, a preoccupation that implicitly ties in to the intellectual responsibility that Peters's text bears, in the words of one editor, as "an unvarnished record of African genius."[66]

On the one hand, I would argue, the description of Peters's early memory as faulty is essential to Odell's narrative in the same way as her description of Peters "as a daughter" to Susanna Wheatley: it allows for a more complete presentation of Peters as American, rather than African or even African American. A lapse in memory facilitates Odell's presentation of Peters as the beginning of a national intellectual history, even as it also threatens to undermine this status. Odell navigates this paradox with the suggestion of a traumatic block. The period between Peters's capture and her transport to Boston, she writes, "was, no doubt, a long one; and filled, as it must have been, with various degrees and kinds of suffering," which "might naturally enough obliterate the recollection of earlier and happier days."[67] This trauma, neatly lodged between Phillis's two "families," rather than extending into her time in the US, is the block that allows for her full "adoption" as American, and that obliterates her past, emotionally, linguistically, and culturally, leaving her genius unchallenged. In fact, as Odell emphasizes in the next paragraph, in the next years "the development of [Peters's] mind realized the promise of her childhood."[68]

On the other hand, though, the issue of memory is vexed given the weight that Peters's text is asked to bear as evidence of "African genius." The issue of memory comes up explicitly again in the context of Peters's poetic practices, as Odell reflects that because Peters "did not seem to have the power of retaining the creations of her own fancy, for a long time, in her own mind,"

Susanna Wheatley allowed a light to be placed at her bedside so that "she might . . . secure the swift-winged fancy" in the course of the night.[69] "It has been suggested," Odell continues, "that memory was in fault in this instance" but "we cannot suppose that Phillis could have made such rapid progress in various branches of knowledge, if she had not possessed a retentive memory."[70] Odell ends, then, by crediting a "peculiar structure of mind—possibly to its activity—perhaps occasioned by lack of early discipline" and stressing again that "this singularity . . . affected her own thoughts only, and not the impressions made upon her mind by the thoughts of others."[71]

This visitation by "fancy" is perfectly in line with both eighteenth-century and early nineteenth-century understandings of poetic composition, which placed authors at some remove from their own compositions. The idea of poetic composition as dream was one that gained wider currency in the years between Peters's initial publication and the publication of Odell's memoir, illustrated perhaps most famously by the composition of Kubla Khan in 1797 and its publication in 1816. Odell's use of the term "fancy," though, displaces any notion of Romantic genius that this image could conjure. As Julie Ellison has shown, by the end of the eighteenth century, Fancy had metamorphosed from its role as "the feminine personification of poetic inspiration" to the much more prosaic position as an "inferior but therapeutic faculty" responsible for "associating, collecting, combining, embellishing, mixing"; in other words, it had moved from creating to adapting.[72] This association of Fancy with characteristics such as mimicry and hybridity coincided, as Eliza Richards argues, with the devaluation of women poets in the antebellum period through similar terms.[73] Fittingly, one of the three poems that Rufus Griswold chooses to include in his entry on Peters in *The Female Poets of America* (1849) is "Fancy: from a Poem on the Imagination," which describes the transformation of a winter landscape into spring through the imagination, an imagination that nonetheless falls short of novel creation.[74] Odell's account of Peters recording her "fancy" before it slips away likewise exists tenuously between notions of Romantic genius and denigratingly feminized imitation.

This confused signification is not surprising given the dueling associations of memory itself. On the one hand, memory is the capacity that proves Peters's ownership of the intellectual labor of her poems. Critics have made much of the prefatory letter "To the Publick" in the 1773 edition of her poems, signed by eighteen eminent (white, male) Bostonian citizens, including Founding Father John Hancock and Governor Thomas Hutchinson, and attesting that "[Peters] has been examined by some of the best judges, and is thought qualified to write [her poems]."[75] Henry Louis Gates, who in his *The Trials of Phillis Wheatley* (2003) attempts to reconstruct what this examination might have looked like, muses "We have no transcript of the exchanges that occurred between Miss Wheatley and her eighteen examiners. . . . Was she perhaps asked for an extemporaneous demonstration of her talent? What we do know is that she passed with flying colors."[76] Although Joanna Brooks has persuasively argued, based on meeting records and epistolary evidence, that it is highly unlikely that any in-person examination took place in politically preoccupied pre-Revolutionary Boston, the idea of a "trial," and memory's role in such a trial, has had a hold on the literary critical imagination in a way that resonates with Odell's anxious reflections on what Peters remembers and what she does not.[77]

Memory, like the question of imitation, was a complex component in Peters's reception long before Odell's memoir. It was central to Thomas Jefferson's infamous evaluation of her work in *Notes on the State of Virginia* (1785), where he in a much-quoted passage declares that "Religion indeed has produced a Phyllis Whately [*sic*]; but it could not produce a poet. The compositions published under her name are below the dignity of criticism."[78] He leads into this statement with a more general reflection on the intellectual capabilities of the races, exemplifying Peters's status as a litmus test for Black potentiality from the early years of her reception. As he begins: "Comparing [Blacks] by their faculties of memory, reason, and imagination, it appears to me, that in memory they are equal to the whites; in reason much inferior, as I think one could scarcely be found capable of tracing and comprehending the investigations of Euclid; and that in imagination they are dull, tasteless, and anomalous."[79] Peters, for Jefferson, exemplifies this failure of imagination through her verse, but presumably did have the capacity to remember, and from this memory to imitate. This early critique of Peters, then, highlights the way that good memory, in the racialized subject, can be construed as a creative limitation that converges with the idea of imitativeness, even as it paradoxically is a necessary asset to proving creative ownership.

Odell's reflection on the "singularity" of Peters's memory-lapses may reflect back on this Jeffersonian understanding of the African's mnemonic skill, and in stressing her difference from this convention, Odell anchors Peters more clearly in the early nineteenth century's nationalist demands for literary composition. At one point, surveying the range of Peters's topics, Odell notes that even in her political poems, she does not write as one "who had been trained to note the events of nations, by a course of historical studies, but one whose habits, taste and opinions, were peculiarly her own; for in Phillis we have an example of originality of no ordinary character. She was allowed, and even encouraged, to follow the leading of her own genius; but nothing was forced upon her, nothing suggested, or placed before her as a lure; her literary efforts were altogether the natural workings of her own mind."[80] Here the assertion of "originality" clearly stands in as a defense for the idea that she was responsible, and solely responsible, for her own compositions, at the same time as the presence of "genius" places her writing beyond the framework of "fancy" that appears earlier in the biography.

Odell's emphasis on Peters's "own . . . habits, taste and opinions" and "her own mind" emphasizes a liberal subjectivity that would have been foreign to an enslaved subject who did not truly possess her body, much less the productions of her mind. Similarly, that which Odell frames as Peters's lapses of memory, both in relation to her early history and her poetic composition, gets the biography into something of a double bind. The sketch of Peters is stuck between the conventional imagination of poetic composition as a gift from the muse, and the demand, in the case of racialized writers, that they extend evidence of their intellectually ability to produce their own compositions. Memory becomes a treacherous subject when the period's poetic convention sees the writer as a mere vehicle, but the political demands of abolitionism require embodied and particularized authorship.

Odell navigates around this bind with a both/and solution, framing Peters's memory as alternately good and bad, intellectually robust, but weak in regards to her own history, placing her within an eternal present of American belonging. At the same time, Odell's use of the term "originality" positions Peters's poetry within the cultural nationalist moment. This era's concern with intellectual property is pressing in relation to conflicts around international copyright and the development of an American cultural canon, but even more so in relation to enslaved authors like Peters, who were reprinted as arguments for self-ownership. In this light, Odell notably hedges around the topic of Peters's manumission, writing that she is unsure if Peters ever really did gain legal independence—she did—a hedging that aligns with the need to place Peters consistently within the white family, and to perpetuate an understanding of her writing as not quite her own, but very certainly and fully America's.

This issue of who can claim Peters, and to what end, has dogged criticism into the present day. As Henry Louis Gates notes, Peters fell out of favor already by the late nineteenth century among the forefathers of Black nationalism, a decline that continued throughout the twentieth century. And the substance of the critique of Peters in more contemporary work resonates strikingly with the old, highly racialized and gendered Jeffersonian complaint: imitativeness. The idea of Peters as too derivative, too neoclassical, too stilted, drowns out even critique of the substance of her work, the idea (based largely on the single short and frequently-anthologized "On Being Brought from Africa to America") that she is an apologist for slavery. Critics such as John Shields and Vincent Carretta have convincingly shown Peters's abolitionist stance across a range of poems, but the idea of her stylistic failures is harder to shake. Contemporary critics are often as hedging in their assessments of Peters as Odell was in 1834, anxious to claim her work and to renounce what fails to conform to hopes and expectations. But Peters confronts all the terms of what would become her stylistic critique in the poetry itself, and her self-presentation is much more bold and uncompromising than any of these assessments would lead us to believe.

WHEATLEY'S EKPHRASIS

As Odell points out in her *Memoir*, and Virginia Jackson has examined at length in *Before Modernism*, Peters herself closely considers memory in her first published poem, "On Recollection." This poem, structured as an invocation to Mnemosyne, the goddess of memory, alternately celebrates recollection as "Sweeter than music to the ravish'd ear" and denigrates it as the "worst tortures that our souls can know," as pleasant in the end only as its subjects have been virtuous. Memory does not carry the intellectual ambiguities that the term held in Peters's own biography; in "On Recollection," memory is only as good as its content, and has no virtue as an ability in and of itself. At the same time, the poem's actual memory is strangely contentless, and as Jackson writes, although the poem opens with a call "to help [the speaker] describe the act of remembering . . . no personal recollections surface in this poem."[81] In the end, the poem is a record of the effects of recollection—generically positive or generically negative—on its subjects, rather than a description of any particularized memory by any particular subjects. Nonetheless, John Shields has argued that in this poem, the "ostensibly sweeping prospect actually bespeaks an intensely personal experience," that is, the transnational horrors of slavery that we know Peters as a historical subject experienced.[82]

Jackson argues for understanding moves like Shields's as "screen memory" and part of "the long history of lyric readings of Wheatley—the long history of making up stories that connect her memory to her experience and her experience to her poetry and her poetry to a representative, feminized 'speaker,'" proposing instead to understand her work as a part of a "collective, undefined, and unfinished history."[83] For Jackson, it is movements such as Peters's fluctuation in "On Recollection" between apparent personal revelation and actual evasion that make eighteenth- and nineteenth-century Black poets early links in the lineage of "the alienated modern lyric subject." Peters offers a prime case study for the connection between the censorships and necessary elisions of writing under slavery, in which (in the words of M. A. Richmond), "what is left unsaid is more significant than what is said" and the subtexts and allusions of "*all* (lyricized) poetry for the past two hundred and fifty years."[84]

Jackson's critique of reading Peters's poetics through "screen memory" is not just that such a memory is a critical manufacture, but that it is, in the Freudian sense, "a less threatening memory" that the unconscious creates to repress a greater pain. "If history," as she writes, "can be narrated as the story of a person, it can be contained and perhaps redeemed," and thereby the appeal of reading "On Recollection" as a personal reflection is that it offers the facile possibility of undoing the singular horror that it (apparently) narrates.[85] Without this possibility, without the poem as a record of individual experience, the readings of Peters that remain are confoundingly abstract, impersonally moralistic, or at most—as Odell might add—the voided result of a traumatic block.

What resonates for me in Jackson's approach is not primarily the broad narrative for the history of the lyric that it offers, but the way that the impersonal as Jackson formulates it lends itself to readings of ekphrasis as a general mode, and to readings of Peters's ekphrastic practice in particular. In her effort to move outside of a critical reading of Peters's verse through personal experience and memory, Jackson turns to Toni Morrison's concept of Black collective "rememory" as first articulated in *Beloved* by Sethe, significantly (as Jackson formulates it) "a literary character in a volume of historical fiction," who muses: "If a house burns down, it's gone, but the house—the picture of it—stays, and not just in my rememory, but out there in the world. What I remember is a picture floating around out there outside my head."[86] This idea of a collective historical memory as an image "out there in the world," accessible in different ways to different subjects, resonates with W. J. T. Mitchell's framing of ekphrasis as a "triangular relationship . . . in which the relations of self and other, text and image, are triply inscribed" or Rancière's understanding of a "third thing that is owned by no one, whose meaning is owned by no one, but which subsists between them."[87] In "On Recollection," the speaker's concern is not any memory, shared or particular, but rather memory as a universal function, the effect that the experience of memory has on a range of subjects. The poem, then, is a kind of ekphrasis of ekphrasis, concerned with affect and experience rather than image description. And this is striking, because even first-level image description, as both Morrison's "rememory" and Rancière's "third thing" imply, is a means of stepping outside of the bounded self. In Peters's poem, that self has already been left behind.

The generalized experience of "On Recollection" may have been a safer place to dwell for an enslaved poet, or just a more possible one. It may be feasible to consider, as Morrison does through "rememory," the collective consciousness of a formerly enslaved population, but to attempt to find a collective imagination in Peters's disparate audience—a collective that encompassed both her own experience and that of her primarily white readers of varying persuasions—would be a daunting project. To an extent, as I have been arguing in this chapter, the idea of America came to take that impossible place, both in Peters's verse and in her later nineteenth-century reception.

With such collective spaces in mind, I would like to turn in these last pages of the chapter to Peters's best-known ekphrastic poem, which also dwells primarily in affect rather than any specific image, shared or particular. In "To S. M., a Young African Painter on Seeing his Works," the speaker addresses Scipio Moorhead, an enslaved Boston artist who scholars have speculated may have painted the portrait of Peters that was copied as an engraving for the frontispiece of her 1773 collection, and then as a lithograph in the 1834 edition. Like Peters herself, the portrait represents a series of firsts: first independent portrait of an African American woman, first American portrait of a woman writing, first frontispiece depicting a woman writer in American history. The portrait, requested by publishers as evidence of her identity, depicts a young African American woman in profile, seated at a desk and writing on a loose leaf of paper, looking off into the distance. The seated posture and abstracted gaze are reminiscent of the style of Bostonian portrait painter John Singleton Copley, but the inclusion of quill and paper was a radical gesture in a portrait of a woman, especially a Black woman. Nonetheless, as Mary Louise Kete writes, the portrait as engraved in the 1773 edition of the book emphasizes the poet's objectification, her body depicted as a painting within an oval frame, the words "Phillis Wheatley, Negro Servant to Mr. John Wheatley of Boston," running around its periphery. The less-commonly reprinted lithograph from the 1834 edition loosens these confines a little: while the image still exists alongside of the same statement of attribution to her owner, there is no frame around her image, suggesting that the book grants access to a person rather than an object, a suggestion that this edition heightens with the inclusion of Odell's biography (see figure 4).

The connection of Peters's portrait to Moorhead is compelling but tenuous, and her poem does little to clarify the relationship. None of Moorhead's work survives, and no contemporary records link Moorhead to the portrait, but Peters did have an acquaintance with both Moorhead and his enslavers. In addition to "To S. M.," textual evidence for this acquaintance exists in the first poem that Peters published after her emancipation, an elegy for Scipio's owner John, whose death resulted in the sale of the enslaved artist by John's wife, and Scipio's disappearance from the historical record.[88] But if we had hoped to find in Peters's "To S. M." more concrete insight into Moorhead's work, her own portrait or otherwise, we would be disappointed. Instead the poem works within the *ut pictura poesis* or sister arts tradition, offering a reflection on the act of creation in which the terms for visual art and poetry increasingly entwine. The general progression of the two stanzas, eighteen and sixteen lines respectively, is to focus first on the act of creation, and then on the artists' creative and spiritual afterlives, as the poem's direct address to the painter gradually opens up to a collective artistic "we." The poem sets up a series of apparent opposites or distinct categories—painting and poetry, day and night, life and death—that its language works to undo. Beneath these apparent opposites are others—Africa and America, enslaved and free—that hinge subtly on the double-meaning of key terms, and that culminate in a more radical vision of Moorhead and Peters as both African and American, both spiritually and materially free.

In a general sense, the poem fulfills what Elizabeth Loizeaux considers as two of the central aims of African American ekphrasis: that of making "present in the cultural arena images of and by black people" and of "identify[ing] artists and, via description and praise, bring[ing] them to view and claim[ing] their importance."[89] In "To S. M.," Loizeaux writes, Peters "allied her poetic efforts in mutual support with those of Scipio Moorehead,"[90] so much so, I would argue, that the roles of poet and painter become difficult to distinguish. The title of the poem implies a direct address to the painter, but from the first lines, this address is flexible, and the language used to describe the addressee's process of creation conforms to poetry as well as to painting. As the poem opens: "To show the lab'ring bosom's deep intent, / And thought in living characters to paint, / When first thy pencil did those beauties give, / And breathing figures learnt from thee to live." "[C]haracters" and "pencils" are the tools of literature as much as the visual arts, and it is only the conclusion of the sentence that establishes the scene more firmly as a visual image: "How did those prospects give my soul delight, / A new creation rushing on my sight?" With this "my," the speaker places themself in the scene of the poem from its beginning, and in the next lines, speaker and object, poetry and painting further interconnect, with the exclamation "[. . .] may the painter's and the poet's fire / To aid thy pencil, and thy verse conspire!" The "thy" here is ambiguous: following the logic of the title, it would seem refer to Moorhead, but it in fact opens up to include both painter and poet, both Moorhead and poetic speaker, in a scene of mutual inspiration. This interrelation between poetry and painting creates a collective space of creativity, in which the speaker's many encouragements to the painter ("And may the charms of each seraphic theme / Conduct thy footsteps to immortal fame!") function equally as encouragements to their own verse.

With this literary and visual entanglement in mind, James Ford proposes that Moorhead's portrait of Peters in fact records a moment of mutual composition and inspiration: that as Moorhead paints Peters, she, contemplatively looking off into the distance at one of his paintings, composes "To S. M." This proposal is based in large part on Peters's pose in the portrait, seated at a writing desk with a pen in her hand, and performs the literal critical effort of placing a physical body into Peters's disembodied verse, the kind of move, common in Peters's criticism, that Virginia Jackson might consider an attempt to personalize the purposefully impersonal. But the imagination of the portrait and the poem as a double gaze is compelling based on the focus of "To S. M." Framing the poem as "both an instance of and theorization of" Black Ekphrasis, a tradition that draws attention to, in Carl Plasa's words, "the rich alternative field of vision that the black gaze opens up," Ford's reading resonates with the intertwining of literary and visual arts in the poem's first stanza, and the focus on the process of inspiration over any specific scene.[91] Further,

FIGURE 4. "Frontispiece," *Memoir and Poems of Phillis Wheatley, a Native African and a Slave. Dedicated to the Friends of the Africans* (Boston: Geo. W. Light, 1834). Courtesy, Emory University Library.

Black Ekphrasis, according to Ford, "prioritizes collectivity over individuality, opacity over transparency, and contamination over purity," a definition that can help to argue for "To S. M." as the opening scene of the genre.[92]

The poem's first bold move is to envision an artistic community between enslaved African artists, but its next, far bolder, is to frame these Africans as also American, and from there to imagine their freedom. Peters achieves this imagination through an apparently conventional conclusion in the "Celestial" sphere, a conclusion that occupies the last lines of the first stanza and all of the second. The speaker transitions directly from a wish for Moorhead's (and the speaker's own) "immortal fame" into "the blissful wonders of the skies," and from there to "That splendid city, crown'd with endless day / . . . / Celestial *Salem* blooms in endless spring." Salem is a term for Jerusalem at the same time that it is a historical city along the same Massachusetts seaboard as Peters's and Moorhead's hometown of Boston, and so these lines introduce both the heavenly realm that dominates the rest of the poem, and the national subtext that grants "Young African" artists a claim to American soil.[93]

The doubling of "Salem" imposes a terrestrial imagination onto the heavenly, which the poem's second stanza extends through a scene that enfolds both spiritual liberation and physical enslavement. Benighting the artist— both Moorhead and themselves—with eternal life, the speaker asks, "On what seraphic pinions shall we move, / And view the landscapes in the realms above?" With this "we," "S. M." and the speaker of the poem come to share the common space of a pronoun in a scene of liberation that is at once a heavenly gift for a lifetime of devoted creative practice, and more implicitly, a freedom from the enslaved state. Slavery comes into play in the poem tacitly through Peters's emphasis on Africa and America, but also in the line above through the double-meaning of "pinions," which denotes both "a bird's wing" and "a manacle, a fetter," or in the verb form "to bind or secure together the arms or legs of (a person)."[94] In a poem that relies so much on an interplay of contrasts that gradually blur—life and afterlife, poetry and painting, speaker and addressee, Africa and America—it hinges, in its crucial second question, on a word that connotes both freedom and enslavement.

The subtextual allusions to slavery suggest that the anticipated liberation of the second stanza is both spiritual and physical, and both are equally the product of the "noble path" of creative work, a wishful thought that may have proven to some extent true for Peters, but likely not for Moorhead. Physical liberation comes into play again with the introduction of the open-ended reference to "Damon" near the end of the second stanza, where the speaker considers the forms that creative production might take in the heavenly realm:

> There shall thy tongue in heav'nly murmurs flow,
> And there my muse with heav'nly transport glow;
> No more to tell of *Damon's* tender sighs,
> Or rising radiance of *Aurora's* eyes,
> For nobler themes demand a nobler strain,
> And purer language on th' ethereal plain.

As Vincent Carretta writes, "Damon is a common name for love-struck shepherds in pastoral poems,"[95] and in this context, the themes that the speaker anticipates abandoning in the afterlife make a certain logical sense: no more poems about the Aurora's sunrise in a realm of "everlasting day," or about Damon's earthly love in a realm of spiritual love. But as James Ford and Ivy Wilson note, the Greek tale of Damon and Pythias offers another gloss. In this narrative, when Pythias is condemned to death by the tyrannical leader Dionysius, he asks permission to settle his affairs at home first, and to leave his friend Damon temporarily in his place. Dionysius grants the leave, but is shocked when Pythias keeps his word and returns, and when both friends offer to die in each other's place. In response, Dionysius grants the two their freedom. Ford reads Peters's possible allusion to this narrative as gesture toward collective bonds in a time of slavery, and an anticipation of a "time when neither she nor Moorhead nor any other Africans must find their individual freedom *at the other friend's expense*."[96] This "ethereal plain," in other words, is also a very terrestrial one.

CONCLUSION

While her nineteenth-century editors and biographers would struggle with the question of Peters's transatlantic bonds, often choosing, as Odell did, to suppress the African and claim the American, it was Peters's continuous return to nationality in her work that made this claim possible at all. But this insistence on Americanness, in Peters's work as in her reception, is always shadowed by the transits of her life, her existence between nations, families, and reading publics, a "no-citizen" to be claimed by all or none. This ambiguous status is amplified by Peters's youth, at only about fourteen when she started writing poetry, and about twenty when her book came out. June Jordan, in tribute to Peters's work, writes, "I believe no one would have published the poetry of Black Phillis Wheatley, that grown woman who stayed with her chosen Black man . . . America has long been tolerant of Black children, compared to its reception of independent Black men and Black women." Lucia Hodgson echoes this sentiment in her consideration of Peters as holding a youthful "pre-political" role, evoking the "liberal myth that every person can become an adult citizen" at the same time that she displaced and postponed "the knowledge that children like herself would not be able to fulfill this process of becoming."[97] In this light, Peters's second book and adult career were always impossibilities. From the vulnerable potentiality of childhood she could both claim and critique America, but not as a politically circumscribed adult. Peters's national focus was always exactly nowhere, effaced once it took on agency, and reclaimed by later critics to represent a different form of (cultural) nationalism.

In the two copybooks at Emory University, kept perhaps partially in Peters's hand, there are, in addition to carefully copied poems and sayings, some small fragments, incomplete poems, and sketchy jottings. On the cover of the first book, to the right of the carefully penned title "Joining Copies," is one such a small fragment (see figure 2). It is a list that reads:

Ignorance
[Virtue?]
Ships
Scripture
Writing
Idleness
Emblems

I am not sure what to make of this collection of nouns, loosely linked but all thematically present both in the content of the copybooks and Peters's verse. I don't know what to make of it, but I am left with the image of Peters sitting at her writing desk, straight-backed with hand poised above paper as in her frontispiece portrait, writing the noun that gave her both her name and her fate, not "America," but "Ships."

CHAPTER TWO

"The Fusion of the Races Among Us"

Summer on the Lakes and
Margaret Fuller's Aesthetic Nationalism

Hailed by Evert Duyckinck, that central champion of literary nationalism at mid-century, as "the only genuine American book . . . published this season," Fuller's *Summer on the Lakes, in 1843* (1844), her first extended "original work," is both a likely and an unlikely candidate for the publisher's admiration.[1] On the one hand, the multi-genre travelogue checks the boxes of many traditionally nationalist concerns: it deals with distinctly American scenes in the form of rural western landscapes, Native American settlements, and frontier camps; it comments explicitly on the supposed traits of the American character and developing nation; and it functions as an antidote to the flood of American travel writing about Europe. Mapping a route through upstate New York, Michigan, Illinois, and back again, *Summer on the Lakes* spans the Northern settlements with a mixture of history and literature, blending descriptions of the national landscape, ethnographic research, poems by Fuller and others, and original fictionalized narratives. But on the other hand, the text is haunted from its inception with transatlantic desire: the trip on which it was based was an affordable alternative to the tour of Europe that Fuller had longed to take in the 1830s and early 1840s,[2] while the dense and allusive writing continuously references the Continental figures and ideas of Fuller's classical education. Even the publication's title gestures toward the lake district where Fuller's English contemporaries might have guided her in another iteration of her travels.[3]

The version of nationalism on display in *Summer on the Lakes* is nuanced, both invested in studying the particularized traits of nationhood, and in highlighting America as a multilingual patchwork of peoples and histories. Perry Miller has argued that Fuller fell increasingly under the sway of the Young America movement's literary nationalism in the course of her career; her reviews of Melville's works and her 1846 essay "American Literature: Its Position in the Present Time, and Prospects for the Future" in which she opens with the statement that "books which imitate or represent the thoughts and life of Europe do not constitute an American literature," support this perspective.[4] That Duyckinck, the literary figurehead for the movement, enthusiastically reprinted *Summer on the Lakes* and later published her *Papers on Literature and Art*, the collection from which this quote was taken, in his Library of American Books series, suggests that the influence was reciprocal.[5] But as Colleen Boggs has shown in her discussion of Fuller's often paraphrastic and partial translations, Fuller's particular form of nationalism was one that relished the country's cultural fragmentation, and that attempted to define aspects of national character as both localized and plural. Fuller, as Boggs argues, "sees cultural relations as iterative and dialogic, not ontological and fixed,"[6] much as Christina Zwarg argues for considering "the problems of pedagogy, translation, and difference" as essential to Fuller's work.[7]

A key means of imagining this dialogue for Fuller is through her ideal of "fusion," which encapsulates both fragmentation and cohesion, calling into play the simultaneously associationist and nationalist aesthetic that was a backdrop to New England intellectual discourse. Though Fuller's criticism of American literature centered on its apparent fragmentation, it was not its diversity as such that she critiqued, but the failure of communication between its distinct parts. In "American Literature," Fuller presents the expansive distances between the American population as a distinct challenge to the nation-building project. After her standard nationalist call for a literature apart from "the thoughts and life of Europe," Fuller moves on to focus on "fusion," a tenuous characteristic that she finds as yet lacking in American life.[8] A true American genius, she writes,

> will not rise till the fusion of races among us is more complete. It will not rise till this nation shall attain sufficient moral and intellectual dignity to prize moral and intellectual, no less highly than political, freedom, not till, the physical resources of the country being explored,

> all its regions studded with towns, broken by the plow, netted together
> by railways and telegraph lines, talent shall be left a leisure to turn its
> energies upon the higher department of man's existence.[9]

Waxing poetic about technologies such as the railroad and the telegraph was a familiar move for political and cultural nationalists, but Fuller's "fusion of the races" is both physical and intellectual, depending on the mapping of communication networks as well as shared cultural ideals. This ideal of cultural cohesion is not based on a negation of difference or of influence, but an assimilation of diverse parts into a whole, a linking that, like the telegraph line, brings parts together but also reveals their points of contact. Fusion, in other words, is an example of the "iterative and dialogic" relations that Boggs sees as instrumental to Fuller's nationalism, which refused to gloss over cultural fragmentation in the name of national unity.

Fuller's fusion shows direct debt to associationism, the philosophy of mind and aesthetics that shaped both antebellum reform efforts and a mode of literary nationalism. Associationism, which holds that mental processes unfold by the association of individual feelings and ideas, influenced the communal thinking of Fourierism, and through it transcendental utopian experiments such as Brook Farm and Fruitlands, which rely on the idea that reforming individual action can radically revise the social whole.[10] In a literary context, Theo Davis has shown the widespread influence of the associationist Common Sense school on American nationalist principles of the 1820s and 1830s, arguing that this philosophy inspires an audience-centered understanding of creation, in which authors depend on a chain of literary types and conventions to produce a cohesive emotional or intellectual response in their readers.[11] As Kerry Larson notes, "while the literary nationalist requires an assortment of ready-made emblems, types, and touchstones connected to a particular place and a particular time, it is their suggestiveness that is most coveted."[12] This mode of nationalism, in emphasizing the work of art as existing in its fullest sense in the minds of readers, "renders the difference between authors and readers hard to see."[13] In Fuller's case, she structures her writing of *Summer on the Lakes* around recurrent stock images and an emphasis on the reader's role. Even her use of the term fusion echoes the associationist principles of John Stuart Mill, whose doctrine of "mental chemistry" understood the mind as creating an active "fusion of the sensory elements in such a way that it gives rise to a new entity which is not a mere sum of its constituent parts."[14]

In Fuller's literary criticism, fusion comes up repeatedly, not only as a spatial or nationalist term, but as an aesthetic ideal. She frames Longfellow, for example, as presenting readers "not with a new product in which all the old varieties are melted into a fresh form, but rather with a tastefully arranged Museum, between whose glass cases are interspersed neatly potted rose trees, geraniums and hyacinths, grown by himself with aid of in-door heat."[15] Longfellow's central fault, according to Fuller, is that "he has no style of his own growing out of his own experiences and observations of nature. Nature with him, whether human or external, is always seen through the windows of literature."[16] In other words, he borrows liberally from the works of others, but is not able to "melt" these "old varieties" into a new form through his own direct observations or feelings. This was a criticism that Fuller brought to bear on not only Longfellow, but also her closest friends and literary allies such as Emerson, and perhaps most obsessively, herself.[17]

Both Fuller herself and her early reviewers were preoccupied with the apparent disunity of *Summer on the Lakes*. In Fuller's journals, she worries of the travelogue that "my mind does not act" on the different parts of the book "enough to fuse them."[18] She called the multi-genre form of the text, which included her own and others' poems, letters from friends, synopses of books about the West, descriptive scenes of travel, snippets of dialogue, and embedded fictional narratives, "a kind of letter box";[19] her sometime companion in the travels, James Freeman Clarke, would call it "a portfolio of sketches."[20] Fuller's contemporary reviewers, even those who were sympathetic, generally shared these concerns about form. Caleb Stetson found "no apparent link of association" between the different parts of her text,[21] while Orestes Brownson, in a generally positive review, includes style among its principle faults, calling the author "wholly deficient in a pure, correct taste, and especially in that tidiness we always look for in a woman."[22] Fuller's friend Lydia Maria Child, whose mixed-genre *Letters from New York* (1841) provided inspiration for *Summer on the Lakes*, wrote to Fuller frankly that "your house is too full; there is too much furniture in your rooms."[23]

Although much modern criticism followed this understanding of the work as a stylistic failure, more recent literary histories have found meaning in the digressive form.[24] Stephen Adams sees in *Summer's* form an answer to Fuller's literary critical call for an American literature that will "make its own laws, and give its own watch-words,"[25] stressing "Romantic experimentation" and the Romantic fragment as contexts for the work.[26] Bell Gale Chevigny writes that Fuller "associated the strictness of literary forms with the confining social forms and . . . resented what both cost her in vitality,"[27] an idea that her more recent biographer also echoes, calling *Summer* "a monument to the non-linear and the anti-cohesive."[28] Jeffrey Steele applies Elaine Showalter's reading of the "gaps" in Fuller's texts more generally to read the "meandering, fragmentary" style as "an index of the cultural pressures inhibiting female literary expression."[29] And Dorri Beam cites Fuller's conversational model in *Woman in the Nineteenth Century* and her constellation of images and "ornamental style" in *Summer* as a means of "keeping . . . associations in play, or alive" rather than fixed in a more apparently stable structure.[30]

Fuller's approach to emulation and the "fusion" of fragments in her pedagogical practices and literary work can provide a sense of how these terms function in her nationalist ideals for American literature. In particular, they highlight ekphrasis, a literary genre that Fuller returned to throughout both her teaching and writing, as a trope for defining the relationship between art object and audience more broadly. In Fuller's dialogic instruction style as well as in the direct address of her writing, the triangulated relationship between speaker, subject, and audience—not the static artwork itself—is a space for the fusion of separate entities, a space where dynamic meaning is created. While in her reviews and her own notes she seems to place the onus of fusion on the authors themselves, in her pedagogy, as well as in *Summer on the Lakes*, she emphasizes the audience's place in enacting this effect, their responsibility to, as she writes in *Summer*, "read me as you would be read."[31] This fluid creative environment, clearly indebted to the reader-centered principles of associationism, enlivens the pieces of other works to create something new, something that goes beyond Longfellow's "tastefully arranged Museum."

This rejection of the static "museum" of "glass cases" and "potted rose trees" in favor of the dynamic public sphere has a clear nationalist subtext, and is also the basic model through which both Fuller's ekphrasis and her aesthetic philosophy, what Kathleen Lawrence calls her "aesthetic transcendentalism," operates.[32] This mode of transcendentalism, "devoted to art and intimately intertwined with . . . intellectual, spiritual, and emotional growth"[33] is interdisciplinary rather than exclusively textual, and is primarily exemplified by Fuller, whose "great mark," as close friend Caroline Sturgis wrote after her death, "was a sense of Art."[34] By describing or reproducing examples of artwork that are enlivened in a public setting, Fuller illustrates how the copied work comes to life through a series of interrelationships, both between sections of the text

"The Fusion of the Races Among Us" 71

as well as the text and its readers. In this focus on the continual reproduction of image and fluid dialogue lies an ideal for the existence of her own work in the world, which she described in a letter to William Henry Channing as the "third thought that is to link together each conflicting two."[35] Concluding that she belongs to "a constellation, not a phalanx,"[36] Fuller implies an association-ist fusion that is more intuitive and organic than strict Fourierist systems, and that maps on clearly to the nationalist mode of *Summer on the Lakes*.[37]

In this chapter, I begin by looking closely at Fuller's pedagogical prac-tice, and argue that the exchanges that she fostered in instructional settings between speaker and audience were essential to her principles of literary creativity and copying more broadly. Though Fuller was often a reluctant instructor who turned to teaching as the most reliable means of supporting her family after her father's death and before her steady literary-journalistic employment, the classroom's modes of attention—absorption, digestion, and recitation—would shape her understanding of her literary work for years to come. Fuller's model of education resonates through the journals of one of her most dedicated pupils from the Greene Street School in Providence, as the nineteen-year-old Mary Ware Allen uses the pages of her mandatory classroom journal to reflect on emulation and expression within the delimited public sphere of the schoolroom. These classroom diaries, which have been discussed only to a limited degree, provide a valuable sense of how Fuller con-ceptualized intellectual exchange more broadly through discussion models such as the Conversations, a series of public meetings for women that Fuller held in Boston after her tenure at the Greene Street School. The focus on imi-tation and reproduction, not as a means to reiterate but to create new knowl-edge, is central to Fuller's pedagogy, and provides a necessary framework for understanding *Summer on the Lakes*.

In light of this pedagogical work, the nationalist fusion of *Summer on the Lakes* emerges as similarly conversational and reiterative, a carefully triangulated construction between speaker, subject, and audience. The trav-elogue's ekphrastic passages emphasize this triangulation, while also serv-ing as central focal points for the disparate images that weave through the narrative. In *Summer*'s poetic interludes, Fuller considers what it means to copy a European work onto an American landscape, and places artistic and national origination in the space between old and new, culture and nature, speaker and audience. Juxtaposition is for Fuller the only means of creativ-ity, but it is also an extremely tenuous one, dependent not only on a carefully balanced series of scenes, but on an ideally receptive audience capable of tying together a dense web of associations. If a successful nationalist fusion depends on an openness among inhabitants, a receptive environment, and a network of communication that facilitates connections, then aesthetic fusion depends on a similar synthesis between author, reader, and work. This is a goal that ultimately may elude Fuller's short narrative, in her time as well as ours.

THE PEDAGOGICAL JOURNAL AS DIALOGUE

The journal may be the ideal transcendentalist literary form, but does not often figure centrally in the movement's literary histories. Both self-reflective and apparently spontaneous, it captures the intuitive aesthetic that Lawrence Buell has characterized as transcendentalism's "literature of the portfolio."[38] But the practical difficulties around publishing work in this format are significant, due to the sheer bulk of the production and the idiosyncrasy and frequent illegibility of personal writing. Women's journals are even less likely to be preserved, published, and written about than those of men.[39]

Margaret Fuller's diaries reflect these difficulties, which are further complicated by her own ambivalent relation to the form. Few of her diaries are preserved, and in editing the *Memoirs of Margaret Fuller Ossoli*, Ralph Waldo Emerson, William Henry Channing, and James Freeman Clarke "mutilated or lost so much of the work that too little survives," too little, certainly, to provide a reliable overview of her life and career.[40] But even before the editing of Fuller's work, the record that she left was relatively fragmentary. The 1842 diary that she kept while visiting the Emersons in Concord not long before the travels of *Summer on the Lakes* is one of the few of her journals to have survived intact, and serves as a record of her dissatisfactions with journal-keeping as a form. The journal stands out among transcendentalist diaries for recording both the world of ideas, in the form of sketches for articles in *The Dial*, and the personal everyday emotional life of the household, which was wracked by the recent death of the Emersons' youngest child. But the record of this social reality was precisely the aspect of the writing that irked Fuller, as she writes near the end of the journal: "Oh, I am tired of this journal: it is a silly piece of work. I will never keep another such. Write thoughts, the sum of all this life, or turn it into poetic form: this meager outline of life has no value

"*The Fusion of the Races Among Us*"   73

in any way."[41] Robert Sattelmeyer argues in this context that "It was apparently the mediating impulse of the journal that she mistrusted, its tendency to interpose between direct experience and inspiration and the shaping of it into literature or thought."[42]

But this mediation between experience and thought is precisely what Fuller valued in the journal-keeping of her students—and, as we will see later, in the record of a journal-based literary work such as *Summer on the Lakes*. The journal-keeping practices of her students provide a strong background to understanding how she regarded the form's potential. The most extensive record of such works is from Fuller's time teaching at the co-educational Greene Street School from June 1837 to January 1839. The journals of four of Fuller's female students—Ann Frances Brown, Hannah Gale, Evelina Metcalf, and Mary Ware Allen—survive in archives and scholars have reprinted short selections from all.[43] Of these, the four journals of Mary Ware Allen, archived at the American Antiquarian Society, are arguably the most revelatory of Fuller's pedagogical method.

Allen, among Fuller's oldest students and her most serious, shared with her instructor an acute self-awareness and an understanding of the journal as a mediator. Almost nineteen when she arrived at the school in 1837, Allen's maturity made itself felt in both her attitude toward the school's instruction and her own progress.[44] She began to attend the school only after refusing a marriage proposal, and her age—at a school where the headmaster, Hiram Fuller, was only 23[45] and Margaret Fuller only 27[46]—meant that while she expressed her effusive admiration of her teachers from the first pages of her journal, she was also more capable than most of taking a reflective and critical attitude toward the school's mode of instruction. She was Fuller's fiercest ally, but also one of the students who wrote a letter of complaint to Fuller after the teacher's blunt criticism prompted a student to flee the classroom in tears. (Fuller later wrote a letter of apology to the class).[47] And Allen also turned her critical eye inward, reflecting on her own writing style and practice as well as the classroom's requirements and assumptions.

Allen's literary self-consciousness manifested itself in part through a continuous comparison of her own mode of expression to the rhetorical models that she studied in the classroom. Granville Ganter and Hani Sarji, in the only extended analysis of Allen's journals, have argued that "as [Allen] discussed the means by which writers achieve the effects of modesty, Allen started to develop a mature, intellectual style of her own, derived from both masculine and feminine rhetorical models."[48] Fuller's course in rhetoric, which used Richard Whately's *Elements of Rhetoric* (1828), was, in Allen's words, the one that most developed her "thinking powers."[49] The influence of Whately's text is apparent throughout Allen's journal, particularly in his central idea that it is preferable to convince rather than to persuade, and that a "gentle and conciliatory manner" toward one's audience is the most appropriate tone for teachers to take.[50] Whately's material stylistic recommendations—including his preference for short sentences, Saxon over Latinate vocabulary, and concrete language—also make their mark on the development of Allen's writing.[51]

Emulation, then, is central to Whately's rhetorical curriculum, but extends well beyond this course in the school's curriculum. The school's almost daily recitations depended on a fair amount of rote memorization, particularly in the foreign languages. And the art classes, as was typical of the period, focused on the replication of artists' illustrations. This course of instruction so voided individual agency that in the last week of Mary Ware Allen's enrollment at the school, the drawing instructor Georgiana Nias, seeing that Allen was to leave significant sections of her final drawing incomplete, simply finished the work for her. As Allen records, with no apparent sense of personal infringement: "This morning when I came into school, I found that a piece that I had but just begun to draw, and feared I could not finish, was lying on my desk, neatly finished by Mrs. Nias. I felt very much obliged to her."[52]

In this sense, the Greene Street School conformed to some degree to conventional models of education, particularly female education, in the republican and antebellum periods. The emphasis on scholastic imitation could produce a spirit of competition between students, but both Fuller and her students seemed to guard against this tendency. As William Huntting Howell observes of republican schooling, "it posits the production of proper individuality in the evacuation of individual difference—the pupil who becomes more like all of the other republicans becomes her best self."[53] This spirit of extreme non-individuation is paradoxically competitive, as students strive toward the same goal that, when achieved, entirely effaces the particularity of their accomplishment. Or as Howell puts it, "Emulation encodes rivalry (and therefore individuation but also, as we have seen, imitation): it is at once the generation of distinction and the erasure of distinction."[54] Allen reflects on precisely this form of competitive non-individuation when she notes in her first journal that "I think much harm has been done by exciting emulation, and a spirit of rivalry in schools."[55] But her positive assessment of Fuller's

"The Fusion of the Races Among Us"   75

methods throughout the journal suggests that this classroom's emulation follows a different model.

Instead of competition, Greene Street cultivated emulation conceptualized through transformative conversation, or what Fuller would later define as "reproduction" in educational practice. If the course of study at Greene Street was not as radically progressive (or ultimately controversial) as that at Alcott's Temple School, where Fuller had taught the year before, or as well-known as the thematic discussions that Fuller would later hold for the women of Boston's intellectually elite families under the rubric of the Conversations, the pedagogical principles followed a similar model. In fact, Hiram Fuller had sought Margaret out as an instructor while she was still teaching at Alcott's school—and had sought to engage Alcott himself as the speaker at the school's dedication—because he saw Greene Street as an heir to the Temple School's philosophy of drawing out students' intuitive knowledge through conversation. Fuller, frustrated with both Alcott's methods and his failure to pay his instructors, accepted the post. Emerson appeared in Alcott's stead at the dedication, giving a speech that anticipated his American Scholar address in emphasizing the potential of education to produce complete rather than hyper-specialized citizens.[56]

But the methods of Fuller's classroom at Greene Street were ones that she would engage through all of her teaching, which was deeply influenced by the ideal of a cumulative dialogue, and replication with variation within that dialogue. Writing was essential to this process. In the first of her Conversations, held shortly after Fuller left the Greene Street School, and recorded from memory by Elizabeth Palmer Peabody, Fuller outlines the aims of the weekly discussions precisely through this language of replication:

> Is not the difference between [2–3 words missing] education of women & of men this—Men are called on from a very early period to reproduce all that they learn—first their college exercises—their political duties— the exercises of professional study—the very first action of life in any direction—calls upon them for reproduction of what they have learnt.— This is what is most neglected in the education of women—they learn without any attempt to reproduce— ... it is to supply this deficiency that these conversations have been planned.[57]

The goal of "reproduction" in this context does not entail the rote imitation of facts, but the creative assimilation and personalized use of knowledge. Reproduction is similar, in other words, to what Allen registered when she recorded in her journal that Fuller did not wish her students to learn their lessons "by heart, as that expression is commonly understood, for . . . it was oftener only getting it by body." Instead, Fuller encourages learning "by *mind*": in being filtered through the intellect, lessons are absorbed and assimilated in a way that they are not when processed simply as physical repetition. And the process that creates the difference between learning "by body" and "by mind" is language, either through the exchange of a dialogue, in the analytic space of the written word, or—ideally—both. In other words, as Fuller stated in the same Conversation, if her pedagogical goal was to be the "nucleus of a conversation" and "a means of calling out the thoughts of others," writing is the second step in the transformation of knowledge, another form of processing that furthers the train of creative reproduction. That our only knowledge of both Fuller's classroom instruction and her Conversations comes from the written records of her most diligent students and peers shows these ideals actualized.

In the case of the Greene Street classroom journals, it is clear that a central aim of the writing is transformative reproduction. On December 19, 1838, Mary Allen opens the first entry of her journal with an undisguised reluctance: "I find it is one of the rules of the school to keep a journal, and though I do not think I shall like to do it, it will be a very useful exercise."[58] But by the very next entry, Allen fleshes out the goals of classroom writing in much more positive terms, stressing repetition and adaptation:

> I have overcome my repugnance to writing a journal, and find it, what I did not expect, a pleasant, as well as useful exercise. It has, as Miss Fuller said to me the other day, when she saw what I had written on the first page, all the advantages of writing a composition without the danger of acquiring a stiff and formal manner of expressing oneself, which is usually seen in common school compositions. Composition! what a dreaded word that is to most scholars, when some subject is given out for them to write on. In vain they rack their poor brains in search of something to write which will be original, and perhaps after repeated efforts they are obliged to give up in despair. Some love to write, and perform their task to the satisfaction of their teacher, but the number is small, and too often they appear with no composition at all. If teachers would oftener do as Miss Fuller does, read an interesting story for their scholars to write from remembrance, it would be more useful as well as pleasanter to them.[59]

"The Fusion of the Races Among Us"   77

Rather than a "composition," which strives to "be original," Fuller's process of journal-writing depends entirely on creative reproduction, as students begin with a recounted lesson or story and "write from remembrance," much as Peabody's records of Fuller's Conversation. In fact, as becomes clear from some of Allen's later entries, students commonly took stock of several days of lessons in one afternoon, back-dating the journal to reflect the day that the lessons took place rather than the day that they were recorded.[60] This delayed recall requires them to process the narratives of the classroom in their own language, and also encourages personal reflection on the meaning or value of the lesson.

As this early entry also suggests, the journals functioned to open a dialogue between teacher and student, a dialogue that itself shaped the boundaries of the record. Allen's new enthusiasm for the journal form, it seems likely, is at least in part shaped by her awareness that Fuller "saw what I had written on the first page." In this second entry, she registers Fuller's pedagogical eye with a directness that is marked throughout the journal, transforming the space of the page into a record of both past and future exchanges. This triangulation of speaker, text, and, audience makes the written text a living document, a fixed point in a fluid personal exchange. This exchange also becomes a point of increasing tension as Allen's writing develops.

Allen's journals show Fuller's careful attention in her penciled corrections of sentence structure and grammar, as well as occasional longer comments. In some entries, Allen records a sentiment that seems designed to provoke a response, and a textual conversation supplements the exchanges of the classroom. For instance, in an entry that underlines the function of nation-building in Fuller's classroom, Allen writes that Fuller had asked each student what most had interested them in the study of Greek history, but "she did not ask me, I know not why, unless it was because I was last, and as she had had all the same answer from all, she thought it not worth her while to hear it again." Fuller's penciled note on the margin comes to her own defense—"I thought I had asked I believe"—followed by, in the next line, Allen's would-be response, clearly structured to be "worth [Fuller's] while." While most of the students, Allen notes, were interested in the revelation of "individual character" through historical accounts, Allen's own focus is considerably more sophisticated: "I have been interested in seeing how much this little nation could do for itself in the beautiful and simple manner in which they expressed the feelings and ideas of their souls, by their mythology, and by their fine arts."[61] Resisting the common response, Allen instead crafts an answer to Fuller's question that shows the influence of Fuller's own instruction, as evidenced by Allen's records throughout the journal. Her retroactively composed reply condenses Fuller's teachings about art as a reflection of national character, but does so through the medium of her own journal's records, producing the creative emulation of a creative emulation, or precisely the type of conversational iteration that Fuller's pedagogy encouraged.

THE JOURNAL OF *SUMMER ON THE LAKES*

Because *Summer on the Lakes* is based at least in part on Fuller's journal from her travels, her own journal-keeping practice and that of her students' provides a lens through which to interpret its structure and modes, but given Fuller's reservations around journal-keeping, this lens also has its limitations. Fuller had reflected critically about her own attempts at the journal form, calling the journal she kept the year before her travels for *Summer on the Lakes* "a silly piece of work."[62] If what Fuller mistrusted in the journal, was, as Robert Sattelmeyer claims, its "mediating impulse," its existence between life and literature, this is a striking frustration to express after encouraging precisely this mediation in the work of her students, and in the wake of her own ostensibly journal-based composition for *Summer on the Lakes*.[63] And it is a surprising frustration, because mediation—between visual artworks and a literary audience, between lived experience and abstract meditations—is a central component of her later work.

I would argue that Fuller's reservations regarding the form lie instead in the personal specificities of journal-keeping, its existence below both the level of abstract thought and more polished literary composition as a "meager outline of fact." Another undated journal scrap, preserved alongside of letters from 1844, implies a frustration with the form not because it is a halfway point to literature, but because it is something entirely apart:

> I think I shall not in the future keep a diary . . .—What avails it—It is little better than a trick to do it—I shall keep the record of my intellectual life in the large book I have provided for the purpose and any secret passages in my affections I may note in a <u>very small book</u> which is to be its companion. And now adieu, thou existence of "buttonings and

"The Fusion of the Races Among Us" 79

unbuttonings" as Byron hath it. Thou tea drinking, errand performing, dreg-requiring existence I will take note of thee no more. What skills this rubbish made in building the Temple—Yet it mouldes as it lies—no volcano can fuse it into marble—Vale—vale, thou record of the days that have no pleasure in them—Vale.[64]

This analysis places personal events and feelings on a lower parallel plane to the more valuable—and ideally, much longer—"record of my intellectual life." And significantly, these personal "affections" are not the initial raw material for abstracted thought or more polished literature, but "rubbish" that "no volcano can fuse . . . into marble." Fuller's choice of the word "fuse" here, which signals her ideal unity in literature, confirms that the fragments of personal life and desire can never amount to the cohesive form that she in her criticism demands of a literary work.

These reflections on journal-writing and literature cast some light on the discrepancies between Fuller's journal of her travels through the West and the publication of *Summer on the Lakes*. While the journal is filed in the Massachusetts Historical Society as "the basis of Fuller's book *Summer on the Lakes*," and while the mixed-genre pastiche of the publication might read as a close translation of a series of journal entries, the relationship between the two texts is relatively thin.[65] In fact, the two closely follow Fuller's own hierarchy of the personal and the literary, the journal a "very small book" of feelings and events somewhat drily recorded, and the travelogue an expansive record that dwells in storytelling and history, with only a loose reference to the same anchoring events. Unlike many contemporary travelogues, such as Sophia Hawthorne's *Notes*, which were only slightly edited versions of manuscript journals or letters, Margaret Fuller's *Summer* takes few cues from her own journal record, emerging only after the travels as a record of research, poetry, and correspondence.

The relationship between the two texts is close to that of an outline to a fully-fleshed work, though there are also several cases of expansive explorations of personal feelings that do not appear in the publication. A mere twenty pages, the journal sketches a schedule of the stops along the way in terms primarily of the individuals visited—almost all of whom are excised from the travelogue—rather than a description of scenes, which dominate the publication. The journal is also a much more linear description of encounters than the expansive, almost three-hundred-page publication, and this shorter, "meager outline of fact" has none of the published text's associationist digressions. It likewise lacks any of this text's experimentation with form, references and summaries of secondary works, letters from correspondents, or poetic interludes. In one case, for instance, the journal's curt line, "On the lake I embarked in a heavy rain," transforms into a long passage at the beginning of the second chapter recording a rainy steamboat ride conversation, in dialogue-form, between three travelers arguing facetiously about the merits of the different earthly elements.[66] At the same time, the full page in the journal devoted to Fuller's dissatisfactions with Chicago—beginning, "I do think it was well nigh the dullest fortnight I ever passed"—does not appear in the publication, in keeping with her ethic of curtailing the personal in the literary.[67]

But although almost none of its precise language and very few of its observations resurface in the travelogue, Fuller seems to have written the journal with a mind toward a public, and as a memetic aid for herself. She titles it neatly, "Being Notes of a Journey to the West, by S. M. Fuller, June 1843," signaling from the first page its elevation above an ordinary journal in its intention toward a public. As she writes: "A few impressions noted down will serve to recall to myself in after days the experiences of this journey. I shall make them with the thought of showing the leaves to a few friends, & shall therefore be silent as to thoughts still half developed or incidents of importance to myself alone" (see figure 5).[68] This opening gesture—which Fuller replaces in the publication with two dedicatory poems—establishes this brief outline as the scaffolding for a document that the author would further trim of "incidents of importance to myself alone."

Like the classroom journals of her students, which take their starting point in efforts to remember the lessons of previous days, Fuller's *Summer on the Lakes* is a remediation of a remediation, a spinning-out of the journal-form that was only ever intended to provide the "recall" that would serve as the basis for original creation. Unlike Mary Allen, who stopped at this second level, and the hope that her classroom journal would "be a kind of satisfaction to me . . . in future," Fuller takes a third step with *Summer on the Lakes*, transforming the journal's "meager outline of fact" into "poetic form."

THE "POETIC IMPRESSIONS" OF *SUMMER ON THE LAKES*

Summer on the Lakes relies centrally on poetic passages to thread the thematic and imagistic sections of the text. Fuller did not typically consider her poetry publishable, and much of her verse exists only in journal form or in letters or

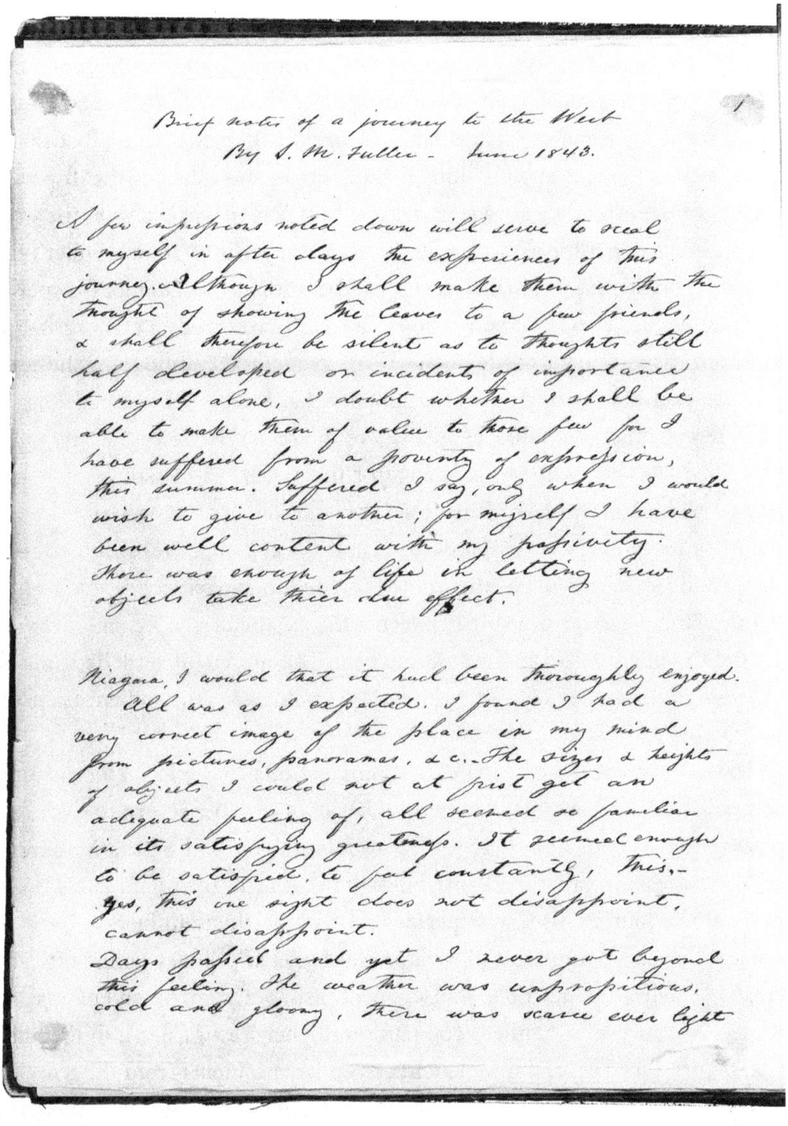

1

Brief notes of a journey to the West
By S. M. Fuller - June 1843.

A few impressions noted down will serve to recal to myself in after days the experiences of this journey. Although I shall make them with the thought of showing the leaves to a few friends, & shall therefore be silent as to thoughts still half developed or incidents of importance to myself alone, I doubt whether I shall be able to make them of value to those few for I have suffered from a poverty of expression, this summer. Suffered I say, only when I would wish to give to another; for myself I have been well content with my passivity. There was enough of life in letting new objects take their due effect.

Niagara, I would that it had been thoroughly enjoyed. All was as I expected. I found I had a very correct image of the place in my mind from pictures, panoramas, &c. The sizes & heights of objects I could not at first get an adequate feeling of, all seemed so familiar in its satisfying greatness. It seemed enough to be satisfied, to feel constantly, this,- yes, this one sight does not disappoint, cannot disappoint.
Days passed and yet I never got beyond this feeling. The weather was unpropitious, cold and gloomy, there was scarce ever light

FIGURE 5. Title Page, "Being Notes of a Journey to the West, by S. M. Fuller, June 1843," Margaret Fuller Papers, Massachusetts Historical Society. Courtesy, MHS.

notes to friends.[69] "All rhetorical and impassioned," she complained of her verse, and on another occasion: "I am dumb and ineffectual, when it comes to casting my thought into a form. No old one suits me. If I could invent one, it seems to me the pleasure of creation would make it possible for me to write."[70] But this failure of form—or experimentation with it—may be precisely what makes poetry the emblem of Fuller's travelogue. Near the end of the third chapter, Fuller writes: "What I got from the journey was the poetic impression of the country at large; it is all I have aimed to communicate."[71] The text's interspersed poems, some of them ekphrastic, are the literary binding that follow Fuller's own conception of "fusion," picking up on and cohering the dispersed themes of the text. They are a least a significant part of what elevates the work from a "meager outline of fact" to literature. These poems trace out Fuller's elusive ideas on literary originality, and track the features that attempt to separate *Summer on the Lakes* from Longfellow's "tastefully arranged" literary museum.

Ekphrasis as a poetic mode is key to Fuller's methods, embodying the complex relationship to copying and originality that infuses Fuller's pedagogical and literary practice. Unlike genres where the reader has access to the scene described only through the language of the poem, ekphrastic works with named art objects emphasize their own remediation, producing a triple image: the work itself, the poet's response to it, and the audience's re-imagination of that response. In this sense, the mode provides an explicit conceptualization of the triangulated relationship between artist, aesthetic subject, and audience central to Fuller's associationist nationalism. The successful work depends on the right juxtaposition of images, but just as crucially, on the audience capable of effecting its "fusion."

The visual art object dominates the composition of *Summer on the Lakes* on several levels. Fuller wrote *Summer on the Lakes* after her return to Concord, placing her writing desk between reproductions of "Del Sarto's Madonna" and a classical sculpture ("Silenus, holding in his arms the infant Pan").[72] The four-month journey itself was permeated with aesthetic influence. Early in the travels, Cary Sturgis, an illustrator and Fuller's "primary confidante and creative catalyst" in "aesthetic transcendentalism"[73] accompanied Fuller as far west as Niagara Falls.[74] Fuller's companion further westward, Sarah Freeman Clarke, produced several line sketches from key moments from the trip that were reproduced with the first publication of Fuller's text. Fittingly then, the travelogue includes not only a long and centrally-placed ekphrastic poem on Bertel Thorvaldsen's statue of Ganymede, but a poetic ode to the American painter Washington Allston on the eve of his death, references to the painter of Native American life George Catlin, and a detailed description of Titian's *Venus and Adonis*.[75]

These images serve as central nodes in the triangulation of author, subject, and audience. But Fuller sets up this triangulation well before her first ekphrastic passage, in the two opening dedicatory poems to the volume that stand in for the author's introduction or address to the reader. The first seventeen-line poem, structured by couplets and a single tercet, introduces many of the issues that dominated Fuller's pedagogy and other writing during this time. Building the poem on the metaphor of nature's seasons as a teacher, Fuller begins with the same central anxiety of Mary Allen's school journals, that she will not be able to properly represent experience in language:

> Summer days of busy leisure,
> Long summer days of dear-bought pleasure,
> You have done your teaching well,
> Had the scholar means to tell
> How grew the vine of bitter-sweet,
> What made the path for truant feet,
> Winter nights would quickly pass,
> Gazing on the magic glass,
> O'er which the new world shadows pass;[76]

Fuller's conceptualization of summer vacation as "teaching" demonstrates the extent to which the habitus of the classroom shaped her understanding of the world. The scholar's "means to tell" carries the promise of future reflection, but ultimately fails Fuller's scholar-subject. As the poem concludes:

> But, in the fault of wizard spell,
> Moderns their tale can only tell
> In dull words, with a poor reed
> Breaking at each time of need.
> But those to whom a hint suffices
> Mottoes find for all devices,
> See the knights behind their shields,
> Through dried grasses, blooming fields.[77]

Jeffrey Steele sees this poem as "remind[ing] us that the 'reality' we find in its pages is a textual construction whose signifiers ('dried grasses') can never totally correspond to the author's experience ('blooming fields'),"[78] but in the context of Fuller's work, this idea resonates with the ideas both of an American literature and an American readership. Language falls frustratingly short of what it aims to represent, but the failure here, rather than being personal or academic, is the fault of the fallen and prosaic era in which the subject composes. "Dull words" are the fate of the "Moderns," who write without the enchantment of a "wizard spell"; this nostalgia for the past is set in the context of the "new world shadows" on which the previous stanza ends. The implicit divide that the poem sketches out, then, is not only between a romantic past and a prosaic present, but also almost explicitly between the old and new worlds, Europe and America.

Fuller's student-vacationer might be seen in this context as a representation of the triangulated author in the modern American context. And while this introductory poem, on the one hand, serves as an apology for the failings of the prose travelogue that follows, it functions just as significantly to place the pressures of interpretation—and creative re-interpretation—onto the reader. In this sense, the poem is both a conventionally modest introduction to a volume, and an appeal to Fuller's ideal readers, "those to whom a hint suffices." The dedicatory verse calls these readers in to engage creatively with the work, and to find the living image or experience behind the paltry linguistic representation. In this poem, then, Fuller sets up the triangulation of image-author-audience that will be vital to her ekphrastic work later in the volume and presents the subject of the work as an image copied and recopied, first through the author's desiccated language, and then again in the reader's reanimating imagination. These "summer days of busy leisure" circulate in multiple iterations, and the author's writing is only their most limited form. If this is a commentary, as the poem seems to imply, on the developing canon of "new-world" literature, it is one that follows nationalist associationism in placing the onus of originality and animation on the reader.

It is also notable in the context of the later ekphrastic passages that what the speaker imagines readers as reanimating is not narrative but imagistic, "knights behind their shields" and "blooming fields." This reliance on repetitive images, woven throughout the text and developing from one another, follows the associationist logic of the book, its allegiance, as Fuller's own, to "a constellation, not a phalanx," in her words. Relying on a loose web of interconnected motifs, rather than an explicitly structured system, Fuller's text is ekphrastic even when it is not, not only because imagery like "knights behind their shields" could easily refer to specific illustrations, but because such images echo in variants throughout the work. It is through such repetition and development that *Summer on the Lakes* strives conceptually beyond the "meager outline of fact" that Fuller derided in her own journals and takes on the ambition of describing the American continent.

"The Fusion of the Races Among Us" 85

Fuller's depictions of the continent, though, are far from independent anthropological sketches. While her own observations form the basis of the book, these reflections are mediated self-consciously by earlier depictions of the scenes in literary and visual culture, or narratives and histories that inform Fuller's observation. In the first chapter on Niagara Falls, Fuller meditates directly on this phenomenon, as she writes, "When I first came [here] I felt nothing but a quiet satisfaction. I found that drawings, the panorama, &c. had given me a clear notion of the position and proportions of all objects here; I knew where to look for everything, and everything looked as I thought it would."[79] In this sense, the pedagogical copy is never far from Fuller's own literary voice, and the travelogue functions at least to some extent, like Fuller's students' journals, as the record of "an interesting story [that] scholars . . . write from remembrance."[80] This visual and linguistic mediation forms the basis of nearly all of Fuller's own sketches.

THE "GANYMEDE DAY"

Such mediation is on full display in the central ekphrastic scene of Fuller's text, which weaves together many of Fuller's dispersed images and grounds the text's ambivalent relationship toward literary nationalism. This poem, "Ganymede to His Eagle, Suggested by a Work of Thorwaldsen's, Composed on the height called the Eagle's Nest, Oregon, Rock River, July 4th, 1843," is an ekphrastic poem that takes a neoclassical sculpture by the Danish artist Bertel Thorvaldsen as its starting point.[81] The Boston Athenaeum had bought and displayed one of Thorvaldsen's several versions of the scene in 1839;[82] Fuller reviewed the exhibition in the second issue of *The Dial* in October 1840, calling the work "as fine as on first acquaintance" (see figure 6).[83] Superimposing onto the American plains this Scandinavian work about a mortal's servitude to the classical gods, within a chapter that centers on both Native American forcible relocation and Fourth of July celebrations, Fuller makes an argument for America's layered cultural ties as a necessary part of the narrative of American literary nationalism. The choice of a Danish sculptor echoes back to the Viking gods in the dedicatory sonnet and anticipates the discussions of Scandinavian immigrants on the plains in later passages, while the image of the eagle gestures toward US nationhood generally and Native American heritage specifically. Both of these gestures argue for an understanding of the US as both European and Native American, or at least as carrying the remnants of these partially transformed cultures within its borders.

The scene around this poem stands out as significant in its centrality to the text of the travelogue, spanning ten pages and weaving together images and themes from other passages in the text, but also in Fuller's personal reflections. In her journal from the period, she records the beauty of the plains outside of Chicago where the poem is set, and writes, "At this spot today, I first drew a free breath, & began to feel at home in the West."[84] In a letter to James Freeman Clarke following her return to Chicago, she writes, "we have passed a fortnight happy as mortals are seldom permitted to be," a sentiment that she later echoes to her brother Richard.[85] And this impression endures, as does the period's association with Ganymede. In a journal entry from July 4, one year after her visit, she marks the day as a significant anniversary: "Last year, this day was the Ganymede day—the full music of soul amid that resplendent beauty of nature. I remember every one of the golden sands of that day—All its pictures of supernatural loveliness pass before my eyes."[86]

Critics have discussed the resonance of this period and of "Ganymede Day" in particular in terms of romantic longing and same-sex desire, terms encoded both in the subject-matter of the myth and Fuller's life at the time. As several biographers and critics have noted, the years leading up to Fuller's travels were marked by intense romantic friendships with women and evidence of conflicted sexual feelings. Caroline Sturgis, a friend who prompted some of Fuller's most searching reflections on love and sexuality, accompanied Fuller on the first part of her travels westward.[87] A heterosexual near-romance came even closer to the setting in the form of William Clarke, the younger brother of James and Sarah whom Jeffrey Steele identifies as the likely model for Ganymede.[88] William shepherded the traveling party from Chicago through the Illinois plains and back again, forming an intimacy with Margaret along the way that never quite congealed into romance.[89]

The myth of Ganymede, in which Jove falls in love with and kidnaps a young, beautiful mortal boy to be his cupbearer on Olympus does resonate with this biographical context, but these resonances are secondary for a writer who so strongly emphasizes the voiding of personality from her work. Mythology, as Steele notes, is an important element of Fuller's writing and teaching because of the ways these narratives "shape both self-awareness and available visions of human potential."[90] But in the poem, Fuller sublimates this personal meaning to a nationalist emphasis that echoes through other sections

"The Fusion of the Races Among Us"   87

FIGURE 6. "Ganymede with Jupiter's Eagle," by Bertel Thorvaldsen, 1817, A44, photographer Jakob Faurvig. Courtesy, Thorvaldsen's Museum, Copenhagen, DK.

of the travelogue. The story of Ganymede may have its inspiration in Fuller's personal intimacies, but particularized longing transforms into a national sentiment, in what Lauren Berlant calls "the revised articulation of national identity in a moment of libidinally charged collective fantasy."[91] *Summer on the Lakes* pivots on this fantasy, mapping out particular towns and localities, but doing so always in the service of binding the parts, and sublimating the fragment to a developing vision of the national whole. The sexualized longing of the Ganymede narrative is not primarily a means of reflecting personal desire, but of encoding different forms of national union in embodied terms.

My reading of "Ganymede to his Eagle" centers on Fuller's ideal in her literary criticism of the "fusion of the races," a fusion that extends both across and down through the surface of the continent. As a mapping project of the country's western expanses, the travelogue enacts a version of the physical linking that Fuller imagines taking place through the railroad or telegraph line, and in that function, it serves as an introduction to the country's diverse inhabitants and geographies. But at the same time that the book offers this expansive lateral connection, it also draws connections downward through the historical surface of the earth, in a movement that resonates with the phenomenon of "deep time," which Wai Chi Dimock glosses as an understanding of the nation as a "complex tangle of relations"[92] in which the "connective tissues binding America to the rest of the world . . . thread American texts into the topical events of other cultures, while also threading the long durations of those cultures into the short chronology of the United States."[93] Literature, as "the home of nonstandard space and time"[94] has a privileged place in "loosening up the chronology and geography of the nation,"[95] and this is a role that Fuller's texts enact with ease.[96] In *Summer on the Lakes* the expansion of linear temporality takes many different forms, but perhaps appears most obviously in Fuller's discussion of Native Americans, from references to burial mounds to her own discovery of arrowheads and tools that direct the reader's attention continuously under the surface of the earth, down through layers of geological time. This temporal layering also appears more implicitly in Fuller's literary and historical references, which superimpose references to neoclassical sculpture, for instance, onto a landscape that is already layered with a pastiche of European immigration and Native settlements.

"Ganymede to his Eagle" is arguably the text's clearest example of the way that Fuller weaves recurrent images through her travelogue to shape a vision of a historically-imbued American present. An ekphrastic poem whose composition is situated very explicitly in the far western reaches of Fuller's travels, on the Illinois plains, the poem undertakes both geographically broad and historically deep versions of fusion, presenting an image of the West by allusively mapping a deep classical history (in a modern European context) onto the American plains. Fuller's poetic symbols bind the dispersive and digressive narrative with their repetition, but as signs they are also intentionally overdetermined and ambiguous. The eagle, for instance, represents American nationality in a narrative that is centrally concerned with defining this character, at the same time that it ties in to Native American histories and classical European mythologies. And in a more implicit sense, it is a Biblical Romantic symbol for personal and artistic ambition, as for instance in Goethe's "The Eagle and the Dove," which Fuller translated in 1837.[97] At the same time, the poem is an artistic imitation whose very point is anti-imitative. Because ekphrasis is an explicitly mimetic literary form—and in the context of antebellum print culture, a highly feminized one—it also offers Fuller a challenging canvas on which to assert something other than imitative borrowing. The art

"The Fusion of the Races Among Us" 89

description that "Ganymede" produces is far from copy work: it takes a European art object as a starting-point for asserting that America needs an art, an education, and a culture adapted to its particular landscape.

The eagle as a symbol in Fuller's narrative appears for the first time in a passage that precedes the poem, in the travelogue's first chapter on Niagara. In this scene, shortly after receiving a tour of the "Americanisms of the spectacle; that is to say, the battles that have been fought there" Fuller sees "an eagle chained for a plaything" near the Falls, which, following the associationist logic of Fuller's writing, prompts her own childhood memory of seeing a captive eagle "in the balcony of a museum."[98] This passage provides a context for Fuller's "Ganymede" poem, as well a reference back to the volume's second dedicatory poem, in which the speaker offers the reader a number of images from her travels, including "an eagle's feather which adorned a Brave."[99] In the passage from Fuller's memory, the many associations of the symbol come together:

> The people used to poke it with sticks, and my childish heart would swell in indignation as I saw their insults and the mien with which they were borne by the monarch-bird. Its eye was dull and its plumage soiled and shabby, yet, in its form and attitude, all the king was visible, though sorrowful and dethroned. I never saw another of the family till, when passing through the notch of the White Mountains, at that moment striving before us in all the panoply of the sunset, the driver shouted, "Look there!," and following with our eyes his upward-pointed finger, we saw, soaring slow in majestic poise above the highest summit, the bird of Jove. It was a glorious sight, yet I know not that I felt more in seeing the bird in all its natural freedom and royalty, than when, imprisoned and insulted, he had filled my early thoughts with the Byronic "silent rages" of misanthropy.[100]

Here, the eagle siginifies largely as it does in the later poem: it is a symbol of America in the shadow of a great national site, a classical figure, a royal emblem, and through the reference to Byron, a more generalized Romantic symbol for poetry. As Jeffrey Steele notes, the eagle, "like Fuller's narrator ... was the victim of a sublime aesthetic that celebrated wildness at the same time that it attempted to appropriate it as a usable aesthetic commodity," an aesthetic that he also sees as enchaining women and Native Americans in Fuller's text.[101] This competing symbolic load—and Fuller's failure to resolve it in any satisfactory way, as she moves on immediately following this memory to a description of the "recluse of Niagara"—is typical of the layering of *Summer on the Lakes*. The chain of memory and association builds up to an image that ties the new and old worlds, with the dedicatory poem and "Ganymede to his Eagle" as textual anchors. The basic narrative of the bird's freedom and imprisonment likewise anticipates the confinements of "Ganymede to his Eagle," which contrasts the eagle's roaming to the young cup-bearer's enslavement.

The first layer of textual context for the introduction of this longer poem is Native American forcible relocation, signaled initially in the dedicatory poem's "eagle's feather which adorned a Brave," and then in the historical description of the landscape that leads into the poem. "Ganymede to his Eagle" appears about halfway through the book's third chapter, in which Fuller and her companions travel along the Rock River in Illinois, a site that bears the vestiges of "some of the latest romance of Indian warfare."[102] This warfare, the Black Hawk War, took place when the Sauk chief of that name returned to his tribal lands in Illinois after the tribe's initial westward removal in 1828. In a series of incursions beginning in 1830, Sauk warriors led by Black Hawk attempted to regain their lands until their final surrender in 1832. Fuller, who may have read Black Hawk's 1833 autobiography as part of her research for the travelogue, refers to the leader by name, and he is the first marker for the romanticized attachment that infuses the landscape throughout the chapter and the poem: "No wonder he could not resist the longing, unwise though its indulgence might be, to return in summer to this home of beauty."[103] Here, the group follows "an Indian trail—Black Hawk's!" and enters a landscape "enchanting, beyond any I have seen."[104]

Though Fuller here and elsewhere bemoans the politics of the western removal of tribes, Indigeneity also functions symbolically in the text as a marker of American identity, and systematic mistreatment of Native Americans does not dampen her celebration of the American present. As Lucy Maddox writes, Fuller's expressed sympathy for the victims of removal politics did not cause her to challenge the view that "in the future [Native Americans] face only 'speedy extinction.'"[105] In the descriptions of the landscape leading up to "Ganymede to his Eagle," Fuller moves flippantly from statements of sympathy with the Native American plight to effusions of nationalism. Fuller's exclamation, "How happy the Indians must have been here! It is not long since they were driven away, and the ground, above and below is full of their traces,"[106] almost directly precedes the book's most patriotic effusion: "It was

"*The Fusion of the Races Among Us*" 91

[the morning] of the fourth of July, and certainly I think I had never felt so happy that I was born in America. . . . I do believe that Rome and Florence are suburbs compared to this capital of nature's art."[107] This juxtaposition does not lean fully into nineteenth-century ideas of the "vanishing" or "dying Indian," as Fuller's statement that "they were driven away" clearly points a finger at particular political forces, rather than a divinely ordained disappearance that allows for and justifies Manifest Destiny. Instead, Fuller's is a seemingly contradictory position that depends on a layering of ideas rather than a clear resolution or ideology.

Fuller's statement that "the ground . . . is full of their traces" provides a direct illustration of this perspective. Framing her thoughts with a paraphrase of the Old Testament phrase, "The earth is full of men,"[108] Fuller continues, "You have only to turn up the sod to find arrowheads and Indian pottery. . . . Here are still the marks of their tomahawks, the troughs in which they prepared their corn, their caches. A little way down the river is the site of an ancient Indian village, with its regularly arranged mounds."[109] The landscape that Fuller discusses is an Indian burial ground, the subterranean world layered both with their tools, and also very literally "full of men." In this sense Fuller participates in what Cecilie Roudeau has described as the early national "writer as geologist," the American artist "who lived at the times when Indian mounds and giant fossils and petrified footprints were being uncovered, glossed over, raved over, turned into national monuments or poetic material."[110] Fuller's excursion into the subterranean, seen in this light, is a historically appropriate movement connecting "deep time" and nationalism, one of the motivations, likely, behind Duyckinck's idea that the travelogue constituted "the only genuine American book of the season."[111] But what Fuller's descriptions of the layered soil suggests so clearly is that even the politically progressive version of these ideas depends on a careful stratification, on the layers of American fossilization staying each in their appropriate place. The liberal mixing of metaphors in *Summer on the Lakes*—the eagle as adornment to a Brave, as nationalist image, as emblem of poetry—requires the Native American to remain safely within his burial mound.

This stratification is apparent in Fuller's defense of Indigenous life and culture in the passage that follows. In her analysis of the analogies to Indian removal in Fuller's 1842 review essay "Romaic and Rhine Ballads," Annette Kolodny describes the "slipperiness of [Fuller's] governing grammatical construction" as characterizing her presentation of "the pervasive discourse of the vanishing Indian."[112] Grammar is similarly revelatory in *Summer on the Lakes*, where Fuller both critiques present Indian removal, and describes Black Hawk's tribe in the past tense: "They may blacken Indian life as they will, talk of its dirt, its brutality, I will ever believe that the men who chose that dwelling-place were able to feel emotions of noble happiness as they returned to it, and so were the women that received them."[113] Told from the security of past events, this defense is only slightly complicated by the more ambiguous tense of the next lines, where Fuller switches to a description of the present landscape: "The whole scene suggested to me a Greek splendor, a Greek sweetness, and I can believe that an Indian brave, accustomed to ramble in such paths, and be bathed by such sunbeams, might be mistaken for Apollo."[114] The ambiguous tense of "might be mistaken," simultaneously past, present, and future conditional, is nonetheless safely cloaked in the imaginative tense of speculation. As an object of fantasy, the Indian can be reanimated on scene in the guise of the classical figures, that like the outlines of his own culture, are representations of American history, ideals, and government.[115] The analogy of the brave to Apollo, likely an allusion to the painter Benjamin West's remark that the Apollo Belvedere resembles a Mohawk warrior, also prepares readers for the ekphrastic scene that follows.

Fuller moves on in the next lines to the image that inspires "Ganymede." She takes her starting-point, though, not in Thorvaldsen's sculpture, but in the American landscape that by association of form recalls the outlines of this sculpture: "The bluff was decked with great bunches of a scarlet variety of the milkweed, like cut coral, and all starred with a mysterious-looking dark flower, whose cup rose lonely on a tall stem. . . . Here I thought of, or rather saw, what the Greek expressed under the form of Jove's darling, Ganymede, and the following stanzas took form."[116] In this landscape, Fuller finds the image of the upraised cup, central to Thorvaldsen's visual depiction of Ganymede. While the poem claims itself "based on a sculpture by Thorvaldsen," this narrative context presents a more complicated picture, framing the apparent artistic original as a copy of the living landscape, a European cultural derivation of a natural American template.

Even the choice of Thorvaldsen as an artist betrays a nationalist bent. Thorvaldsen, who spent most of his career in Rome, was mentor to many of the young American artists who traveled to Italy in the 1820s and 1830s, including most prominently Horatio Greenough.[117] Thorvaldsen's popularity may owe something to the popular nationalist idea that he was said to be a descendent

"*The Fusion of the Races Among Us*" 93

of one of the Viking explorers who settled briefly off the North American coast around the turn of the first century, or as Thoreau records in *Cape Cod* (1865), this explorer, Thor-finn, "is said to have a son born in New England, from who Thorwaldsen the sculptor is descended."[118] Narratives of the pre-Columbian Viking "discovery" of the US were popular among the Boston intellectual elite in the nineteenth century, and have a clearly nationalist and racially motivated slant, claiming a Northern European heritage in light of Southern and Eastern European immigration, and imbuing America with a deeper historical past that provides a Euro-American challenge to its Indigenous heritage.[119] Fuller's choice of Thorvaldsen as an artist, then, provides a loaded association in this landscape that was until very recently inhabited by Native Americans, and symbolically extends the Northern European site of first contact further West.

But this nationalism is tempered by a nostalgic longing that infuses much of the poem. While Goethe's 1789 poetic interpretation of Ganymede focuses on the moment of the boy's capture in the eagle's claws, Fuller's version, like Thorvaldsen's statue, is much more static.[120] It imagines a time after the boy's initial abduction, when he with "A goblet of pure water in his hand, / . . . / A willing servant to sweet love's command,"[121] waits impatiently to be brought back once again to Jove. As he implores:

> Hast thou forgotten earth, forgotten me,
> Thy fellow bondsman in a royal cause,
> Who, from the sadness of infinity,
> Only with thee can know that peaceful pause
> In which we catch the flowing strain of love,
> Which binds our dim fates to the throne of Jove?[122]

Focusing on a moment of lovesickness and abandonment that is not a part of most versions of the tale, Fuller's poem emphasizes longing and Ganymede's wish "To wait, to wait, but not to wait too long."[123] And the Eagle, "the emblem of sovereignty of the United States"[124] in the words of one critic, is not an incarnation of Jove, but like Ganymede, a servant to this "Olympian king," Ganymede's "fellow bondsman in a royal cause."[125] In imagining the Eagle as not divine, but as Caleb Crain writes, "an intermediary,"[126] Fuller constructs a triangulated relationship within the already triangulated structure of ekphrasis.

Given the eagle's status as a national symbol, and Jove's as a "monarch," Euro-American, and specifically Anglo-American dependence is a dominant subtext in the poem.[127] This is a sense that is strengthened both by the context of Fuller's broader writing and the chapter in which the poem appears. Fuller's description of Ganymede's transitional longing strongly recalls the language that she uses elsewhere to discuss America's continued cultural reliance on Europe in the early national and antebellum periods. When Ganymede reminds Jove at the end of the poem of his mortality—"I am not yet divine, / Long years of service to the fatal Nine / Are yet to make a Delphian vigor mine,"[128] he echoes Fuller in her role as critic, describing an American literature that is separate yet servile: "Books which imitate or represent the thoughts and life of Europe do not constitute an American literature. . . . We are not anxious to prove that there is as yet much American literature."[129] Caught between servitude and independence, this early national version of the Ganymede-figure cannot yet strike out on his own, and gives no sense, through the continued longing on which the poem concludes ("Answer the stripling's hope, confirm his love") that independence is eminent.[130]

Likewise, the chapter that frames and follows the poem describes in large part what Fuller sees as the emulative and overly-dependent failings of women's education on the plains. "Everywhere," she writes, "the fatal spirit of imitation, of reference to European standards, penetrates, and threatens to blight whatever original growth might adorn the soil."[131] The result is women who are maladapted to their particular climates, who "can dance, but not draw; talk French, but know nothing of the language of flowers; neither in childhood were allowed to cultivate them, lest they should tan their complexions."[132] They are drawn to servitude rather than independence, but unlike the Indigenous people whose lives in the text function only to gesture toward an American past, the refusal of these eastern transplants to adapt is a refusal of their racial and national destiny. Their isolation on the plains underlines the formulaic futility of their servitude to another culture. Like the abandoned Ganymede who "A hundred times, at least, from the clear spring, / Since the full noon o'er hill and valley glowed" has "filled the vase which our Olympian king / Upon my care . . . bestowed,"[133] their repetition of earlier traditions constitutes a pathological gesture, an empty form, drained of its practical function.

Inserted between descriptions of Native American relocation and Euro-American resettlement, then, "Ganymede" is a record of two different forms of a nostalgic longing, both of them misdirected. Fuller represents Black Hawk's homesickness for his tribal lands as understandable but problematic—"No wonder he could not resist the longing, unwise though its indulgence might be"[134]—not only because his return to his homeland brought warfare and ultimately further losses to his people, but because, as she writes elsewhere in the travelogue "the power of fate is with the white man, and the Indian feels it."[135] Though Fuller repeatedly seems to be taking a strong stance for Native claims—as when she writes, just before this statement, "I scarcely see how they can forbear to shoot the white man where he stands"[136]—she simultaneously undermines this stance by statements that assume the inevitability of the white man's inheritance and are almost Jacksonian in their tone.

Fuller's representation of East Coast and Euro-American transplants in the West similarly frames their nostalgia for the forms of the past as understandable but ultimately misdirected. In an uncomfortable parallel, Fuller implicitly posits that if Native Americans need to accept the inevitability of their westward dislocation, Euro-Americans need to do the same, abandoning along the way ill-suited fashions such as piano music and the trend of "copying New York or Boston"[137] in educational practice. Like tribal resistance, such nostalgia is ultimately a dislocation, and ignores the exigencies of history and climate. Both of these forms of longing are encompassed in the dramatically futile image of Ganymede pining for his captor. Fuller herself seems to heed this call in her writing: in a narrative that elsewhere reproduces full letters and poems by friends, this section curtails the copying impulse. Near the end of the chapter, she reflects on the storytelling and "unstudied lore" of a friend, likely her travel companion (and possible source of inspiration for "Ganymede") William Freeman, and concludes, "But I will not attempt to transplant it. May it profit others as it did me in the region where it was born, where it belongs."[138]

Of course, the equation of Euro-American longing for eastern fashions, personal creativity, and Indigenous American longing for seized homelands is both radically incongruous and willfully ignorant of the place that agency plays in these dislocations. But this is the convolution of Fuller's politics—that she is both explicitly sympathetic to the Native plight on an individual level at the same time as she subscribes to the ideology that made tribal dislocation possible. Westward expansion is the force that will allow for the ideal of cultural fusion that Fuller lays out as literary critic in "American Literature," when "all its regions studded with towns, broken by the plow, netted together by railways and telegraph lines."[139] In "Ganymede" and its contexts, the images that Fuller relies on to conceptualize the American continent are not just those of a westward expansion, but of a downward movement through histories that are still only partially buried in the land.

This downward mapping takes place not just through the insistence on the Native American as past-tense artifact, but also through the historical framing of more recent waves of American immigration. Following the visit to Eagle's Nest that inspired her Ganymede poem, the traveling group celebrates the Fourth of July with "free and independent citizens . . . among whom many a round Irish visage dimpled at the usual puffs of Ameriky."[140] This celebration, with its "queer drumming and fifing"[141] contrasts in its acclimation to the landscape to the image of settlers wearing "satin shoes to climb the Indian mounds."[142] But like the deep history of this heritage, Fuller's vision of immigration to the continent depends on both a geographical and historical expansion.

This imagination emerges most clearly near the end of *Summer on the Lakes*, through a description of cultural blending in Milwaukee. This passage, like the poems that initiate the volume, also directly addresses the reader, calling for their participation in a nationalist imagination:

> Do not blame me that I have written so much about Germany and Hades, while you were looking for news of the West. Here, on the pier, I see disembarking the Germans, the Norwegians, the Swedes, the Swiss. Who knows how much of old legendary lore, of modern wonder, they have already planted among the Wisconsin forests? Soon, soon their tales of the origin of things, and the Providence which rules them will be so mingled with those of the Indian, that the very oak trees will not know them apart,—will not know whether itself be a Runic, a Druid, or a Winnebago oak.[143]

Fuller claims for the American continent not just the present lives but the past cultural histories of the people who inhabit the land, conceptualizing immigration as a movement that expands westward at the same time that it travels downward, a nationalism that is at the same time deeply transnational. In other words, she images very literally Dimock's description of deep time as "a set of longitudinal frames, at once projective and recessional, with input going both ways, and binding continents and millennia into many loops of relations."[144] Migrant populations alter not just an area's present cultural moment, but that culture's imagined history and its own origin stories. The tales of immigrant and Native American groups "mingle" with the landscape to emphasize the fluidity of the American identity: like the oak trees, Americans take on a collective past, even as the faces of Swedes, Swiss, and Germans are distinct.

"The Fusion of the Races Among Us" 97

This is Fuller's ideal of "fusion" enacted, where, as in Fuller's own text, European cultural references help to craft a new American present of multinational stories that overlap in shared national language, a concept that lies somewhere between complete assimilation and modern transnationality. On the one hand, fusion echoes the general ideal of the melting pot, and the vision of America—particularly its frontier—as a space of where nationalities and histories merge. In fact, fusion was a term that was used to describe the process of the melting pot in prominent instances.[145] And while there were degrees of assimilation in what writers through the nineteenth and twentieth centuries assumed in the idea of the melting pot, Fuller's vision is more varied for instance than Crevecouer's of a few generations earlier, who asserted that the American, "leaving behind him all his ancient prejudices and manners, receives new ones from the new mode of life he has embraced, the new government he obeys, and the new rank he holds."[146] Fuller's discussion suggests a more ethnically diverse if not exactly inclusive vision of nationality, while her idealized descriptions of Norwegians on the frontier in their national dress[147] suggest an understanding of assimilation that is less imitative, and less complete than melting. At the same time, Fuller's representation falls short of Randolph Bourne's later and more fully transnational understanding of America as a "transplanted Europe" in which "its colonies live here inextricably mingled, yet not homogeneous. They merge but they do not fuse."[148]

Summer on the Lakes ends as it began, with the direct address to the reader that typifies Fuller's brand of nationalism. Titled "The Book to the Reader, who opens as American readers often do, at the end, with doggerel submission" this poem emphasizes what has been implicit in Fuller's addresses to audience throughout: that this is an American book, by an American author, intended for an American audience. And if her opening dedicatory poems address the associationist mode of reading that she hopes her audience will indulge, one that relies on animating the stock emblems of her work, this last poem further conflates the distinction between the author and the reader, ending on a request to "read me, even as you would be read."[149] In line with this conflation, the final clause of the poem's title is ambiguous, referring either to the author or the reader, Fuller's own doggerel verse, or the reader's submissive reading practices. The poem—both through this title and its extended metaphor of berry-picking and jam-making—is more serious than its light, wholesome theme would imply. The title is gently teasing in its attitude toward its impatient readers, but in the context of a work that expresses continual disillusionment with the crass pragmatism of Americans, and what it presents as their frequent focus on the end rather than the means, the barb has a decided sting. And though Fuller in her introductory poems reaches out to readers to approach her text as she would have it read, in this last poem, she anticipates the worst. In the context of a largely plotless work, where Fuller's stated aim is to leave the reader with a "poetic impression," the joke is on the reader who skips to the end, and has clearly not absorbed the lesson of reading Fuller on her own terms.

The poem relies on the extended metaphor of eating blackberries—either in their wild, thorny form in the summer fields, or preserved with "housewife skill"—as respectively direct and mediated experience. The first is "A sweeter fruit . . . / Of wild, gay feelings, fancies springing sweet—" but also entails the tearing of dresses and hands. The second, for when "you cannot go yourself" is preserved "with foreign sugar." If this jam is a symbol for Fuller's text—both its second-hand travels and its transnational intertextualities—the response is not generous, and the teasing tone of the title flips to the author herself. The poem conjures an imagined critic, who deems the jam "pretty good," but continues:

> the best pleasure such a fruit can yield,
> Is to be gathered in the open field;
> If only as an article of food,
> Cherry or crab-apple are quite as good;
> And, for occasions of festivity,
> West India sweetmeats you had better buy.[150]

The speaker then confirms this taster's criticism as uncontroversial fact, pronouncing the mixture of native fruit and foreign sugar, this "dish of homely sweets," less pleasing than both the purely native or the purely foreign product. But the poem nonetheless ends on this entreaty by the speaker:

> Yet try a little with the evening-bread;
> Bring a good needle for the spool of thread;
> Take fact with fiction, silver with the lead,
> And, at the mint, you can get gold instead;
> In fine, read me, even as you would be read.[151]

This bid for generosity is in fact a bit more than that, inviting readers not just to see the work in its best light, but to increase its value, to transform silver and lead to gold. Readers in this framework pick up where the work leaves

"The Fusion of the Races Among Us"   99

off by threading the spool and taking an active part in the story's unfolding. Even a much more generous reading of Fuller's authorship—for instance, John Matteson's gloss of Fuller's "wild" text as the fresh-picked fruit—ends on the similar idea of the poem presenting "a challenge to readers to make themselves as deliberately unrefined as Fuller has made herself, to venture as boldly into the traps and wonders of her text as Fuller has explored the environs of Lake Michigan."[152]

This call to engagement ends on much the same note as Fuller's dedicatory poems began, and suggests the ways that she as an author saw mediation, imitation, and creation as interacting in the production and consumption of a work of art. Her own artistic product is made with "foreign sugar," under the influence of work such as Thorvaldsen's and Goethe's, among her other international digressions. This transnational influence is not a crutch but a conscious aesthetic choice: the white sugar, unlike the native "maple juice," "spoils not the fragrance of the fruit" with an overpowering flavor.[153] This distinction emphasizes what is already clear from a reading of Fuller's work: its mode of nationalism does not function through unmixed native scenes or language, but through mediation and influence. It is "by the best receipts compiled" rather than a wholly original production.[154] The collaborative triangulation of artist, art objects, and audiences in the end produces a fluid and experiential work more dynamic than that of innocent experience. That the poem's critical persona—not the speaker—has reservations about the product means only that they do not approach it as Fuller's ideal reader, on whom the speaker lays the onus of creation, the fusion of silver and lead to gold.

Whether Fuller found the ideal reader that her writing so clearly staked its success on is up for debate. The fragmentary form of the work, as I noted at the beginning of this chapter, was the subject of critical confusion and distaste. At the same time, she found a sympathetic reader in Evert Duyckinck, who was able see the broader outlines of her nationalism. The book also reached some general readers, selling a respectable seven hundred copies, more than Emerson's *Nature* or any issue of *The Dial*.[155] Several reviewers commented on its relative accessibility, and its move away from the dense thorniness of transcendentalism.[156] Horace Greeley, the editor of the *New-York Tribune*, who had been following Fuller's career since her work on *The Dial*, considered *Summer* "unequalled, especially in its pictures of the Prairies,"[157] offering proof of Fuller as "one of the most original as well as intellectual of American Women."[158] Greeley's admiration for the book brought to fruition the final stage in Fuller's career, as he offered her the positions of literary editor and eventually European correspondent for the *Tribune*.[159] Even Edgar Allan Poe, the most critical of critics, also seemed to see some of Fuller's aims, admiring the book's "graphicalilty" in its descriptions of the West.[160]

In some ways, though, the most fitting legacy of *Summer* may be on the landscape itself and the mapping of Fuller's imaginary setting onto the actual scene. The site of the "Ganymede Day" that made such an impact on Fuller's life now bears her own name and a legacy that conforms to her own ambitions. According to popular lore, she composed her poem to Ganymede under what was known as "Eagle's Nest Tree," and she dubbed a nearby spring as "Ganymede Spring," a name it still bears locally. In the same vicinity, a piece of land in the Rock River is called Margaret Fuller Island in honor of her visit. And in the 1898, the area became the site of the Eagle's Nest Arts Colony, a retreat founded by Chicago-based sculptor Lorado Taft. One of the artists associated with the colony would later erect a statue to Black Hawk on Eagle's Nest Bluff.[161] This development of the central scene of Fuller's narrative has a certain poetic justice. In making her textual mark on the physical American landscape, Fuller effected precisely the kind of collaboration between reader and writer that *Summer* advocates.

CHAPTER THREE

"Folded up in a Veil"

Sophia Peabody Hawthorne's Familial Ekphrasis
and the Antebellum Travelogue

Sophia Hawthorne is known to literary history primarily as the wife of Nathaniel Hawthorne, the sister of Elizabeth Palmer Peabody, and the editor—some have said prudish censor—of Nathaniel's posthumously published work. But as a trained and exhibited painter, and visual copyist of landscapes, her single published work, a travelogue of the Hawthorne family's movements through Europe from 1853 to 1860, offers revealing insights into questions of American artistic originality from the perspective of a simultaneous insider and outsider to the conversation.[1] Sophia's art descriptions, which take up the principal part of the Roman and Florentine sections of the travelogue, show the nuance and detail-orientation of the painter's eye as well as a developing understanding of the visual copy as central both to the preservation of works of the past and the creation of "original" works. The travelogue, whose professed purpose is to help others to enjoy "the illustrious works of the Great Masters in Architecture, Sculpture, and Painting," aspires to these same dual functions of preservation and origination. The text's arguments for the creative potential of the copy allude not only to Nathaniel but to family friend Ralph Waldo Emerson, both of whom were directly imbricated in public conversations around a national literature. In this sense, *Notes in England and Italy* (1868), though the single published text by an author who insisted on her own unprofessional status, reflects many of the conflicts and concerns of the broader American literary culture in the years leading up to the Civil War.

Notes complicates the gendered categories of original/copy and public/private that were an important part of the antebellum vocabulary of artistry. As Claire Badaracco writes, Sophia was part of "that last generation of the women of pre-industrial American society . . . where girls were educated in front parlors, 'reading' was commonly understood to mean *elocution*, 'composition' was *making copies*, and 'writing' was primarily an exercise in journals and copy-books."[2] Antebellum women writers—from Frances Osgood to Lydia Sigourney to Fanny Fern—were strongly associated with such mimesis. Literature and popular culture likewise feminized the character of the visual copyist, and the era's discourse associated women with the private sphere of the family.[3] To some extent, *Notes* works from within these categories, and as Annamarie Elsden suggests, Hawthorne understands her writing as "a way to 'copy' what she sees on her travels and transmit it to readers at home."[4] But at the same time, the travelogue challenges the boundaries of what it means both to copy and to exist in a privatized space, carving out a space for itself, and for women's writing more broadly, that also extends into original creation and the public sphere.

Ekphrasis, a central aspect of the era's Grand Tour travelogues, lays bare American anxieties about originality and offers Sophia, a lifelong copyist married into literary nationalism, a testing ground for replication that is both publicly anodized and privately allusive. The interplay between reader, author, and text in *Notes* crystallizes in passages that challenge apparently derivative description, both inscribing and concealing the private life of the Hawthorne family and friends within the public space of ekphrasis. Sophia had from her youth written hundreds of pages of journal writing that was circulated among an audience of family and friends but not formally published, as part in what Noelle Baker calls "a 'third sphere' of public discourse, a social realm that mediates 'private' and 'public' spheres."[5] A sort of "third sphere" also emerges in the published *Notes*: by alluding to private, partially effaced events through a public commentary, Sophia creates a document that is both a familial and an artistic record, both a private and a public document. The ekphrastic descriptions of *Notes*—and the excisions and emendations that these descriptions underwent as she prepared the journal for publication—reveal not just a concern for the divisions between copy and original, but a preoccupation with the often needling or idiosyncratic distinctions between "public" and "private" material. The resulting document works fragmentary glimpses of private life into publicly accessible art descriptions, disturbing the boundary between these spheres.

Reading *Notes* in relation to the manuscript journal on which it is based, it becomes clear that editing—the activity for which Sophia has been most maligned in relation to Nathaniel's work—allows her to transform a direct nonfictional account into an original aesthetic production.[6] Her editorial hand excises direct references to family members and friends, overwriting them with descriptions of artworks. She shifts phrases for effect as much as for meaning. And she replaces the personalized, direct references to her children by a more general address to an audience. Sophia's editorial alterations are not merely expressive of an overdeveloped propriety, as has often been argued of her editorial work on Nathaniel's journals, but show the creative potential of copying with a difference.

This chapter first traces Sophia's discussion of her own writing through the trope of the veil, a trope that calls into play Nathaniel's canon and its representation of the woman writer. Through this trope, Sophia represents her own text not as the body beneath the veil, but the veil itself, hiding more than it reveals, and preserving a private essence within the public sphere. I then turn to the nationalism that has often been a framework for the travelogue more broadly, and consider Sophia's art descriptions—and her shifting relations to copyists and copying in the course of the writing—within this framework. References to Emerson support a conception of reiteration and repetition as a creative space, and the text's relation to copying and the copyists of the Roman and Florentine galleries grows increasingly positive. Ultimately, the travelogue preserves and recreates both the works of the Great Masters and Hawthorne family history, suggesting the transformative potential of what was one of the era's most common forms of women's writing.

THE BAGGAGE OF WOMEN'S TRAVEL WRITING

A few pages from the end of *Notes*, on a final return to Rome with her family, Sophia mulls over the ways that these midlife travels have altered her youthful, idealized image of the city and its imperial history. Sophia's travels in the 1850s with her husband and children "destroyed [her] fancies" of Rome, complementing the vision of militaristic glory with a darker, more destructive reality, shadowing the natural and artistic beauties of the city with the constant threat of malarial death. But despite this disillusionment, Sophia remains entranced, and on the family's final carriage-ride through the city, she considers this contradictory attraction: "What, then, is this Rome that *will* hold sway over mankind, whether or no, in past and present time? I have an idea, but it is folded up in a veil, and I cannot take this moment to answer my question."[7] Though the text does not return to the question, the other objects that the travelogue has described as being veiled—paintings and the doorways to churches—suggest an answer. Descriptions of art and architecture take up the bulk of the Italian sections of the text, and these descriptions, like Sophia's most private sentiments, are often obscured.

If meaning "is folded up in a veil" in Sophia's text, ekphrasis is the veil that enfolds it, and the task of uncovering falls to the reader. In describing a Madonna by Raphael, after noting that the painting "surpasses entirely all the copies in oil and all engravings" Sophia complains of her own ekphrastic attempts: "This work transcends any power I possess of conveying it to the mind of another. My words seem poor rags, with which I endeavor to clothe the idea—heaps of rags—the more I try, the larger the heaps."[8] Her writing— which dwells primarily on the expression on the faces of the mother and child rather than any concrete markers of color or form—obscures as much as it reveals, but goes on nonetheless, in this section spanning two pages of "rags," to build up a veiled meeting space for reader and author. Here as elsewhere, Sophia switches in her writing between the first person singular and plural, concluding the description with a more generalized summary: "We may find some lesser or greater shortcomings in others; but Raphael cannot be criticized."[9] Calling into play the creative participation of the reader, the text's ekphrastic moments function as a "third sphere" between private and public, which opens up to an audience to fill its literary gaps. The potentiality of this space is, like Rome itself, alluring, mysterious, and at times confusing. Italy, in Sophia's inconclusive conclusion, preserves its mysteries precisely because "the answer" lies not in the unidealized Roman that the text unveils, but rather in the folds of the veil themselves.[10]

Sophia's self-positioning as author in this passage exemplifies what critics have identified as the conflicted relation to public spaces in women's writing of this period. Richard Brodhead, for instance, conceptualizes the opposing demands of the public and private spheres for mid-nineteenth century American women authors through the symbol of the Veiled Lady. This popular antebellum performer was both "a creature of physical invisibility," completely hidden by her veil, and one of "pure exhibitionism,"[11] whose work on stage brought her continuously before the public to answer its questions with apparent clairvoyance. Similarly, the rise of mass print brought female writers into the public sphere in unprecedented ways, even as it broadcast an understanding of the women's sphere as "dephysicalized and deactivated domestic privacy."[12] The Veiled Lady is for Brodhead a symbol for the bestselling authors and entertainers of mid-century, public figures like Harriet Beecher Stowe and Susan Warner whose books both propagated and were enabled by a vision of the home as a private space of leisure. These celebrity figures and their works represented to their readership "a public embodiment of a fascinating private life,"[13] an unprecedentedly accessible vision of individual subjectivity. Sophia, in figuring her (first-person, and implicitly personal) text as a veil that readers may themselves uncover, participates in this symbolic tradition.

Fittingly, Brodhead's starting point for analysis is Nathaniel Hawthorne's *The Blithedale Romance*, a novel whose Veiled Lady, the character Priscilla, has long inspired critical parallels to Sophia. Sophia certainly confronted the contradictory demands of a public existence both before and after her marriage,[14] but unlike Nathaniel's veiled clairvoyant performer, who as Brodhead writes, is talentless, "a victim of her display" exploited by her handlers, Sophia made her own (albeit conflicted) decisions about the extent of her public appearance.[15] In her youth, she saw her older sister Elizabeth Palmer Peabody struggle to support the family through careers in teaching, writing, and publishing, all the while remaining in the shadow of the figures her writing promoted. Sophia, afflicted throughout her lifetime with debilitating migraines that had been exacerbated by childhood mercury "cures," was to a large extent freed from these financial demands.[16] But given the literary circles in which her family moved, and her later marriage to one of America's most celebrated authors, she was never far removed from publicity.

For Sophia, though she had exhibited as a painter, uncomfortable publicity often took the form of the more personally revelatory writing, a discomfort that was exacerbated by Nathaniel's well-known reservations about women writers. When her sister Elizabeth read to her wide circle of friends journal entries that Sophia had sent home from Cuba in the early 1830s, Sophia chided her and reported feeling "as if the nation were feeling my pulse."[17] The letters, which were eventually bound by the family into a three-volume, 785-page "Cuba Journal," were never published, although Elizabeth had encouraged

Sophia to edit them for the *American Monthly*.[18] When Nathaniel and Sophia first met, he borrowed the volumes for more than a month, copying passages into his own notebooks, and on their return pronouncing Sophia "the Queen of Journalizers."[19] He nonetheless supported her reticence toward publication later in their relationship, praising her in 1856 for having "never prostituted thyself to the public" by appearing in print, and opining that authorship "seem[s] to me to deprive women of all delicacy."[20] When Nathaniel's editor James Fields approached Sophia in 1859 about publishing her English and Italian letters and journals, she continued to insist that Nathaniel alone was "the Belleslettres portion of my being."[21] But published or not, Sophia was an undeniably public literary figure, and after her husband's death in 1864, did print sections from these travel notebooks in addition to Nathaniel's American and European journals. Two passages from her British letters first appeared in the September and October 1869 *Putnam's Magazine*, and then the full *Notes* was released by the same publishing house later that year.

Notes is particularly salient from the perspective of Sophia's conflicted public persona, because if women writers often found their public and private selves conflated, the travelogue exaggerated this conflation. A travel narrative not only purports to publicize the autobiographical experience of an author, it does so in the very public context of the cities, monuments, and museums of international destinations. Whatever the limited public roles of their authors, these works are primarily studies of public space. The numbers of women's travelogues dramatically increased in the course of the nineteenth century. Before the 1820s, women's travel outside of the US was for the most part what Mary Schriber characterizes as "accidental,"[22] undertaken to accompany male family members, who most frequently traveled for work rather than leisure. The invention of steam-powered ships in the 1820s encouraged women's leisure travel, even independent of male escorts; the luxurious "steam palaces" of the 1860s furthered this trend. Women's writing remained "accidental" in style even as the travel that occasioned it became increasingly purposeful. Only 27 women's travelogues were published before the Civil War, in contrast to the 168 that appeared after the War. The books of this earlier period are characterized by informality; they are "letters written by homemakers for private consumption, and later cobbled into travel books" rather than the professional newspaper or magazine correspondences that emerged later in the century.[23] The very informality of this work highlights the intimacy of its writers with their audiences, and heightens the voyeurism of more general readers in consuming private letters and journals. As if to mitigate this exposure, authors often prefaced these travelogues with modest protestations of their reluctance to publish, and placed responsibility on friends and family members for engineering the move.[24]

In this same vein, many women's travelogues from the antebellum period negotiate public space through the lens of domesticity. Travel writing was often a means of reflecting back on the "home"—both the private domestic circle and native country—from the luxury of distance. In this sense, many of these works challenge the strict binaries between public and domestic, inserting reflections on home into descriptions of their destinations, and reflecting on the differences between foreign and native perceptions of private space. These reflections could be either liberating or limiting.[25] In some cases, even as women traveled abroad, their accounts of these travels were shaped by the home and conceptions of their "proper province."[26] Sarah Haight describes her domestic camp in the Egyptian desert, while Harriet Beecher Stowe dwells on the "bed room, dining room, sitting room" of Robert the Bruce's caves.[27] This domestication of public spaces comes in direct contrast to the frequent sexualization of travel and foreign lands in the travelogues of male writers. If Italy, for instance, was allegorized by male travelers on the Grand Tour as both "frivolously beautiful" and the "feminized" object of sexual conquest, for female writers, the land's domestication became a means of ensuring readers of the traveler's protection from sexual threat.[28]

Sophia's *Notes*, from its first pages, participates in many of these generic conventions, though she may have been less reluctant to publish than she led her audience to believe. The preface, for instance, begins with a stock protestation of unwillingness to publish that ties the author's voice firmly in the private sphere and suggests the extenuating circumstances of her publication:

> I think it necessary to say that these "Notes," written twelve years ago, were never meant for publication; but solely for my own reflection, and for a means of recalling to my friends what had especially interested me abroad. Many of these friends have repeatedly urged me to print them, from a too partial estimate of their value; and I have steadily resisted the suggestion, until now, when I reluctantly yield.[29]

Sophia's descriptive writing was much admired among her inner circle; Nathaniel wrote to William Ticknor during the family's time abroad that "Mrs. Hawthorne altogether excels me as a writer of travels."[30] But there is evidence that it was Nathaniel, rather than Sophia, who most strongly "resisted" the publication of *Notes*. When Fields proposed the publication in 1859, Sophia asserted dramatically that "nothing less than the immediate danger of starvation for my husband and children would induce me to put myself between a pair of book covers."[31] A contemporaneous letter to Elizabeth, however, points to Nathaniel as the source of resistance. In discussing Fields' proposal, Sophia writes dutifully of her decision "not to argue the matter any further with Mr. Hawthorne" and to "postpone all my own possibilities in the way of art."[32] This deferral provides an answer to the open question that the preface inspires: why, after twelve years, did Sophia "reluctantly yield"? Critics have traditionally pointed to the financial straits of the years after Nathaniel's death for an answer, and Sophia's ambiguity in the preface may have intended to hint in this direction. But the letter to Elizabeth suggests that personal artistic fulfillment, deferred during Nathaniel's lifetime, was at least equally at stake.[33]

Certainly, the way that Sophia represented private and public life in *Notes* was carefully considered and curated. For Sophia, the experience of an art object enfolded within it the familial and personal trappings that influenced her perception of the work. This influence is clear from the Italian journals on which Sophia based the Roman and Florentine sections of *Notes*. These journals record images of the children alongside of sketches from great works, and descriptions of the children likewise accompany passages of ekphrasis.[34] In the published *Notes*, the author curtails these private interruptions, to the extent that Edwin Miller complains that "her descriptions constitute a rather prosaic and impersonal travelogue. . . . When Sophia was writing about the home, she was at her best."[35] A close examination of the descriptions in *Notes*, however, reveals that Sophia is precisely "writing about the home," if only indirectly. The volume is dedicated to "Elizabeth P. Peabody" from "her sister, S. H.," and the name that appears on the title page is simply "Mrs. Hawthorne." More explicit familial references get absorbed in the descriptions of images themselves, haunting artworks in ways that point at the private significance of public works. The last lines of the preface draw these connections out: "If [these *Notes*] will aid any one in the least to enjoy, as I have enjoyed, the illustrious works of the Great Masters in Architecture, Sculpture, and Painting, I shall be well repaid for the pain it has cost me to appear before the public."[36] The focus of the text is on the "Great Masters," but it is Sophia herself who feels painfully exposed. Family makes only a secondary appearance in *Notes*, but it is to family that the work is dedicated and doubtless in part because of these connections that the travelogue went through eight editions in the fourteen years following its publication.[37] At the same time, artworks are the primary means by which this private space gets articulated, suggesting that ekphrasis's seemingly narrow and mimetic function couches much broader goals.

THE ART OF THE TRAVELOGUE

Ekphrastic descriptions were a major component of antebellum travelogues, but critics, following the assumptions of nineteenth century writers themselves, have often treated this element as a more or less transparent (and often somewhat boring) description of objects. In the preface to her 1841 travel narrative, Catherine Maria Sedgwick writes that "I was aware that our stayers-at-home had already something too much of churches, statues, and pictures, and yet that they cannot well imagine how much they make up the existence of tourists in the Old World."[38] Sedgwick's terming as "familiar things" the "churches, statues, and pictures" that by the 1840s only an elite minority of Americans had seen firsthand speaks both to the strong market presence of the travelogue and to the public's sense of the stock representation of these objects. Accordingly, critics have tended to see ekphrasis as easily glossed description that does not participate significantly in the theoretical concerns of the travelogue as a whole. Alfred Bendixen and Terry Caesar, for instance, both see nationalism as the unifying preoccupation of American travelers from the nineteenth to the twentieth centuries, but do not consider the almost universal factor of art description in these terms.[39] And although theorists discuss poetic ekphrasis in terms of gender—or an aesthetic competition between masculine text and the feminine art object—they have not extended this formulation to the more prosaic terrain of travel writers translating an object for a reading public.[40] Sophia's art-centered travelogue formulates the issues of nationalism and originality with particular focus, given the place of her family and friends' roles in American literary nationalism, and her own work as a copyist of images.

Nationalism is also at play in aesthetic descriptions of people and places. Like many travel writers of this period, Sophia used the travelogue as a means to stress the practical and political backwardness of Europe, making constant implicit and at times explicit comparisons to the more modern American norms. In the sections on Italy in particular, the filth and poverty of the towns and the people is a constant refrain, as Sophia writes from Bolsena: "We, of the other side of the Atlantic, have not the remotest idea of how dirty a person can be, who has not been washed for nearly three thousand years! . . . It is only in Europe that one can see a dirty face, and it is necessary to come Europe to comprehend it."[41] Sophia often links this dirt to disease, and particularly the threat of malaria; as she writes later in this section, after describing a grimy Etruscan palace, "the stealthy demon of malaria is stealing up the heights; and soon the people will all fall victim to it."[42] (Sophia was, as she recorded this statement, nursing her daughter Una back from a malarial fever.)

But even further, the ingrained dirt of the towns and the people connotes a more abstract political and historical taint such as that which Sophia admits in discussing her late disillusionment around Roman honor and glory. In that passage in Bolsena, for instance, Sophia notes that the stones of the palace "must be impregnated with evil, which could not be burnt out," a reference perhaps to the Etruscan practice of human sacrifice, which the Romans would later adopt.[43] She references this practice more concretely earlier in the travelogue when referencing the slave labor that built the Coliseum, "where unspeakable atrocities once amused assembled thousands"; "Then it is necessary to suffer to *produce* beauty as well as *to be* beautiful. Alas for the blood and toil and misery and crime out of which these glories sprang!"[44] That central conflict of American literary nationalism, the shallowness of the country's Euro-American history, reads from this perspective as a boon.

Notes moves forward in part through a drive to disinfect for an American public the original spirit of Renaissance paintings from this historical grime, to offer a version of beauty without suffering. In Sophia's accounts, many of these artworks are illegible, poorly maintained, or hidden, and attempts to restore their surfaces only botch them further. The work of the copyist, visual or textual, in Sophia's text is therefore to disseminate the lost or damaged original to a broader, and in her text implicitly American public. The copy is always dependent on the reference point of an original, but also capable of replacing this reference point in cases where the original is damaged, lost, or inaccessible. This preservationist function appears first in the preface to *Notes*, which states its aim to "aid any one in the least to enjoy, as I have enjoyed, the illustrious works of the Great Masters."[45] Similarly, in cases where visual copies are faithful, Sophia embraces their utility in the task of artistic dissemination. As she writes of one fresco room in Perugia: "A young artist was sitting there, copying the groups and single figures with a lead pencil, in an extraordinary manner, and with the utmost fidelity. He, and others as accomplished and faithful, should be commissioned to save in imperishable lines the vanishing masterpieces of fresco-painting."[46] The fragility of fresco and the clumsiness of nineteenth-century preservation techniques—*Notes* also often references botched restoration jobs—makes the good copy the most reliable means of salvaging the painted works that are fading before viewers' eyes.[47]

In spite of the preservationist value of the copy, Sophia is in earlier gallery entries critical of replication and imitation that extends beyond this function. Her critique of the Pre-Raphaelite painters reflects this skepticism, as she notes that they replicate external elements of style, while eschewing essence: "all the religion is left out, all the holy fervor, sincerity, and simplicity."[48] This failing has to do directly with the spirit of the age, and the decline of the connection between religion and art, or as she writes: "If painters now were holy men, and dedicated their genius to heaven, perhaps angels and cherubs would still live to their imagination, and so to our eyes, through their pencils. But what watery, theatrical, unspiritual, impossible angels we have now-a-days!"[49]

The failing of the Pre-Raphaelites is the same failing that makes for a bad preservationist copy, but also leaves open the possibility for a copy to surpass the original. Copyists, like modern "unspiritual" painters can produce a bad painting that convincingly replicates a form, but misses the essence of a work. The "faithful" artist commissioned to undertake the preservation of a great work must operate by channeling the spirit of the original work, or as Sophia writes, they "should be informed with the feeling and the secret of the soul that wrought the wonder, or they only hide the masterpiece they pretend to repeat."[50] This goal heightens the stakes of the copy beyond the faithful execution of form—and many copyists subject to Sophia's criticisms fail even at this.[51] But more compellingly, some artists outperform the originals that they set out to imitate, and in so doing, create a work that transcends its descriptive qualities. Sophia encounters several such artists, including one at a large Nativity scene by Gherardo della Notte, whose copy "had the depth of an abyss in it, and the dazzle of light from the Holy Child was truly spiritual, far finer in effect than that of the original picture."[52]

The ability of a copy to transcend its original suggests that even the preservationist copy can take on the characteristics of an independent work, and in fact, Sophia's attitude toward copying grows more liberal in the course of the text. Her harshest reflections on the work of bad copyists occurs early in the Italian sections, and her admission of a copy that was "far finer" than the original occurs almost at the end of the travelogue. At the same time, latter sections of *Notes* introduce the idea that her most admired "original" artists were themselves capable of replication. The first time the text introduces the question of a master having imitated another's work in his own, Sophia dismisses it just as quickly. Certain figures, Sophia writes, were "so much admired by Raphael that he is said to have imitated them in his sibyls of the Santa Maria della Pace, in Rome. But it is pretty bold saying that Raphael imitated any one."[53] Nonetheless, this "bold" suggestion becomes increasingly persuasive in the course of the travelogue.

Some pages later, Sophia recounts a story about the sculptor Horatio Greenough, although this time in terms that reveal a more expansive sense of what the copy can be: "According to Mr. Mozier, of Rome, Greenough never originated the slightest thing, but copied the antique, and embodied detailed descriptions of antique statues, now not extant, and put into marble painted figures, like these cherubs. Here are these, at any rate, perfectly familiar to me through Greenough's group, which I saw so many years ago in Boston, and always supposed his own conception. No one ever told me they were copies."[54] Although Sophia in this statement, as the last, maintains a careful distance from the accusation of copying—the suggestion attributed to a single figure, with "no one" else having mentioned it in the years since she first saw the figures—she is less careful about policing the variety of practices that fall under the single idea of copying. The term seamlessly encompasses replicas of existing work; interpretations of lost works, based on written descriptions; and sculptural interpretations of painted work. The last two of these practices involve a translation from one medium to another, and so are only copying practices in a much looser interpretative sense than the first. This medial translation implicitly calls into play Sophia's own ekphrastic text—Powers's second form of copy is a form of reverse ekphrasis, from text to image—and begins to break down the boundaries between copied and original work, even as Sophia is careful to avoid weighing in on Mozier's judgement.

This expanding sense of the copy culminates in the last sections of the text to the point that Sophia frames both Raphael and Michaelangelo directly, and even offhandedly, as copyists. She begins an entry from Florence with the statement, "I stood long at the gate of the Baptistery this morning, and I saw why Raphael studied and copied those figures. He drew from them some of his ineffable grace."[55] Whereas earlier in the text, even to suggest Raphael's imitation seemed "bold," here his copying—and his artistic gains from this imitation—are presented as a matter of course. Later on in Florence, near the end of the travelogue, she goes even further: "I saw in the Institute a figure by a very early master, like Michel Angelo's Judge in the Sistine fresco. Could he have appropriated it? Michel Angelo and Raphael took with royal hands whatever they pleased, from right and left, and then made their spoils entirely their own; and they were so rich, and their genius so plastic, that they could do this without invading their originality. As Mr. Story said, 'It is only the weak who fear to be helped.'"[56] At this late point in the writing, appropriation, far from being a "bold" suggestion, is a given, and is evidence for rather than against "originality."

The blurring of these terms complicates their traditional hierarchy and reflects Sophia's own history and ambitions as a visual copyist, and ultimately as a writer. The seeds for the pilgrimage to Italy that *Notes* records were planted thirty years before, when the young aspiring artist completed a copy of a landscape painting by Washington Allston. Declaring it the first time she had "felt *satisfied* with a copy" Sophia described the process of this painting as not simply a reproduction of forms, but as a "bodying forth the poet's dream—*Creation!*"[57] The work made the twenty-six-year-old Sophia a minor celebrity in Boston, and eventually brought to her home studio Allston himself, who praised the copy and laid out for Sophia his advice for a young artist's education: apprenticeship in England and Italy, which would include both drawing from nature and from masterworks. But for Allston, steeped in a neoclassical tradition that valued history painting as the highest form of the medium, the advice to copy other works was only the means to the end of creating "original" compositions.[58] Sophia's conceptions were more mixed: most of the works she produced in her lifetime were copies, but she held the creation of "original" work—images that she had seen neither in nature or in other artworks—as an aesthetic ideal. When she for instance painted eight small landscapes for an 1833 Salem fundraiser, she wrote proudly to her sisters that "Four of them I created!!!!!!!"—meaning that she had imagined and improvised the compositions.[59] At the same time, her exclamation that the Allston copy embodied "the poet's dream—*Creation!*" implies a distinction between copy and original significantly more conflicted than Allston's. Rather than seeing the copy as simply a stage in the progression toward mature artistic work, Sophia appreciated gradations of quality within the category, and understood the copy as capable of expressing a form of originality, even possibly surpassing its original subject.

Sophia holds her own prose in the travelogue to the same standards that she applies to the visual copyist. The analogy between the visual and the textual copy is, in her manuscript journals, very literal: her descriptions of images are often accompanied by, and explicitly refer to, sketches that also copy some detail of the artwork.[60] That these textual descriptions enter into some of the same conflicts that Sophia lays out for the visual copy, then, is not surprising. *Notes* is in its most basic sense conservationist, recording descriptions of works that often seemed on the verge of disappearance; as Annamaria Eldsen suggests, "the written word of Sophia's text may be her attempt to transcend time's destructive power and offer to a reading public 'lines' that will not fade."[61] As part of the task of conservation, these descriptions efface their obvious personal contexts, much as "faithful" visual copies channel the works that they emulate at the expense of individualist expression. But Sophia's writing also aspires to something like the "*Creation*" that she saw in her Allston copy, a personal intervention that distinguishes the copy from its source.

A fitting metaphor for the originary potential of both Sopia's textual and visual copy-work emerges in an unassuming description in *Notes*, tagged at the end of a day of sightseeing in Florence. "In the University halls," Sophia writes, "we saw a very singular work. I supposed it to be an engraving of Raphael's *Belle Jardinière*, but the custode told us that it was all composed of almost microscopically small words, written with a pen."[62] A word-painting that is both a visual replica of Raphael's original painting of the Madonna and Child with St. John the Baptist and its own "singular" artwork, the pen drawing is an original copy in its own right. As an image comprised of words, it also provides an elegant metaphor for the originary ekphrasis that Sophia undertakes in *Notes*. The journal entry ends abruptly on this last line, and Sophia does not describe what the "small words" that make up the image spell out. But this withholding too is fitting: like her own ekphrastic text, which conceals beneath its surface the intricacies of family life, and which gives up only the larger outline of her descriptive copy, the image of Raphael's *Belle Jardinière* presents its external form to casual viewers and hints only "microscopically" at the run of its internal text. This curated interweaving of public and private is precisely what defines the work as "singular."

If the best copies can be "far finer in effect than the original picture," it is by making some alteration to their source. Looking at the alterations of Sophia's text, both her deviations from a literal ekphrastic description and the changes she made from manuscript to print volume, provides a sense of the means to her own originality. Such an examination reveals the extent to which the private life of *Notes* seeps into its ekphrastic passages, and Sophia's adept manipulation and incorporation of family life—a life that the Hawthornes had explicitly sought to curtail from the public eye—into the space of her ekphrastic description. By highlighting with ellipses and other markers her decisions about what to excise or alter in the published volume, she signals her acute awareness of both the public/private and original/copy divides. *Notes* is a record of the "works of the Great Masters" for the general public, but it is equally a record of family and friendship couched and made consumable for a larger audience, a "record for my children's sake, hereafter," as Sophia confesses near the end of the travelogue.[63] Ekphrasis is for Sophia a means of confronting both public and private spaces, copied and original works, and staking out a place for herself as a writer and artist that is inclusive of both ends of this spectrum. By inhabiting in *Notes* an aesthetic middle ground, Sophia directly challenges the notion that aesthetic questions must be phrased in divisive terms.

MR. E'S "REFLECTIVE" MUSE

The figure in *Notes* who first highlights this attempt to exist between categories is defined by some of the same contradictions as Sophia's text. A family friend and supporter of Sophia's creative work who had strongly gendered views on artistic originality, Ralph Waldo Emerson is key to introducing the terms of analysis for Sophia's ekphrasis. Emerson appears in four thematically significant passages in *Notes*, the only person not actively participating in the travels to feature so centrally. The reiterated references to "Mr. E." or "E.," as he is called in the published text, emphasize his personal significance to Sophia, while his public persona renders these references legible to Sophia's readers. The references actively develop an understanding of copying and originality, terms that were both subtexts to Sophia and Emerson's relationship and touchstones in his writing. As a recurrent figure in *Notes*, Emerson helps to define the "singular" potential of the copy in Sophia's own text.

Emerson first entered the Peabody family circle in 1822, when the recent college graduate gave Greek lessons to Elizabeth, who was then teaching in Boston.[64] Elizabeth's relationship to Emerson is well-documented. After the first awkward introduction as pupil, she became close to Emerson and his second wife Lydian through her work with Bronson Alcott's school in the mid-1830s.[65] She became Emerson's equal in Greek as well as an important intellectual ally, and was a frequent summer visitor to the Emersons' home in Concord. On such visits she helped to organize his lectures and advised him on publishing, with which she had greater familiarity.[66] At her short-lived bookstore in Boston, she hosted the final meeting of the Transcendental Club, as well as distributed and eventually published copies of *The Dial*.[67] While the aims of Elizabeth's work were more social and reformist than Emerson's—she saw in his championing of the individual the threat of "egotheism" among the "weak brother and sister Transcendentalist[s]"—they were cut from the same intellectual cloth and held a deep mutual respect for each other's ideals.[68]

Sophia's relationship to Emerson is less well-documented, but was much more than an extension of her older sister's friendship, and dwelled significantly in issues of creativity. She maintained an independent correspondence with Emerson into her late life and was his neighbor in Concord on two separate occasions: in 1842, when the newlywed Hawthornes rented the Old Manse from Emerson, and from 1860 until Nathaniel's death in 1864, when the family returned from Europe and lived in the Wayside.[69] Though Emerson was conservative in his views of female artists, writing that creative genius "dangerously narrows the career of a woman" and that "only the most extraordinary genius can make the career of an artist secure and agreeable to her," he was adamantly supportive of Sophia's endeavors, including her attempts to craft original compositions.[70] He admired her skill at copying, writing, for instance, of a copy of the Washington Allston painting *Lorenzo and Jessica* that it was "admirable, and of a Chinese exactness of imitation," but he encouraged her even more in creating independent compositions.[71] In 1836 he wrote, "I learn with great pleasure that you are attempting an original picture on a great subject. Of this I hope soon to hear much more. I shall heartily rejoice in your success. You must postpone everything to it, but your health."[72] Two years later, he reiterated the encouragement: "I can never quarrel with your state of mind concerning original attempts in your own art. I admire it rather."[73] Sophia sent him drawings in the 1830s, and in 1840 sculpted a Roman-style portrait medallion of Emerson's beloved brother Charles, who had died a few years earlier. Emerson was deeply impressed by the "striking likeness" which Sophia had produced from memory, and had eight copies in plaster cast for family members, calling it in a letter to Sophia "the gift of a Muse" and praising her "genius."[74]

Emerson's consideration of copying and originality in Sophia's work reflects the terms' unclear definitions in literary nationalism, and the way that that they were alternately used to denigrate or praise his own production. A scathing 1847 review of Emerson's *Poems* in the *Southern Quarterly Review*, for instance, begins by calling him "an American Carlyle, in the same way that we have the American Walter Scott in Cooper, and the American Dickens in Neal. . . . It is a grave mistake, however, to take pride in such resemblances, as if any portion of the merit of the originator of any style of writing, belonged to his copyists. What in him may be proof of genius, in them is sure proof of the lack of it."[75] Other readers came to nearly opposed perspectives, as the author of the *Blackwood's Edinburgh Magazine* review that appeared the same month.[76] That author praises Emerson precisely in terms of originality, stating that if he were called to elect an American writer whose works "displayed the undoubted marks of original genius" he would select Emerson; the author is "quite sure that no French or German critic could read the speculations of Emerson without tracing in them the spirit of the nation to which this writer belongs."[77] This assessment, read alongside the contemporary assessment of Emerson as a "copyist" of Carlyle speaks to the complexities of a writer who both wore his transatlantic debts on his sleeve and proclaimed that Americans "have listened too long to the courtly muses of Europe."[78] Long before the publication of "Quotation and Originality" in 1859, "an essay which made an eloquent and lengthy case for the acknowledgement—even the acclamation—of cultural unoriginality," Emerson's approach to artistic originality caused controversy—or at least confusion.[79]

Sophia's references to Emerson in *Notes* function both to highlight and cultivate the concept of literary originality. On the one hand, they align with Emerson's somewhat confused placement within discussions of literary nationalism, as well Sophia's own conflicted considerations of artistic originality. The allusions provide Sophia with an intellectual backdrop for considering the nature of the copy and the potential power of "copied" descriptions in her own text. At the same time, the point of the references is just as much in Emerson's presence as it is in his perspective. The power of Sophia's own aesthetic copies lies precisely in the personal references to well-known figures that Sophia works, almost imperceptibly, into the larger text. Emerson, and Sophia's personal access to Emerson, is part of the currency that grants *Notes* its value as "original."

Sophia's first reference to "Mr. E." in *Notes* alludes clearly to his published writings in order to discuss the distinction between the copies and originals on which they are based. Following a description of Raphael's *Staffa Madonna*, Sophia contrasts the original to Cephas Thompson's well-respected copy, which she had recently seen in Rome:

> Mr. Thompson's copy is good, but what can be said of Raphael's creation? How could wise and great Mr. E say such a preposterous thing as it was just as well *not* to travel as to travel! And that each man has Europe in him, or something to that effect? No, indeed; it would be better is every man could look upon these wonders of genius, and grow thereby. Besides, after Mr. E had been to Europe himself, how could he tell? Would he willingly have foregone all he saw in Italy? It was mere transcendental nonsense—such a remark."[80]

Moving seamlessly from a discussion of the painting and its (inferior) copies into a discussion of the gains of travel, Sophia clearly equates travel and the experience of originals. Emerson, as a strawman in this passage, allows her to affirm her own (and her text's) dedication to the original work. At the same time, Emerson appears from the first as a figure of both public and private significance. The reference to Emerson's famous statement in "Self-Reliance" that "the soul is no traveller; the wise man stays at home" could leave readers with few doubts about the identity of the subject.[81] But the irreverent tone and even the seemingly stiff title—"Mr. Emerson" was the name by which Emerson's wife Lydian addressed him—affirm Sophia's familial intimacy. "Mr. E." is simultaneously a public and private currency, and by aligning him with the copy, Sophia aligns travel, and implicitly her own travel writing, with originality.

Two later passing references perform a similar function of positioning Emerson as an owner of copies and the first-person narrator as distanced from the simply reiterative copy. Sophia notes after describing a bad copy of Michelangelo's *Three Fates* that "Mr. E. has a copy, but I cannot recall it vividly enough to compare it to Michaelangelo's."[82] Though the statement seems to withhold judgment, in the context of Hawthorne's larger discussion of art it does exactly the opposite, as original works of art are often remarkable precisely for the impression that they leave in their absence.[83] Once again, Sophia aligns Emerson with the copy in order to imply the larger ambition of her own text, part of which is precisely to grant original access to figures such as "Mr. E."

"Folded up in a Veil"   119

Similarly, in describing a self-portrait of Raphael, Sophia writes that he had "cheek and chin 'clean as Apollo's' (as Mr. E. said of his brother Charles's)."[84] Here as in the last statement, Sophia's private access to a figure whose public persona has already been established in the first reference is an important part of the point. But at the same time, Emerson's reference to his brother by way of Apollo, and Sophia's description of Raphael's portrait through this same analogy writes into existence a progression of clean-faced copies that are "like" but not identical, emphasizing the creative buildup of replication over any one original or source. This effect is further exaggerated by the existence of another "clean cheek" in Sophia's medallion portrait of this same brother Charles, which Emerson had so highly praised. The "singular" contribution of Sophia's own document in the market of travelogues lies in access to figures such as Emerson, but also in this image of replication as a hyperreality that loses its grounding in an original object. Sophia's descriptions, here as elsewhere, function to upend the traditional hierarchies of original and copy in unbinding the replicated object from a clear precedent.

A final, longer passage extends this idea of reiteration, taking Emerson's ideas about the reiterative nature of history as the foundation for a creative conception of copying. This scene is ambiguous, imaginative, dense with wordplay, and in a very literal sense, not about Emerson at all: the manuscript journals reveal that this "E.," unlike the others, refers to Sophia's sister Elizabeth, the only reference to her beyond the book's dedication. But the passage is markedly Emersonian, alluding to the writer's work to establish the creative potential of copying, and the existence of an alternative "E." only further emphasizes the scene's dizzying replications. The setting is the historical battlefield on Lake Trasimene, in which the Hannibal's Carthaginian army defeated the Roman forces during the Second Punic War. This landscape, in Sophia's description, has been transformed through time to a peaceful, hilly setting that still carries resonances of the massacre:

> We were served with a generous dinner, of which the poetical part was of course fish from the classic lake, which we ate reflectingly. I felt as if I were a person in an ancient history of Rome. Hannibal's elephants were close at hand. The tent of Flaminius was pitched near by—alas for him! Memories of war, defeat conquest, alternated with the deep peace of the present moment, with the vines and olives and fig-trees, the flocks and herds—the undisturbed grain waving, the birds singing roundelays, the smooth waves lapsing to drown the distant tumult of war; so real and

profound the peace, so more and more ghostly and vanishing the battle. While I dreamed over the purple twilight, the moon rose opposite our windows. First a heap of clouds took fiery hues, like the reflection of a burning city, though rather more pink than red; and then the gold rim of the moon marked a clear arc of a circle over the mountain. When it rose a little higher, a column of silver struck down from its full orb into the depths of the lake, and soon the whole atmosphere was flooded with white radiance. A still vaster peace rose with the moon to possess the earth. I will write to E. as the muse of history, before I sleep.[85]

This passage, which marks the abrupt end to the entry titled "Lake Thrasymene" in *Notes*, relies centrally on visual reflection as a metaphor for the intermixing of past and the present. From the first sentence, when the family eats a fish that has been brought up to land "from the classic lake," the levels of experience—water and land, past and present—begin to intermix. Hawthorne's pun on "reflectingly" prompts her feeling "as if I were a person in an ancient history of Rome." The landscape's memories of war, and the present state of peace, hold the backdrop of another reflection, that of the rising moon "into the depths of the lake." The "white radiance" makes its stamp on the sky, the lake, the mountain. And though the manuscripts reveal that Hawthorne's cryptic last sentence references Sophia's sister as the source for the ambiguous "E.," the publication reflects both Emerson and Elizabeth, a doubling that is in line with the content of the passage. The muse of history, as she appears in Emerson's "History," would be at home in this fusion of past and present; what she recalls, and what the passage seems to be alluding to here, is Emerson's idea that "the creation of a thousand forests is in one acorn, and Egypt, Greece, Rome, Gaul, Britain, America, lie folded already in the first man."[86] At the same time, the section is also appropriately addressed to Elizabeth, who was not only Sophia's primary correspondent but had also been the guiding force in Sophia's early education, Punic Wars and all.[87]

Sophia uses the description to consider issues of artistic originality. If the family eats "reflectingly," they are also reflections of people "in an ancient history of Rome." The copy that they create is far from perfect, mingling present with past rather than simply preserving the latter. The tent of Flaminius may be "pitched near by," but rather than dwell on this image, Sophia shifts to a hybrid mental space and the sense that "memories of war, defeat, conquest, alternated with the deep peace of the present moment." Neither past nor present are unaffected by one another; the bright hues of the sunset are "like the reflection of a burning city," but Sophia concedes they are "rather more pink than red." This is a moment "like" the past, but never quite identical to it, a copy that ends up producing difference in the culminating "still vaster peace" that replaces the original war. The allusion to Emerson's "History" works to strengthen this connection between history and artistic originality. Though the essay's foundation lies in stressing the importance of past events to the present moment, it culminates in the assertion that "genius borrows nobly," and that "originality" can only exist in the interpretation and reformulation of past thought. Sophia's layered perspective of the battlefield enacts precisely this reformulation.

A subtle alteration from the manuscript journal to the published text also confirms the imagistic emphasis of this section. In *Notes*, the final line expresses Sophia's aim to write her letter "before I sleep," but in the manuscript, this last line reads, "before I retire from this marvelously beautiful picture."[88] The initial wording of the draft affirms Sophia's consideration of the landscape in painterly terms, and reframes her extended description of Lake Trasimene as a form of ekphrasis. And like the rest of Sophia's ekphrastic passages, this is one in which Sophia's own family—Una sketching, Julian gathering shells, Rose picking flowers, Elizabeth receiving a letter—is intimately implicated.

SOPHIA'S FAMILIAL EKPHRASIS

After Nathaniel's death, publisher James Fields encouraged Sophia to write her husband's biography. Sophia's response reveals her perception of the family's relation to the public: "I can neither write a book, nor would I, if able, so entirely set in opposition to my husband's express wish and opinion as to do so. . . . The veil he drew around him no one should lift."[89] She went on to edit and publish his notebooks, specifically, she wrote in the 1870 preface to *Passages from the English Note-books*, to "gratify the desire of his friends and of literary artists to become more intimately acquainted with him" in a form that would respect his "extreme reserve."[90] Her formulation of Nathaniel as veiled—a formulation that she used on several other occasions—is telling.[91] Nathaniel is, like his own characters Priscilla and the Reverend Hooper, both in the public eye and apart from it. In *Notes*, as we saw in her final description of Rome, Sophia again references the trope of the veil, and in this image she couches the biography of the Hawthorne family that she had resisted crafting outright. In Sophia's hands, the "churches, statues, and pictures" that Catherine Sedgwick in 1841 had termed as "familiar," become etymologically so, reflecting family in ways that transform mimesis into original description. The aestheticized and depersonalized family descriptions that result are a means of exploring the veil rather than lifting it, while creating a work that stakes "originality" in the middle ground between public and private life.

In the Sophia Hawthorne Papers in the Berg Collection, a small pocket diary from 1859 presents the record of daily life from January, when the Hawthornes were in Rome, to the next fall, when they had traveled back to London. The commercial planner, its dates and holidays printed in French, allows only half of a small (approximately 5 × 3 inch) page for each day's entry. Within these curtailed rectangles, Sophia records in terse lines the prosaic familial events of each date. As such, the diary functions as a parallel universe to the published *Notes*, which expostulates expansively on artworks, people and places seen, but often neglects to mention how exactly these spaces are traversed, and in the company of whom. The diary's brief records—written in tiny script, frequently up to the border allocated to each date—provide immediate insight into the day-to-day concerns of a parent and individual, in opposition to the more aesthetic preoccupations of the artist in *Notes*. Entries are numbingly similar, typically comprising a line or two about the weather, some note about each family member's health, and a brief line about the social and cultural events in which the family participated. A representative entry from January 26 demonstrates the dominance of personal and physical concerns to these daily accounts: "Splendid day. Una not well, so that I wrote to Mrs. Story that she could not drive. But at two she wanted to walk, and Papa took her to the Forum. Miss Shepard came from her chamber at noon. My shoulder was very bad and my cough. I feel brisée. I read Frederic the Great" (see figure 7).[92] The most common accounts of bodily suffering center on herself and on Una, who during this year recovered slowly from a violent bout of malaria, but Sophia also recounts the ills of the nurse Ada Shepard, and the youngest child, Rose. This pocket diary show weather and health to be in a constantly fluctuating and equally unpredictable balance, the results of which largely determine the daily landscape of family life.

None of this attention to daily mundanities appears in the published *Notes*, but the travelogue does signal its reliance on the earlier, unpublished journal (also in the Sophia Hawthorne Papers in the Berg), underlining the distinction between private and public revelations, original and copied works. The inconsistency of Sophia's editorial marks, however, implies that she is more invested in pointing out this distinction than in upholding it. For instance, some excisions from the journals and letters on which *Notes* is based are marked with ellipses or a series of asterisks in the published text, but many other excised passages are not. An examination of the journals reveals that most of the differences between the print and the manuscript texts—flagged or not—are minor, consisting most often of extended, direct descriptions of friends or family whose inclusion in the published document Sophia likely saw as too personal.[93] The inconsistency with which Sophia marks these minor differences demonstrates not an ingrained respect for the line between original and copy, but a desire to make this line visible. As she was editing Nathaniel's journals in 1866, Sophia wrote to James Fields that "what I cannot copy at all is still sweeter than the rest. The stars in their courses do not cover such treasures in Space—as do the dots I substitute for words sometimes."[94] The "dots" in *Notes* thus signal the existence of this "sweeter" space and, as Marta Werner and Nicholas Lawrence have argued in the context of Nathaniel's edited journals, these ellipses "point to aporias in the text that are themselves figures for her understanding of the soul." Ellipses, like veils, reveal an understanding of selfhood in which "the self, an occulted mystery, is readable only through signs of absence."[95] Sophia's editorial gestures, insofar as they are guides to readers, are self-conscious markers of the terms—private/public, original/copy—that are at stake in consuming the work.[96]

These terms are readily apparent in Sophia's presentation of family. Hawthorne family members populate the pages of *Notes* only fleetingly; they appear as single initials (or in the case of Nathaniel as "Papa" or "Mr. H."), making occasional commentary on aesthetic objects, but for the most part following as silent companions on Sophia's artistic pilgrimages.[97] Though each of the family members plays only a small supporting role in the travelogue as a whole, they strain constantly in couched forms at the borders of the text. Embedded references to Nathaniel are particularly prevalent. Some passages point specifically to "papa's" celebrity and the types of access that this celebrity grants the family, and by extension Sophia's readership. In Lincolnshire, for instance, Nathaniel gives an antique bookseller his card, after which this man insists on guiding the Hawthornes through his formidable personal collection of relics and art objects that includes several drawings by Raphael, Rembrandt, and Cellini. The opening of this private collection and the recognition of Nathaniel's standing are entwined, as an exchange between Sophia and the

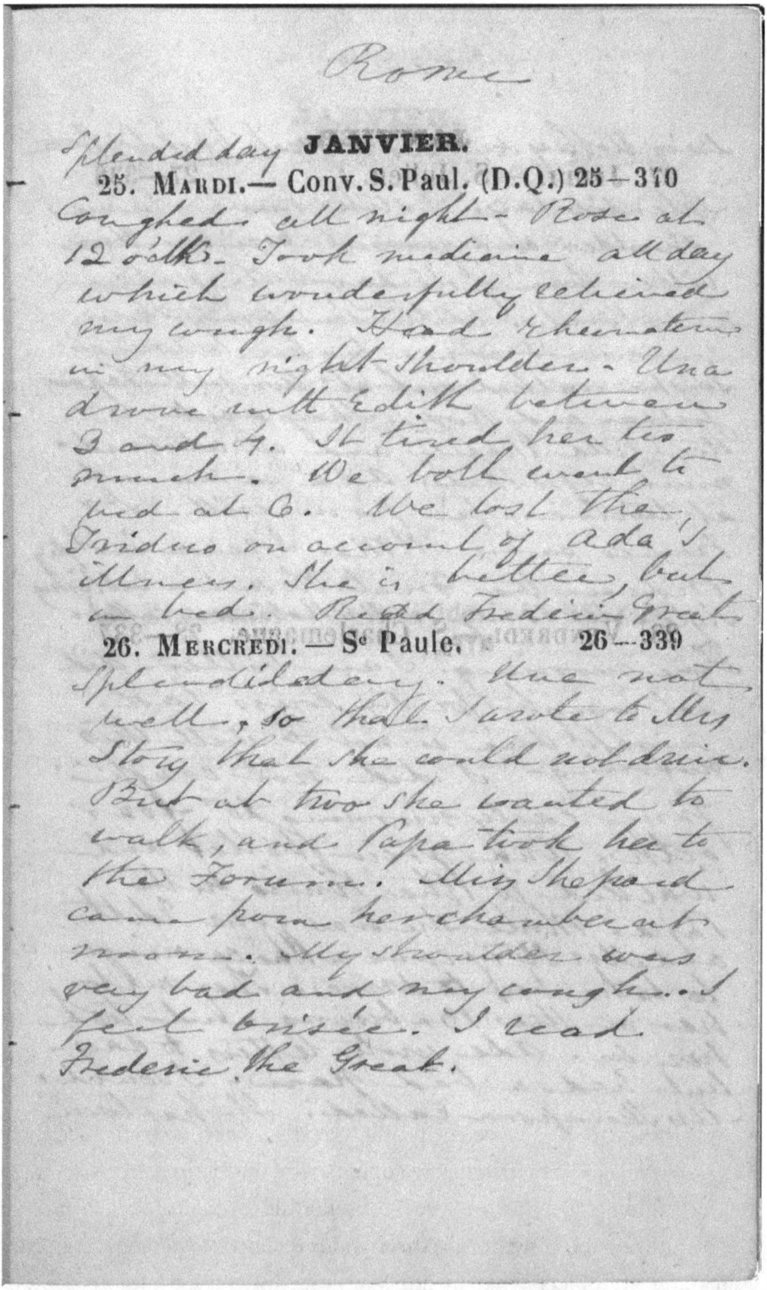

Rome

JANVIER.
Splended day
25. MARDI. — Conv. S. Paul. (D.Q.) 25 — 310

Coughed all night — Rose at
12 o'clk — Took medicine all day
which wonderfully relieved
my cough. Had rheumatism
in my right shoulder — Una
drove with Edith between
3 and 4. It tired her too
much. We both went to
bed at 6. We lost the
Trideus on account of Ada's
illness. She is better, but
in bed. Read Frederic Great

26. MERCREDI. — Sᵉ Paule. 26 — 339

Splendid day. Una not
well, so that I wrote to Mrs
Story that she could not drive.
But at two she wanted to
walk, and Papa took her to
the Forum. Miss Shepard
came from her chamber into
room. My shoulder was
very bad and my cough.. I
feel brisée. I read
Frederic the Great.

FIGURE 7. January 26, 1859, Diary, Sophia Peabody Hawthorne Papers, Berg Collection, New York Public Library. Courtesy, NYPL.

bookseller's wife hints: "I asked Mrs. P whether she were as much interested as her husband in these [art objects], and she said she was not, but preferred to read. And then she remarked, pointing to a brilliant red-bird in a missal that I was turning over: 'That bird is almost as red as the Scarlet Letter!' She said this in a private, confidential little way, and made no other allusion to the authorship."[98] While Sophia's text never openly broadcasts its space as privileged, it doesn't need to; her allusions in a "private confidential little way" are, like those of the bookseller's wife, more than clear enough. These allusions complicate the idea that the travelogue is a purely public document of generally accessible spaces, and in highlighting these private collections, makes its own claims for what it can provide of "original" content for its readers. At the same time, the use of visual cues in this passage provides an analogy for Sophia's own transformative ekphrasis. Just as the bookseller's wife gestures from the "brilliant red-bird," to the "Scarlett Letter," to its author, Sophia uses the visual description of *Notes* to point toward family, enmeshing her own familial "originals" into the space of the ekphrastic copy.

That family and intimate life should be written into artworks is in line with Sophia's practice, from the beginning of the travelogue, of personifying works in a more general sense. This practice begins well before the Italian journals, as she writes for instance in Scotland, of a "marble figure of a little child, whose father is the sculptor"; "The original baby-form lay asleep, draped in only its beauty and innocence, and a lady who saw it was so much affected by its repose and loveliness, that she wished it for her own, and the father actually sold it for a hundred guineas, and carved this one in place of the other for himself." [99] The blurring of people and portraits continues into the Italian sections, when Sophia for instance writes of the paintings of the Borghese gallery, "I looked at every one of the eight hundred pictures, in twelve rooms, and at some of them carefully . . .—and yet I have merely introduced myself."[100] At the Villa Ludovisi, she similarly describes encountering a sculpture room: "I have now become perfectly acquainted with Julius Caesar, Hadrian, [and] the good Trajan . . . . How little I once thought I should ever see these persons!"[101]

If Sophia routinely personifies images, particularly portraits, she also aestheticizes people, particularly family members. Sophia's descriptions of Nathaniel are an important part of this aestheticization: he rarely has a voice in *Notes*, but Sophia often comments on his appearance. In one passage describing diners at a Scottish boarding house, Sophia compares their aesthetic merits much as she might compare a series of adjacent paintings:

"The table was exactly full, and I saw hardly one comely person. Two young gentlemen in gray, and a young clergyman at the top of the table, were good-looking, but only one individual in the room was eminently handsome."[102] This "one individual" is almost certainly Nathaniel, to whom Sophia turns next in conversation. The passing reference serves to rally readers together around the famous—and famously beautiful—figure who likely inspired much of the text's audience, at the same time as it establishes a knowing connection between Sophia and these same readers. At the same time, Nathaniel's representation as alternately "handsome," or on another occasion "an Artist of the Beautiful" readies the ground for the even more explicit aestheticization of other family members.[103]

The Hawthorne children, like Nathaniel, appear much more prominently in the manuscript journals than in the publicized text. In many cases, this presence takes the form simply of a specification of appearance, as in this entry from March 25, 1858 describing the family's visit to the Villa Ludoviso in Rome: "Upon entering the gate, avenues and enchanting vistas opened on every side, but we went first to the Casino of Sculpture. [We were six—my husband, Una, Miss Shepherd, Julian, and Bud]."[104] Sophia's brackets mark the text that is later edited from the published document. Because of such excisions, the plural first-person pronoun that remains in the first line of the text echoes vaguely throughout *Notes*, a generalized "we" that rarely specifies its precise participants. The children take much more defined form in the original manuscripts. In the first Roman manuscript journal, for instance, a full-page pencil drawing of a young girl in a knee-length dress figures on the cover page of the book, subtitled "Rose in Rome/Palazzo Lazarani/Percean Hill" (see figure 8). On the other side of the page, the faint outline of a pencil drawing of a young boy, perhaps Julian, remains, the vestiges of a concerted erasure.[105] Another entry—which includes Sophia's sketch of the Piazza del Popolo—is interrupted by the name "Rose," written in a slightly unsteady and juvenile hand. Sophia's parenthetic comment follows: "(Mademoiselle Bouton de Rose just requested to insert her name, and here it is for all who are interested in her little autograph)."[106]

These remnants of family life dissolve from *Notes*, replaced by artworks that implicitly offer evidence of the children's lives. The recurrent descriptions of Madonna and Child that populate the travelogue obliquely reflect on Sophia's own maternity, but artworks also betray more specific descriptions of individual family members.[107] For instance, Julian's general outline takes shape from his fitting of an antique vest: "Lord Burleigh must have been slender, for J could not button it round his waist."[108] On a visit to the gallery of the Sciarra Palace, Sophia similarly describes Titian's Bella Donna in terms that image Una: "A folded mass of auburn hair crowns the head, and falls behind the throat. As U. stood near I perceived what artists have meant when they called U.'s hair 'Titian hair,' for it was precisely like the Bella Donna's."[109] The prioritization of ekphrasis is such that when Sophia goes on with her description after the reference to Una ("The eyes are dark and rather small, and their expression and that of the perfect mouth are not amiable") it is clear that she has moved back to a discussion of the Titian painting. Moments such as these showcase Sophia's "originality," enabling her to revel in both the artwork and her own creation.

Rose is similarly aestheticized. In the published text, she appears only as "R.," but in the manuscripts, her name is subject to Sophia's maternal whimsy: she is alternately Rose, Rosebud, Bud, Baby, and Bouton de Rose. The variations on "rosebud" suggest that she was the inspiration for Sophia's representation of her children through rose "portraits" when describing a meadow scene in England: "We gathered here from a wild eglantine three roses—one a shut-bud, but showing the lovely pink petals—another not quite half opened, and a third just ready to unfold, but curved over the stamens. We named them after three children we know, and they are the prettiest of portraits."[110] This nickname also recalls Sophia's extended description of Guido's Beatrice Cenci portrait, particularly its fixation on the "rose-bud lips, sweet and tender," that betray "no cry, nor power to utter a word" (see figure 1).[111] The silence of the painted innocent neatly echoes the speechless artistry of Sophia's own children: described only through works of art, their speech is curtailed in the text to the snippets of childish commentary on the works that are at the center of Sophia's travelogue.

These transformations demonstrate the extent to which ekphrasis for Sophia moves beyond rote description and into "familiar," or familial, things. Ekphrasis is not merely the reiteration of well-worn territory, as Catherine Sedgwick implies, but the creative transformation of the public art object into a space that likewise can function as a private family record in the "hereafter."[112] Through these moments of transformation, it becomes apparent that Notes's preoccupation with copy and original is tied up precisely in the creative power of ekphrasis. The domestic backdrop of Notes's ekphrastic moments forms the subtext for thinking about how the textual and visual copy in Sophia's

FIGURE 8. "Rose in Rome," Henry W. and Albert A. Berg Collection of English and American Literature, The New York Public Library. Journal. Rome, beginning March 17, 1858. (Mar.–Oct. 1858: v. 1). Courtesy, NYPL.

travelogue can take on the characteristics of originality. The use of ekphrasis as a means of concealing and revealing family also acknowledges Sophia's earlier injunction to James Fields that the "veil" not be lifted from Nathaniel. This insistence is, in other words, both a creative and a protective act.

CONCLUSION

In a section from the Roman journals, Sophia comments that "over every rare and famous masterpiece in the churches these Romans hang a veil, so as to get a paul for removing it; though I should like to think it were to preserve the painting from dust and light, which might fade the colors."[113] Sophia presents two possible understandings of the veil here: the one (cynical) view that it exists only to bring profit to those who have placed it there, the other (idealistic) possibility that it is placed to protect from the damage of exposure. (She does add, in relation to the Domenichino fresco in question, that the priest who unveils it "seemed neither to expect or await a fee—honor be to him ever!").

Her own travelogue could be read according to these same terms of exploitation and protection. In some senses, *Notes* shows Sophia both keeping the veil intact and getting a paul for removing it. The popularity of her travelogue depended heavily on its thinly veiled familial subtext, but its publication does little to offer any novel revelation. The barrier that Sophia casts over her private space, then, acts both to compel a readership and to protect the members of an inner circle. The most significant aspect of this binary, though, is not her text's tenuous existence in the space between exploitation and protection, but the role that she as an author has in creating this space. In the passage describing the Domenichino fresco, Sophia summons the unveiling priest by "pulling at the curtain" herself.[114] While *Notes* continuously insists on the frustrating inability of language to unveil the people, places, and objects of Sophia's Roman encounters, this tugging at the edges suggests an awareness of her role in initiating revelation. Unlike Nathaniel's passively unveiled Priscilla, Sophia is the agent, however hesitant, of the act of unveiling.

The difference that Sophia's perspective makes for conceptions of her own writing and women's writing more generally is subtle but important. Sophia saw her own undertaking as both derivative and potentially original, both copy and singular, both public and private. This undefined place in the literary landscape could be—and continues to be—troubling. One contemporary reviewer of the travelogue praises Sophia for covering "with originality"[115] many of the topics that Nathaniel himself had documented in his published journals, but is clearly uncomfortable with the execution of this innovation in Sophia's descriptions of art, taking to task the "poetical" embroidery surrounding Guido's Beatrice Cenci: "To see in the Cenci's 'white, smooth brow, without cloud or furrow of pain,' the hovering of 'a wild, endless despair,' is to see much more than is evidently visible on the canvas, or than is certainly apparent in the description."[116] Sophia's ekphrasis moves far from the bounds of the literal description that a might reader anticipate from a travel narrative, into the more nebulous realm of the "poetical." *Notes*, which relies on strict dichotomies at the same time that it thrives in the spaces between them, invites such confusion. But so, too, does ekphrasis more generally, which exists by its very nature in the undefined middle ground between the perfect copy and the freestanding work, the ideal medium for an ambivalent author. That it should be such a popular one at precisely the time when publication summoned ever more ordinary Americans—many of them women travelers—is no coincidence.

CHAPTER FOUR

Longfellow, *Michael Angelo*, and the "Middle-Class" Curator

> Longfellow is artificial and imitative. He borrows incessantly, and mixes what he borrows, so that it does not appear to the best advantage. He is very faulty in using broken or mixed metaphors. The ethical part of his writing has a hollow, secondhand sound. He has, however, elegance, a love of the beautiful, and a fancy for what is large and manly, if not a full sympathy with it.
>
> –Margaret Fuller, "American Literature: Its Position in the Present Time, and Prospects for the Future" (1846)

Margaret Fuller's short analysis of Longfellow in her most explicit contribution to the literary nationalist debate, the essay "American Literature," is striking for its definition of the terms that dominate both nineteenth and twentieth century criticism of the poet. Her judgment of Longfellow as "artificial and imitative" resounds with Whitman's categorization of the poet as an "adopter and adapter."[1] Poe, in the reviews that make up his half of the infamously overblown "Longfellow War"[2] takes the idea of aesthetic imitation one step further, accusing the poet of "the most barbarous class of literary robbery."[3] Fuller's judgment of Longfellow's problematic "mixing" (both in his blending of sources and his incongruous metaphors) also resonates with Poe's assessment that Longfellow's use of imagery "wavers disagreeably between two ideas which would have been merged by the skillful artist in one."[4] Recurring incongruities such as these are the source for Poe's resounding judgment that "[Longfellow] has no combining or binding force. He has absolutely nothing of unity."[5] Fuller's backhanded blow to Longfellow's "manliness," and the faint praise of "elegance" meanwhile, echoes Whitman's understanding of the writer as the "universal poet of women and young people,"[6] and Poe's charged encapsulation of his reading public as "negrophilic old ladies of the north."[7]

These are among the harshest assessments of Longfellow's contemporary readers, but they are the ones that have haunted his demotion to the status of a minor genteel writer in the twentieth century. When George Santayana and Van Wyck Brooks in the early decades of the twentieth century began constructing the canon of American literature that would culminate in F. O. Matthiessen's *American Renaissance* (1941), they developed a critique of Longfellow from the terms that Fuller, Whitman, and Poe had set. Longfellow's femininity—which connoted simultaneously imitation, fragmentation, and meek domestication—was at the center of this critique. For Santayana, Longfellow's writing was "*grandmotherly* in that sedate *spectacled* wonder with which it gazed at the terrible world and said how beautiful and wonderful it all was."[8] For Brooks, Longfellow is one of the "prudent women" of the first generation of American writers, who prepared a house for inhabitation by making it "cozy and cheerful" but did not have enough force to really "revivify a people."[9] This writing is essentially domestic, structured as "stories he was telling his children" and envisioning its public as a "larger world that was an extension of his household."[10]

The basic focal points of this critique—imitation, disunity, femininity, and the interconnection of all of these characteristics—echo through even more favorable modern Longfellow criticism. The Longfellow Wars and the question of the poet's influences occupy critics as diverse as Virginia Jackson, Christoph Irmscher, and Mary Louise Kete. That the pendulum has swung in relation to the value of "imitation" is evidenced by Jackson's elucidation of Longfellow's literary sources, Irmscher's reevaluation of Longfellow's sense of his own "originality," and Kete's framing of Longfellow as a "sentimental collaborator."[11] "Unity," meanwhile, a term that has largely fallen out of the vocabulary of post-New Critical readers, lives on as a term in critical reactions to Longfellow's "broken" canon. In the introduction to the 1988 Penguin edition of Longfellow's *Selected Poems*, for instance, Lawrence Buell's notes that the "would-be masterwork" *Christus* shows "unevenness and disunity."[12]

Similarly, Fuller's jab at Longfellow's masculinity has an afterlife in the work of Irmscher and Eric Haralson, who see Longfellow less as a writer lacking in manly "force" than as, in Haralson's words, a progressive advocate of "a cross gendered sensibility" and a "sentimental' masculinity."[13]

Longfellow's writing on visual art, particularly his posthumously published dramatic poem, *Michael Angelo: A Fragment* (1883), provides a unique opportunity to examine these terms as they interact within the body of the poet's work itself. Within Longfellow's canon, the visual arts and material objects have long been considered as metaphors for the poet's understanding of his own literary work.[14] In this vein, readings of *Michael Angelo* have focused on the work as biographical or anti-biographical, as either "a spiritual autobiography"[15] or "a study of everything Longfellow was not."[16] Michelangelo is for Longfellow an important figure for self-conscious artistic evaluation because the same terms that circulate in their positive form around that artist in the nineteenth century—masculinity, grandeur, originality—circulate in negative reversal around Longfellow, as femininity, fragmentation, and derivation. The biographical readings of the play all seem to latch onto this truth: that Michelangelo becomes a proving ground for Longfellow, a means of sorting out and analyzing these terms late in his career. But as I argue, this organizing process works neither to frame Longfellow's canon with a Michelangelesque grandeur, nor to set in contrast their respective artistic modes. Longfellow's Michelangelo is, unlike the Michelangelo of many writers in the eighteenth and nineteenth centuries, not a figure of exclusions but of inclusions, embodying the contradictions that circulate around the terms of gender, artistic unity, and originality. As such, Michelangelo may indeed provide a late-career perspective on Longfellow's work, but it is a view that complicates rather than simplifies.

Through Michelangelo, Longfellow theorizes his own definition of artistry, which hinges particularly on what we might discuss today as the distinction between art and craft. Longfellow's definition, though, falls far from the period's stock readings of either Michelangelo's art or his own, which emphasize the extremities of both artists: Longfellow as plagiarist, as populist, as sentimentalist; Michelangelo as emblem of aesthetic originality, as genre-defining high artist, as sensualist. These definitions are neat reversals of one another, but in *Michael Angelo*, Longfellow builds the character of the Renaissance artist on a liberal blend of all of these terms. The aesthetic theory that emerges from the contradictions of this protagonist controverts any easy distinction between high art and craft, and questions the critical apparatus that presumes to draw such distinctions. Longfellow's Michelangelo makes a virtue of notions such as the fragmented, the unfinished, the derivative, and the transient. As such, the character is an embodiment of Fuller's critique of Longfellow's "mixing" and of her related barb at his status as "middle class."

Margaret Fuller, in an 1845 review of *Poems*, calls Longfellow a "middle-class" poet, a label aimed to reflect the poet's middle-ground position between the high-cultural elite and the disposable pulp writing of the lowbrow.[17] Though Fuller's use of the term was clearly critical, we might recover the label more neutrally to point out the borderlands that Longfellow occupies: between masculine and feminine norms, between original invention and outright plagiarism, between the genteel and the proto-modern. To see Longfellow as "middle class" is both to understand his democratic appeal and to recognize the fragmentary, underdefined, and overdetermined nature of this state. In the same review, Fuller writes that "Mr. Longfellow presents us not with a new product in which all the old varieties are melted into a fresh form, but rather with a tastefully arranged Museum, between whose glass cases are interspersed neatly potted rose trees, geraniums and hyacinths"[18] positing the poet's writing as not fully cohesive, its multiple parts not "melted" but "arranged" in the artificial environment of a greenhouse-museum. This image of the greenhouse was not unique to Fuller, but a common image for expressing anxiety about the crude nationalist "forcing" of American literature, which picked up on the era's frequent equation of new national literature with the continent's wild natural expanses. The following year in *The North American Review*, for instance, C. C. Felton critiqued the most strident advocacies of the Young America movement by arguing that "national literature cannot be forced like a hothouse plant."[19] In Fuller's image, then, Longfellow's writing falls into line with a simplistic mode of nationalism that advocated for the North American wilds as the subject of a new canon, but ended up in a domesticated, staid, and unsynthesized version of a natural form.

At the same time, Fuller's framing of Longfellow as museum-curator opens up his work for consideration through a nineteenth-century culture newly driven by collecting and by the burgeoning space of the museum gallery. The imagination of Longfellow's museum drives my readings of quasi-ekphrastic works like *Michael Angelo* and the poet's larger canon. The story of the visual arts in nineteenth-century America—and especially of the middle class's experience of the visual arts—cannot be told apart from the space of the museum. Early in the century, Americans experienced the museum primarily through the European galleries and exhibition spaces of the Grand Tour, which the upper class and upper middle class then disseminated more broadly through travelogues and letters home. After the first quarter of the nineteenth century, internationally focused collections and galleries began to appear within the United States, beginning with private collections, and then with university and gallery collections such as the ones donated to Longfellow's own alma mater, Bowdoin, in 1811 and 1826. But both European and American collections, however ambitious in scope, had their foundations in the eclectic home collections of images and artifacts popular for centuries in sometimes extensive curiosity cabinets. These collections were by their very nature incomplete and fragmentary, particularly in the early and indiscriminate period of collecting that characterized the mid-nineteenth century. By 1870, pioneering American collector James Jackson Jarves could still say, "We cannot speak of art museums as a matter of fact in America."[20] At mid-century, collections were even more in flux, often unsystematized spaces bringing together natural history artifacts, informal performances, copies or casts of artworks, and original artistic "masterworks." These galleries are, as Lawrence Levine argues, emblematic of the historical permeability of what we now consider as high or low cultural spaces. Museums of the era often had unclearly defined objectives, and only in the last quarter of the nineteenth century did "sacred language and religious analogies" enforce a certain hushed attitude toward art spectatorship.[21]

In this sense, the "mixed" and culturally unsystematized nineteenth-century American museum provides an important context for Margaret Fuller's understanding of Longfellow as "middle-class." If, as Levine argues, early to mid-nineteenth-century citizens "shared a public culture less hierarchically organized, less fragmented into relatively rigid adjectival boxes than their descendants were to experience a century later," Fuller's "middling" of Longfellow does not propose a distinct category but a cultural realm defined by inclusivity. [22] To be a "middle-class" poet is to be neither a creator of "mock poetry" who is solely "fed by their own will to be seen of men," nor a poet of "the Pantheon, from which issue the grand decrees of immortal thought."[23] But it is also, because the middle class in this framework has no inherent characteristics of its own, to be both. Longfellow's work is less "tastefully arranged museum" than tastefully disordered, its diversity of influences suggesting that Longfellow does not hold himself tensely between extremes of high and low, as Fuller suggests, but rather participates in the far ends of both of these categorizations. Longfellow's "middle class" is not a cultural vacuum, but a space of cultural excess, a space where commercialism and disinterested aesthetics, craft and art, can overlap. This excessive sense of the "middle class" offers a vocabulary for discussing fragmentation in both the form and the content of Longfellow's work.

Fragmentation is a clear component of Longfellow's framing of the national. Longfellow participated explicitly in literary nationalist debates through the early decades of his career, from essays such as the 1925 Bowdoin graduation address "Our Native Writers" and the 1832 "Defense of Poetry," to the caricature of Cornelius Matthews from the Young America movement in the prose pastoral *Kavanaugh* (1849). One common way of mapping Longfellow's nationalism is as becoming increasingly international in the course of his career, moving from an acknowledgement of British influence to a broader invitation of world literatures into the American canon.[24] But even the very early "Our Native Writers" shows a resistance to isolationist tendencies in defining American letters, and *Kavanaugh* points to the ludicrousness of Matthews's concept of national literature as the raw translation of an American nature. For Longfellow, even the most clearly nationalist efforts to survey the American scene were highly mediated, or as Fuller might say, "tastefully arranged." In the narrative poems *Hiawatha* and *Evangeline*, his most explicit works of national mapping, Longfellow relied not on his own direct experience of the settings, which he had never visited, but on visual sources such as George Catlin's depictions of Native American life and John Banvard's panorama of the Mississippi River Valley.[25] And in *Michael Angelo*, the cracks between different media and sources are exaggerated enough that the act of mediation becomes an important subject of the work itself.

We might understand this method of composition through what Jay Bolter and Richard Grusin have called remediation, the incorporation of one medium into another in a manner that reshapes both media. This incorporation can stress immediacy, where the goal is a seemingly unmediated experience; or hypermediacy, where the goal is to call attention to the lines between media; or, as is most often the case in the twentieth century new media with which the authors are primarily concerned, some combination of the two. But as they note, remediation has been around for as long as media themselves, and both ekphrasis (the incorporation of a visual medium into a textual one) and the citation from other sources are forms of remediation. In the case of Longfellow's canon, almost all of his work depends on some form of remediation, but *Michael Angelo* is unique in the extent to which it stresses hypermediation, or its own media fragmentation. This hypermediation is, I argue, a means for Longfellow to signal his own self-conscious choice of an aesthetic between extremes, in the unfused space of what Margaret Fuller calls the "middle class."[26]

In this chapter, I first trace Longfellow's habits of home collection, which demonstrate his investment in the material object (whether of art or craft) and his understanding of its function as a personal and historical marker. Next, I look to three ekphrastic poems that puzzle out the boundaries between art and craft. The definition of these terms that emerges from these poems ultimately leads into *Michael Angelo*, an ambitious work that resists the simplifying gestures of much earlier commentary on the artist in favor of his representation as part stonemason, part divinely ordained artist. Longfellow's resistance to drawing boundaries—whether between craftsmanship and artistry, femininity and masculinity, or imitation and originality—is the factor that most clearly defines *Michael Angelo*. It is also this factor that can allow us to reclaim Fuller's assessment of Longfellow as "middle-class" in constructive terms, not as an aesthetic purgatory, but as a conscious self-positioning between aesthetic extremes.

LONGFELLOW AT HOME

In this section, I look at Longfellow's personal and domestic relation to the collection of visual objects as evidence of an aesthetic driven by eclecticism and association rather than strict classification. This aesthetic, I argue, shapes his ekphrastic work, which self-consciously probes the categories of art and craft. Longfellow's biographical and literary relation to the visual arts and crafts is usually read through the lens of one of three closely related ideas: a concern with materiality, an interest in the history and tradition of the crafted object, and a connection to the conspicuous consumption of nineteenth-century bourgeois "gewgaws." While all of these relations to the object are evident in Longfellow's biography and work, his poetry transforms these objects from markers of consumption to historical and sentimental sites, objects that call into play the specific effects of their histories. Longfellow's encounters with the visual arts betray an interest in the aesthetic potential of the eclectic collecting in which he himself participated, calling into question critical perspectives that locate him solely as a "competent redistributor of cultural goods" in opposition to the role of "godlike creator of unique meaning."[27] Longfellow's domestic museum, as his ekphrastic poems, muddies the lines between these categories.

Longfellow's home collection had its roots in the Age of the Museum in America, which began not in international art tourism, but in a national interest in traditional handcrafted American objects such as ceramics. At the end of the eighteenth century, local historical societies began to form with the goal of collecting and preserving American antiquities including books, manuscripts, and household objects. At the fore in 1791 was the Massachusetts Historical Society (MHS), followed by the New York Historical Society in 1804. An institution of somewhat broader reach but similar goals, the American Antiquarian Society formed in 1812. In the course of the 1820s, more local societies followed in Maine, Rhode Island, New Hampshire, Pennsylvania, and Connecticut. Groups of serious individual collectors of antiquities also grew in the first half of the century, especially in New England, where a longer local history facilitated the discovery of collectibles. After the Civil War, a number of societies, including the Daughters of the American Revolution (DAR), encouraged individuals in their collecting efforts.[28]

Longfellow's work and life closely follows this interest in the handcrafted visual object. A writer in *The Atlantic Monthly* shortly after his death suggested that the writer's poetry was responsible for the recent rise in "the graphic and constructive arts and music" because "his appropriating genius drew within the circle of his art a great variety of illustration and suggestion from the other arts."[29] Historical perspective may have tempered this assertion: today, it seems clear that Longfellow was a small part of a larger movement drawn to the "suggestion" of the visual arts, broadly defined. By the time that he began attending Bowdoin College as an undergraduate in 1822, the school had secured the first donations to build a campus museum, the first such a collection in the nation.[30] Longfellow's letters home from his first visit to Europe, shortly after graduating from college, frequently mention art and artists. After he had established himself as a writer, Longfellow was actively involved in the illustration and visual layout of his works, suggesting images to the editors of his many illustrated volumes. His writing itself has often been considered strikingly imagistic, and passages of his most famous works are inspired by paintings. Artistic appreciation and collection formed an important part of

Longfellow's domestic life and lived on in his sons Charles, whose collection of Japanese decorative arts contributed to the aesthetic of his parents' home, and Ernest, a painter who illustrated a posthumously published edition of his father's collected poems.[31]

The art of Longfellow's domestic life was the subject of a 2007 Maine Historical Society exhibit, "Drawing Together: The Arts of the Longfellows," which presents the visual culture of three generations of the Longfellow family. These works showcase the values often associated with the poet's canon as a whole: domesticity, community, history, and craftsmanship. But the eclecticism of the exhibition also indicates the permeability of aesthetic categories—and textual and imagistic boundaries—within the Longfellows' domestic space. The show includes work encompassing embroidery samplers, oil portraits, architectural plans, children's drawings, adults' drawings, sculptures, and maps. Some of the works are collaborative, like drawings initialed by both mother and daughter, or large drawings undertaken by both Longfellow sons. Both the poet and his wife Fanny took drawing lessons with the professional artist Francis Greater, who also illustrated Longfellow's poem "The Skeleton in Armor." Ernest Longfellow, who would later become a professional painter, produced childhood drawings that were submitted to serious scrutiny, as the poet-father annotated each with date, subject matter, and the graphic problem confronted.[32] Other childhood art projects were inspired by well-known works, like the spooled drawings that reproduced the aims of John Banvard's panorama paintings of the Mississippi River Valley, which also influenced Longfellow's own work in *Evangeline*.[33] The intermingling of text and image is likewise evident in the local subject matter of many of Longfellow's own carefully rendered drawings of the landscapes or houses in the environs of Cambridge, which embody the dictum expressed at the end of his "Gaspar Becerra"(1850): "O thou sculptor, painter, poet! / Take this lesson to thy heart: / That is best which lieth nearest; / Shape from that thy work of art."[34]

The interaction of text and image is also sustained in many of the creative projects that Longfellow undertook specifically for his children. Among the works in the poet's archives in the Houghton Library are the extensive illustrated stories that the poet wrote for his children. These tales—humorous, densely illustrated, and often indirectly didactic—reveal much about Longfellow's family and the function that art played in this part of his life. Longfellow's illustrated stories for his children, such as the sagas "Little Merrythought," "Peter Piper," and "Peter Quince" showcase the interaction of the visual and verbal narrative. In "Little Merrythought," the series's protagonist is a tiny man composed of a turkey's wishbone, something between a pet and a companion for Longfellow's children, who appear as thinly veiled characters. Longfellow at various points considered editing the series, which he worked on from 1847 to 1855, for publication, but it exists today only in manuscript form. "Peter Quince" and "Peter Piper," likewise unpublished, center on the misadventures of well-meaning but slightly buffoonish protagonists, often in the context of international travel, one of Longfellow's favorite literary subjects.[35]

The decision not to publish ultimately places Longfellow's illustrations in his home collection of (original) art objects rather than in his (mass-produced) literary bibliography, in what Nelson Goodman calls the autographic rather than the allographic.[36] But such categorizations provide little real guidance in thinking of the place of visuality in Longfellow's life and work. The diversity of his home collection, which features both original objects and reproductions, closely parallels the mid-century American museum. Longfellow's home in Cambridge was known to both friends and strangers for its beautiful material objects, and visitors in his lifetime were—as they still are, now that it is a house museum—granted tours of the possessions. For some, such objects connoted solely material wealth. Emerson, for instance, wrote in his journal in 1853 of his reluctance to visit Longfellow in his home: "Longfellow, we cannot go & talk with; there is a palace, & servants, & a row of bottles of different coloured wines & wine glasses, & fine coats."[37] The "different coloured wines" in the Longfellow home were undoubtedly part of the status-conscious collection of mid-nineteenth-century America, but such objects were also a personal means of interacting with history. In Longfellow's office, for instance, prized objects included markers of both sentimental and commercial value: Thomas Moore's and Coleridge's quill pens; fragments of Dante's coffin; first editions of various works; and crayon portraits of Emerson, Sumner, and Hawthorne. Christoph Irmscher argues that these objects formed not a high-cultural "shrine," but were symbolic of Longfellow's understanding of literature, in which writing was "achieved in patient dialogue with those who had come before."[38] These objects, far from being simply status symbols, stand as personal and historical markers, connecting Longfellow to creators of the past and the present, presiding over the scene of his writing much in the same way that intertextual references and passages permeate the text of his writing. Contemporary photographs and commentary from visitors indicate that the office collection was less "tastefully arranged Museum" than it was an often disordered space of influence and association in which Longfellow's children also played.[39]

The reading public came to associate Longfellow and his work with this varied home collection—as did the poet himself. A sort of contemporary visual culture sprang up around the home and its contents. In addition to the numerous photographs of the poet in his study—often sitting almost incidentally off to one side, or dwarfed by the objects in the room—prints of the poet in his home were common, especially by the 1870s, when the poet's own immortalization as national treasure was complete.[40] A nineteen-page profile of the writer in the November 1878 *Scribner's* includes no fewer than twelve large illustrations—all of them of a room in the house or its surroundings. Though the article devotes only a few paragraphs to Longfellow's historic home (which had briefly been Washington's headquarters during the Revolutionary War), a connection between an artist's work and his domestic space introduces the profile and contextualizes the illustrations: "We find in all biographies that all writers, even the greatest, are influenced by their surroundings."[41] Other articles note Longfellow's "*penchant* for pipe collecting," architectural details of the building, and particular artworks in his collection. An ekphrastic newspaper poem, "On a Portrait Owned by H. W. Longfellow and Painted by Tintoretto," celebrates the poet as sharing the sight of the painting with "lesser mortals." (The authenticity of the painting has since been disproven.) Longfellow was conscious enough of this documentation that he clipped many of these articles and assembled them, alongside of handwritten entries on notable events taking place in the home, in a scrapbook labeled "Craigie House." He also carefully archived the contents of his various home collections, keeping notebooks, for instance, of both alphabetically-organized wines in the cellar and paintings throughout his home.[42]

This eclecticism—a careful attention not just to paintings, but to pipes and wines—is the dominant characteristic of the home collection. Longfellow's own participation in this wide spectrum of art-craft collecting, and his poetry's participation in the same variety, can get lost in reading Longfellow entirely against the grain of originality. Critical appreciation of the imitative nature of Longfellow's verse—which Virginia Jackson aptly calls "so thoroughly derivative that it becomes authentic, so artful that it becomes natural"—often argues for understanding Longfellow's production as craft.[43] Longfellow's couched "borrowings" are an important source of the work's widespread resonance with mass audiences. Framing Longfellow as "less as an 'original' creator than as the competent redistributor of common cultural goods, whose relationship with his audience was based on a system of exchange, both monetary and emotional,"[44] clearly aligns him with nineteenth-century conceptions of craft.[45] Literary historical readings of Longfellow that emphasize his economic savvy in copyrighting and his position among the first American professional writers perform much the same function, as the early nineteenth-century definitions of art and craft depended largely on whether one was reliant on economic "systems of exchange": artisans were, while artists were not. So, while a positive emphasis on Longfellow's derivations and literary practice offers a constructive critical shift, to argue that Longfellow conceived of his poetry exclusively in craftsman's terms limits the work's broader ambitions.

The equation of Longfellow's work with craft is problematized not only by the more open attitude toward art-craft distinctions apparent in the poet's home collection, but by the complications of his ekphrastic canon. The ekphrastic work offers a vision of artistry that supplements the diligent workmanship of "craft" poems like "The Village Blacksmith"(1842) whose protagonist "Each morning sees some task begin, / Each evening sees it close." There is more to Longfellow's work—and to his artistic self-presentation—than the redistribution of such "common cultural goods," and his ekphrastic canon shows earnest thought around categories such as craft and fine art, emulation, and originality. Critical readings of these works are rare by both Longfellow's contemporaries and modern critics. Of less obvious nationalistic or historical import than sweeping narratives such as *Hiawatha* or *Evangeline*, these ekphrastic poems–most often short lyrics—are easy to dismiss as ornamental museum pieces, genteel constructions of cultural capital. But beyond this facade, these poems test the boundaries between artistic classes, and also suggest an alternate manner of construing the idea of collection at this historical point, emphasizing a fragmentary, cyclic history rather than a clear teleology of artistic development.

THE POETRY OF COLLECTION

Longfellow's home, the Craigie House in Cambridge, is a museum that embodies the idea of cyclic history in a clearly nationalist context. The poet initially rented a room there as a young professor in 1837, attracted to a history that included its use as George Washington's headquarters during the Siege of Boston. When he married into the wealthy Appleton family in 1843, he received the home as a wedding present from his father-in-law and continued to live there until his death in 1882. George Putnam's *Homes of American Authors* (1853), a volume that includes essays on the homes of Ralph Waldo Emerson, Catherine Sedgwick, and Washington Irving, also prominently features the Craigie House. The sketch begins with a description of the house's "association with the early days of our revolution."[46] These associations, the author writes, inhabit the poet's mind and ultimately influence the course of his poetry: "For ever after, his imagination is a more lordly picture-gallery than that of ancestral halls."[47] In turn, Longfellow, too, influenced the house: "He who has written the Golden Legend knows, best of all, the reality and significance of that life in the old Craigie House, whose dates, except for this slight sketch, had almost dropped from history."[48] The celebrity of Longfellow's writing preserves the house in cultural memory, as under his ownership it "has again acquired a distinctive interest in history."[49] Longfellow's fame curates, preserving a piece of American history that otherwise might have been lost, even as his writing is shaped by this same history into a rich "picture-gallery." Relying on the nineteenth-century conception of memory as a storehouse of images, both house and intellect become museum spaces whose collections overlap. By providing a new chapter in the history of the house, Longfellow imbues what is now known as the Craigie-Longfellow House with enough cultural capital to continue to function as a museum that showcases not just Longfellow's tenure in the home but that of those generations of inhabitants that preceded him. The poet's ekphrastic work may have fallen short of shoring up an aesthetic legacy akin to the biographical one, but shows a similar appreciation of layered history, and aspires to a similar curatorial power.

The historical witness of artistic objects infused Longfellow's poetry as much as his life. Longfellow's writing on (primarily) European art functions as an alternate home collection, an accumulation of the works that could not or would not be collected on the poet's travels. In "The Old Bridge at Florence," "Kéramos," "Giotto's Tower," and *Michael Angelo*, Longfellow brings together site-specific works and spaces that many Americans had not seen firsthand. These poems reveal Longfellow's perspective on how such objects might be categorized, assembled, and understood. His literary collection presents a logic as clear as that of any material collection, but the understanding that underlies this collection is uniquely inclusive. While the trend in American art collecting and exhibition moved increasingly toward the creation of a comprehensive narrative for any given group of collected works, Longfellow's poems embrace instead the fragmentary, rejecting cohesion in favor of the suggestive part. Longfellow's poems, rather than providing a teleology of artistic development, emphasize the fragmentary nature of artistic production and artistic history, inviting readers to see their own time as a moment in the narrative, rather than its ultimate culmination.

The ekphrastic sonnet, "The Old Bridge at Florence" (1875), written after what would be the poet's last visit to Europe, marks the monument as a historical witness within Florence that extends an affective connection to audience.[50] The first lines register the bridge's origin ("Taddeo Gaddi built me. I am old, / Five centuries old.") and the rest of the work unfolds the experiences that this structure has stood through, including the battles between the factions representing the Holy Roman Emperor and the papacy and the later expulsion of the Medici from Florence. The sonnet's final, awkwardly sensual lines—"And when I think that Michael Angelo / Hath leaned on me, I glory in myself"— underline the importance of historical touch, even across centuries. The bridge has no physical markers of its own and is described through the poem only as "old," its shape outlined through the imprint of the creator that opens the poem, and the form of Michelangelo that closes it. The inscription of this historical touch is more central to the work's significance than any architectural feature, just as Thomas Moore's quill pen carries its significance entirely in its former owner's fingerprint. The value of these objects for Longfellow, as both poet and owner, lies not in the specificity of their crafted features but in their connection to varied historical and aesthetic moments.

At the same time, Longfellow's choice of cultural monuments calls to mind the intermixing of commerce and high art typical of his poetry. "The old bridge" is the literal translation of the site more commonly known as the Ponte Vecchio, the bridge that since its reconstruction by Gaddi in 1345 has housed the shops built into its structure. In Longfellow's time as in our own, these are jewelers, as the twelfth line suggests: "Florence adorns me with her jewelry." That the bridge, which in the first eleven lines Longfellow describes entirely in terms of historical endurance, is also a central site of commerce, points to the intermixing of artistic categories, and intermingling of past with present, that occurs throughout Longfellow's work. As a monument, the bridge is both a historical site marked by Gaddi's artistic pedigree and Michelangelo's leisured leaning, as well as a modern-day center of the jeweler's craft.

Longfellow, Michael Angelo, and the "Middle-Class" Curator 145

Commerce, artistry, and history are likewise intertwined in Longfellow's most sustained ode to craftsmanship, "Kéramos"(1877). A narrative poem following a Maine potter through an international survey of ceramic traditions, "Kéramos" is obscure today, but was considered culturally relevant enough at the moment of its composition that *Harper's* offered Longfellow $1,000 for the rights to publish the ten-page poem in the December 1877 edition of the magazine. Composed on the heels of the 1876 Centennial Exposition in Philadelphia, at which American potters had made a weak showing, "Kéramos" was written as a call to arms for American craftsmen. The poem had an afterlife in excerpt form in American ceramics periodicals, and played its small part as a motivational piece to the potters themselves, who in the last two decades of the century refined their skills and gained international renown.[51]

But the poem also exemplifies Longfellow's crows-eye aesthetic as a writer and arts collector, presenting a non-hierarchical pastiche of fine art and craft works. Throughout the poem, in which the speaker follows the potter-protagonist through an envisioned international journey across different ceramic traditions, the work's themes center around originality and individual conception. "All are made of clay" is a continuous refrain, and the creation and destruction of pottery is a well-worn metaphor for the natural cycles of birth and death.[52] The unoriginality of the trope of man as clay is fitting, as originality is far from the poem's purpose or the purpose of the potter's art. This art is made by "no hand" but guided rather by the "Creator."[53] Though the speaker lavishes description on objects and places, many of the craftsmen creating objects, including the poem's protagonist, are anonymous. A passage near the end of the poem underlines this anonymity:

> Never man,
> As artist or as artisan,
> Pursuing his own fantasies,
> Can touch the human heart, or please,
> Or satisfy our nobler needs,
> As he who sets his willing feet
> In Nature's footprints, light and fleet,
> And follows fearless where she leads.[54]

This perspective on both "artist" and "artisan" favors tradition and natural form over original conception, at the same time as it points out, then conflates the distinction between art and craft. Longfellow's request to the editors of

Harper's that the poem be illustrated not with human figures but with images of the vessels and plates described aligns well with this deemphasis of the individual.[55] *Harper's* ultimately published the poem alongside of images of brawny craftsmen, attractive onlookers, and global landscapes, which speaks instead to a more traditional sense of (masculine) artistry as located in a specific person and location.

Examples of the blending of art and craft, original conception and imitation are fundamental to the structure of the poem. The first stanza opens with the potter's song, a varying refrain that through the poem will offer a philosophical background to the concrete sights and scenes of the poem ("Turn, turn, my wheel! All things must change / To something new, to something strange") but that also produces the travel that makes these scenes possible:

> Thus still the Potter sang, and still,
> By some unconscious act of will,
> The melody and even the words
> Were intermingled with my thought,
> As bits of colored thread are caught,
> And woven in nests of birds.
> And thus to regions far remote,
> Beyond the ocean's vast expanse,
> The wizard in the motley coat
> Transported me on wings of song,
> And by the northern shores of France
> Bore me with restless speed along.[56]

The poem is part appropriation of the potter's song, part record of the journey on which the song "transport[s]" the speaker; the work as a whole is an "unconscious act of will" and seamless "intermingling" of song and thought, the speaker and the potter's joint account of an international ceramic tradition. This account, in turn, credits the intermixing of the arts for producing ceramic excellence. The workshops of Gubbio "In perfect finish emulate / Faeza, Florence, Pesaro."[57] One Italian ceramicist "caught / Something of [Raphael's] transcendent grace, / and into fictile fabrics wrought / Suggestions of the master's thought."[58] In Florence, the "more fragile forms of clay" are "Hardly less beautiful" than the frescos of Lucca della Robbia.[59] The images on the Imari porcelain of Japan are "The counterfeit and counterpart / Of Nature reproduced in Art."[60] Imitation, throughout the poem, is both distinct from its original, and entirely equal to it, both its "counterfeit and counterpart." Longfellow's work effaces the aura of the original and the hierarchy between replication and creation.

At the same time, the eclectic collection that "Kéramos" surveys presents a couched commentary on nativist collection—both literary and aesthetic—of this period. As J. Lockwood writes, late-nineteenth-century American collecting practices were often driven by much more than aesthetic sensibility: "In saving china, collectors often imagined themselves to be recovering a story of Anglo supremacy and to be defending it against the threat of foreigners as well as the threat of lower-class rural Anglos, both of whom were considered incapable of stewarding the nation's historical treasures."[61] Much American collecting was centered on the ceramics of the northeast states, Northern Europe, and Asia, which had provided England and America with its first models for porcelains. Collecting was by its very nature nostalgic, reflecting back on an apparently simpler pre-industrial era. "Kéramos" undercuts this aesthetic in the breadth of the ceramic genealogy that it presents, describing potters not just in Holland, China, and Japan, but also in Italy, Greece, and Egypt, and proclaiming that "The human race, / Of every tongue, of every place, / . . . / Are kindred and allied by birth, / And made of the same clay" (19). But the poem elides the country most important to American ceramics collectors, England, from its catalogue. Like Longfellow's own increasingly transnational form of literary nationalism, "Kéramos" is not limited to British or American models. The poem's editor considered the omission a failing, suggesting that Longfellow include some references to Wedgewood ceramics, a popular American target for collection; Longfellow replied that he did not see any way of "treating picturesquely" such works in the context of the poem.[62]

In setting itself apart from nationalist nostalgia, the focus of "Kéramos" is not retrospective, but forward-looking, albeit driven by a cyclic perspective on history. This is a perspective that the potter's song, which begins its refrain, "Turn, turn my wheel!" helps to emphasize. The work of the past informs and creates the work of the present, as the last lines of the poem stress: "Behind us in our path we cast / The broken potshards of the past, / And all are ground to dust at last, / And trodden into clay."[63] Longfellow presents the value of the art of the past as lying not in its wholeness as a preserved and categorized object, or a "tastefully arranged museum," but in its existence as a part, a "broken potshard" that makes up a piece of the "clay" of the present. Far from the preservationist aims of the traditional collector, the narrator of "Kéramos" understands the value of past artistry through the processes that it instructs rather than the unscathed objects that it passes down. The poem's emphasis on the permeability of influence and the fragility of the individual art-object makes for an unusually motley collection, one that provides little cohesion beyond the cyclical movement of the potter's wheel.[64]

The representation of craft and art in "The Old Bridge at Florence" and "Kéramos" emerges in part through the earlier works of "Giotto's Tower" and *Michael Angelo*, in spite of some superficial divergences. By calling attention to the artists' names in the titles of these works, Longfellow introduces artistic individuality as a central concern, an idea that "Kéramos" and "The Old Bridge" clearly evade. *Michael Angelo* in particular emphasizes a biographical concern with the individual creator. But both *Michael Angelo* and "Giotto's Tower" openly question the power of the isolated artist and depict creation as a collective rather than an individualized process. These poems anticipate the "broken potshards" of Kéramos through a focus on fragmentation and a sense that the art of the present consists through a reconfiguration of the past. Both works, like "Kéramos" and "The Old Bridge," embrace the cross-pollination of craft and fine art.

"Giotto's Tower" (1867) reads as a celebration of fragmentation.[65] Robert Gale, for instance, summarizes it as a celebration of the essential completeness of the famously incomplete Campanile in Florence, begun at the end of Giotto's life in 1334 and left unfinished at his death in 1337: "Many sweet, restrained, uncomplaining persons devoted to answering the requests of the Holy Spirit lack nothing but a halo such as artists paint above saints' foreheads. So it is with Giotto's tower."[66] But Longfellow's version of Giotto's Tower is perfect because of, not in spite of, its apparent lack. The sonnet's first octave introduces this idea through its reversal: figures who fall short of perfection precisely because of their apparent flawlessness, who "are in their completeness incomplete." The restrained structure of these lines performs the self-containment of their subjects, who are too simplistically whole:

> How many lives, made beautiful and sweet
> By self-devotion and by self-restraint,
> Whose pleasure is to run without complaint
> On unknown errands of the Paraclete,
> Wanting the reverence of unshodden feet,
> Fail of the nimbus which the artists paint

Around the shining forehead of the saint,
And are in their completeness incomplete![67]

The earnest Christians of these lines "fail of the nimbus" of sainthood not because of any lack on their part but rather because of a too-great "completeness." What they "want" is not any addition but an absence, "unshodden feet," and the sacrifice that this absence implies. Instead of making such sacrifice, they are turned inward with "self-devotion" and "self-restraint," deriving "pleasure" from the idea of self-denial, of running "without complaint / On unknown errands." The lines themselves enact this self-enclosure through the ABBA structure and end-stopped rhyme scheme. Similarly, the opening line's apparent question ("How many lives") becomes an exclamation by the final line ("in their completeness incomplete!"), breaking down the promise of a dialogue or exchange beyond the solipsistic speaker. Like the "beautiful" lives, these lines are characterized primarily by measured restraint.

While these devices are familiar features of the sonnet-form, the final sestet of the poem marks a dramatic shift. Focusing on the perfect imperfection of the tower, this section challenges self-containment in both form and subject:

In the old Tuscan town stands Giotto's tower,
The lily of Florence blossoming in stone,—
A vision, a delight, and a desire,—
The builder's perfect and centennial flower,
That in the night of ages bloomed alone,
But wanting still the glory of the spire.[68]

The interlacing rhyme scheme, the feminine rhyme of lines 9 and 12, and the dashes at the end of lines 10 and 11 open up the form of this sestet, loosening the structure of the preceding octave. The subject likewise opens, from the "self-restraint" of the previous section to the organic "blossoming" in stone of the tower. Giotto's tower is described not in terms of beauty, as the aspirants of the previous octave, but in terms of growth and potentiality. It "bloom[s]"; it is a "desire" and a "vision," rather than a static object. The history of the Campanile tells a similar story: after Giotto's death, his design was picked up by Andrea Pisano, who in his tenure as builder was faithful to Giotto's original plans. Finally, Francesco Talenti took over the building in 1348 and completed it in 1359, though he altered Giotto's design by omitting the tower's proposed spire.[69]

The tower, then, is literally incomplete, but nonetheless "perfect"; it reverses the terms of the previous stanza, and is complete in its incompleteness. The tower, overhung always by the shadow-structure of the unconstructed spire, has a parallel in the saint of the octave before, who carries an immaterial "nimbus" to signal his "perfection." The tower is "Giotto's" because his blue-prints form its foundation, but it is also the tower of the "builder," who made the choice to leave the completion of structure in the minds of viewers. Long-fellow's poem, which in its title seems to defend single artistic authorship, in fact questions the validity of understanding the isolated artist-creator as the source of "perfect" art, and opens up the idea of perfection to include the collaborative and the unfinished. Within the schema of "Giotto's Tower," the sacrifice of some part of the ideal design creates a form of completion that goes far beyond material understandings of conclusion.

In *Michael Angelo*, Longfellow continues to use the fragment to question the nature of originality and individuality, in the artistic and, by extension, literary canon. The subject of *Michael Angelo* ensures that Longfellow's debate occurs against basic cultural assumptions about artistic production, particu-larly about the European high-art canon. Lene Østermark-Johansen, in her study of Michelangelo's nineteenth-century reception, calls this figure "the great individual who becomes the receptacle for a wide range of other people's projections."[70] Longfellow's "projection" is unusual for the nineteenth century in its embrace of the complexity of Michelangelo's work, including its literary and visual loose ends.

COLLECTING MICHELANGELO

High-profile postbellum American art collectors, in striking contrast to Longfellow-as-literary-collector, were concerned with presenting a teleolog-ical view of art history, and by showing through their works a narrative of gradual artistic advancement, leaving out works that did not contribute to this storyline. In this period, a mode of collection and exhibition that func-tioned by exclusion gradually superseded the cabinet of curiosities model. When wealthy collectors like James Jackson Jarves and Thomas Jefferson Bryan began buying the works that would eventually form the first signifi-cant collections of European Renaissance painting in America, they collected with a newly-defined sense of purpose. Though the collections were spotty in quality, their aim was toward providing "something like a history of the progress of painting."[71] Just as American ceramics collectors focused on certain types of works in creating a narrative of national identity, art collectors aimed to narrate specific stories. Jarves's collection of early Italian Renaissance paintings, for instance, told the now well-known story of the development of certain aesthetic characteristics—linear perspective, chiaroscuro, anatomical study—into the High Renaissance. Such narratives necessarily had the effect of limiting the eclecticism of galleries and aiming toward, if not always arriving at, an idea of wholeness.

At the same time as this mode of art collection was taking hold, critics and translators were making new strides in the compilation and publication of Michelangelo's poetry. The nineteenth century was, as Østermark-Johansen writes, "*the* century when Michelangelo became a text, in addition to his previous reputation as a painter, sculptor and architect."[72] The first English biography of Michelangelo, by Richard Duppa, appeared in 1806 and inspired Anglophone interest in the artist's poetry. Titled *The Life and Literary Works of Michael Angelo Buonarroti*, it reprinted the entire Italian first edition of the poetry, published twenty letters, and included a handful of commissioned translations by Robert Southey and William Wordsworth. By 1869, the biography had been through five editions. In 1840, John Edward Taylor published a monograph on the poems alone, translating thirty-five into English prose, and introducing the whole with a hundred-page essay. John S. Harford's voluminous 1857 biography likewise highlighted poetry, and included translations of nine madrigals and twenty-two sonnets. No fewer than eight Italian editions of Michelangelo's poetry were published during the nineteenth century, one of which, Cesare Guasti's 1863 text, was widely available in England. Later in the century, both Dante Gabriel Rossetti and John Addington Symonds worked on translations.[73]

These textual collections of Michelangelo also reflect the interest in narrative cohesion that increasingly shaped art collection. Works that "upset [the Victorian] image of [Michelangelo] as the divine, grand and melancholy artist"[74] were either left untranslated or polished into a nearly unrecognizable form. The apparent lack of polish in the poems—which manuscripts show to have gone through extensive revision—was often seen by editors and translators as "yet another instance of the artist's *non-finito*: a difficulty with finishing his works which surely could not be intentional" and so were "corrected" with a filling in of gaps.[75] The lighthearted or cynical aspects of the canon, including long burlesque poems in *terza rima* and *ottava rima*, were not translated into English in the nineteenth century.[76] Michelangelo's homoerotic sonnets were not faithfully translated until the end of the century, and with this work came an accompanying shift of narrative on the part of the translator, Symonds, who "saw in Michelangelo a potential source for the exploration of 'sexual inversion' and its manifestation in the individual."[77]

The nineteenth century was also the century in which Michelangelo's visual works became accessible to a much broader English-speaking audience, although responses to this canon likewise suggest a very partial and targeted embrace of the work. The bulk of Michelangelo's visual canon—consisting of monumental marble statues, architectural works, and frescos—defied collection and circulation in a way that the verbal work did not, but some images found entry into a newly classified public space. Today, a quarter of Michelangelo's graphic work resides in three English collections, a shift that took place in the course of the nineteenth century, as both drawings and manuscripts passed from private to public hands. The Royal Collection at Windsor, the British Museum, and the Ashmolean Museum in Oxford all contain significant collections of work that were at the time considered an indisputable part of Michelangelo's canon.[78] The reception of these works by British audiences, though, indicates an unspoken bias echoing the one toward the literary work. In spite of the large number of sketches and partial architectural designs in public British collections, critics of Michelangelo's work such as Symonds and John Ruskin almost always preferred to discuss the relatively polished drawings. Critics paid less attention to the looser and more apparently incomplete sketches and studies, even as biographers professed the importance of these works to understanding Michelangelo's process. The same aesthetic biases in both cases pushed editors and critics toward considering only works that conformed to a uniform conception of the artist.[79]

The ideal of uniformity also informed Michelangelo's American reception. Emerson typifies the desire to see the artist in terms that stress the cohesion of his canon. He formalized his own views on the artist in an early lecture titled "Michel Angelo Buonaroti," (1835) which emphasizes the unity of Michelangelo's life and art, his universality, and his independence from outside influence. The introduction to the lecture outlines the span of Michelangelo's life in these terms:

> There are few lives of eminent men that are harmonious: few that furnish
> in all the facts an image corresponding with their fame. But all things

Longfellow, Michael Angelo, and the "Middle-Class" Curator   153

> recorded of Michel Angelo Buonarotti agree together. He lived one life:
> he pursued one career. . . . Every line in his biography might be read with
> wholesome effect.[80]

Michelangelo's interest as a subject of biography lies foremost in his story's unity of effect, the manner in which the moral perfection of his life conforms easily to the physical perfection of the artwork. While Emerson presents a very generalist vision of the artist—he admits in his introductory remarks that to many in the audience "much more is known than I know" of the artist's life and work—this generality is in fact key to the cohesion of his argument.[81] The narrative that he creates depends on the absence of any details that might disrupt the ideal of perfect unity.

The desire to see in the canon a unified effect did not always produce the adulation that infuses Emerson's response. In some cases, the extremity of the criticism swung in the other direction, while a perspective on the canon's cohesion remained fixed. Few writers fleshed out this dramatically polarized approach to the artist more completely or more famously than John Ruskin, whose analysis of Michelangelo in his lecture "The Relation Between Michael Angelo and Tintoret" (delivered 1870–1871, printed 1872) provides a good background to Longfellow's treatment of the artist in *Michael Angelo*. The contexts through which the two discuss the artist are similar, and yet the ends at which they each arrive diverge sharply. Both writers are centrally concerned with the opposition of craftsmanship and fine art. Both are equally concerned, at least implicitly, with the accessibility of the artist's work to audiences. But if the analogy for Ruskin's lecture is the Oxford gallery collection that he purports to bring to a broader public, the analogy for Longfellow's work is the older, more eclectic public gallery that is by its nature democratically inclusive.

Ruskin claims to have composed his lecture to encourage Oxford students and even "strangers visiting the Galleries" to take advantage of the University's recently acquired collection of Michelangelo drawings, but this apparently democratizing purpose is superficial at best.[82] The speech not only did nothing to encourage an admiration of Michelangelo—Edward Burne-Jones "wanted to drown himself in the Surrey Canal" after a private reading of the papers—but Ruskin's analysis of the artwork casts doubt on his alleged aim of encouraging a viewership. He notes, for instance, that deep aesthetic flaws damage many works to the extent that they "ought never to be exhibited to the general public" and even those works remaining are best seen only by artists:

"Incipient methods of design are not, and ought not to be, subjects of earnest inquiry to other people."[83] Ruskin's lecture, then, is not primarily directed at a general public, but rather targets those few who "ought" to reference the works in question.

Even for that select group, Ruskin finds little positive knowledge to be derived from a study of Michelangelo's work. Many of the writer's criticisms of Michelangelo center on his apparent lack of technical skill. Ruskin understands the years from "1480 to 1520" as a "deadly catastrophe" in the world of art, led by the triumvirate of Raphael/Michelangelo/Titian and only eventually countered by Tintoretto who "stands up for a last fight, for Venice and the old time."[84] Bad workmanship, following Ruskin, is a central fault of this earlier group, and he takes Michelangelo to task for his execution of works either "hastily and incompletely done" or shoddily completed so that "the best qualities of it perished."[85] This artist "lived in [the] world of court intrigue" (as opposed to Tintoretto and his peers, who "lived as craftsmen") and criticized oil painting (which Ruskin considers the highest form of art) because he "had neither the skill to lay a single touch of good oil-painting, nor the patience to overcome even its elementary difficulties."[86] In attributing Michelangelo's most significant failings to technical deficit, Ruskin emphasizes the division between what he sees as courtly but incompetent fine art, and humble but proficient craftsmanship.

The final paragraphs of the lecture confirm this polarized understanding of art practice. If Michelangelo's failure as a craftsman is evidenced by the destruction of his works by time, the mark of the accomplished craftsman lies in being threatened by the vagaries of human judgment. Ruskin ends his digressive lecture with a long description of Tintoretto's *Paradise*, "the most precious work of art of any kind, whatsoever, now existing in the world."[87] This huge oil on canvas, he warns, is "on the eve of final destruction," as a result of impending reconstructive work in the council chamber where it is housed in Venice.[88] The contrast to Michelangelo's work in the Oxford collection is implicit: while this artist's loose sketches are sheltered within the preservationist realm of the museum, Tintoretto's supreme craftsmanship is at the mercy of the outside world, sheltered only by the political mundanity of the council chamber. The lecture ends with an appeal to readers to offer this work the same protection that they have granted what is deemed fine art, to recall "the treasures that we forget, while we amuse ourselves with the poor toys."[89] Instead of encouraging listeners to visit Michelangelo's work, the piece concludes by

Longfellow, Michael Angelo, and the "Middle-Class" Curator 155

encouraging them to sequester Tintoretto's, to remove this work from the dangers of the public realm that can threaten even good craftsmanship.

Collection, craftsmanship, and artistry are for Longfellow as for Ruskin central terms in the consideration of Michelangelo's work, but these words take on a radically different meaning in Longfellow's play. Rather than place Michelangelo solidly in the category of either craft or high art, Longfellow questions the cultural assumptions that give rise to these divisions. Michelangelo occupies the space, alternately, of each category: he was nursed by a stonemason's wife, but also claims the aristocratic heritage that the drama connects to the fine arts. The play embraces time's destructive touch and the artist's tendency to leave works incomplete as an invitation for a new generation of artists, rather than as evidence of a shoddy artistic practice. Longfellow's vision of artists in *Michael Angelo* is better understood through an older, more democratic museum than through Ruskin's Oxford gallery, in which art is "little likely" to be either "useful or dangerous to my pupils" since "no student has ever asked me a single question respecting these drawings, or, so far as I could see, taken the slightest interest in them."[90] Longfellow's play, unlike Ruskin's lecture, is populated by visitors: critics who discuss Michelangelo's work, and friends who move through the artist's life. Both problematize one-sided characterizations of the artist's life. Inclusive rather than exclusive, *Michael Angelo* incorporates many biographical versions of the artist into its narrative, and in so doing invites a more rounded if less focused understanding of the life and work. Longfellow's drama, though it remained in a desk drawer until after his death, ultimately granted the kind of accessibility to the artist that Ruskin's writing only professed.

MICHAEL ANGELO'S OPEN COLLECTION

The critical treatment of Longfellow's *Michael Angelo* provides a good starting point to a reassessment of the text. The work is, of course, a drama, but even Longfellow's earliest critics were dismissive of its status as "real" drama. Written in blank verse, and supplemented with only the thinnest of stage-settings, the play focuses almost entirely on character development and has little narrative drive. With its emphasis on long, abstract monologues and its complete absence of any stage direction, the play is difficult to imagine as a performance. As a reviewer in *The Spectator* writes in 1883: "with all its merits—and it certainly contains fine passages—it is dramatic only in form."[91] Other reviews, such as the 1884 acknowledgement in *Lippincott's Magazine*, refer to the work more often as "poem" than drama.[92] Horace Scudder's biographical introduction to *The Complete Poetical Works* assumes the insignificance of the dramatic frame, to a personal end: "The caution against mistaking a poet's dramatic assumption for his own character and expression is of less force when applied to one in whom the dramatic power was but slightly developed; and the whole poem of *Michael Angelo*, taken in connection with the time and circumstances of its composition, may fairly be regarded as in some respects Longfellow's *apologia*."[93] In this reading, the dramatic scaffolding of the play, because "but slightly developed," simply holds up a thin scrim through which we are amply justified in reading the facts and feelings of Longfellow's late life.

Contemporary criticism reiterates this tendency toward biographical readings of the play. Charles Calhoun's 2004 biography of the poet discusses *Michael Angelo* briefly, considering it as a reflection of Longfellow's "own situation as an artist facing death."[94] Christoph Irmscher's 2006 book of essays on the poet, *Longfellow Redux*, also depends significantly on biography, but takes an opposite tack in its analysis of *Michael Angelo*. Devoting a full five pages to the play, the longest sustained discussion since its publication, Irmscher finds in the central protagonist a figure who "attracted and appalled" Longfellow, but who in spite of their similar life stages at the time of the play's composition, is more anti-type than model. As Irmscher writes, "Michelangelo is, in a sense a study of everything Longfellow was *not*—an artist consumed by, made desperate even, by his desire to have the 'labor of his hand' match the grand, innovative conceptions in his head."[95] Irmscher frames Longfellow as a writer who felt no shame in literary borrowings and never strove for a modern notion of aesthetic originality, in contrast to Michelangelo, who embodies precisely these ideals of "innovative conception."

In both of these readings of the work, Michelangelo is a stable signifier of high art, devoted to originality as an artistic ideal. And yet it is precisely this stability that Longfellow's *Michael Angelo* takes to task. The discrepancy between Calhoun and Irmscher's nearly opposed readings lies only in whether the critics take Longfellow to subscribe to a stable set of "high art" ideals—and certainly the pendulum in recent Longfellow criticism has swung more to Irmscher's side, with critics increasingly favoring a more inclusive craftsman's ideal in discussing Longfellow's "derivativeness." This perspective on Longfellow's work as located to one side of debates about originality and metrical innovation is an overwhelmingly positive one, freeing criticism of Longfellow and poets working in a similar mode from an undercurrent of defensiveness. It locates Longfellow as "middle-class" in a manner that does not demand apology. My aim in reading *Michael Angelo* is to submit the figure of the Renaissance artist to this same nuanced scrutiny. In an examination of Longfellow's Michelangelo, the stable reading of the artist as original, monumental, and unified so prevalent in nineteenth-century artistic criticism quickly unhinges. His role, instead, is strikingly similar to the in-between "middle-class" place that recent critics have found for Longfellow. The poet's greatest accomplishment in *Michael Angelo* may have been to redefine this unlikely artist-figure as an emblem for his own literary craft. Placing Michelangelo between the fluid categories of art and craft, unity and fragmentation, history and contemporaneity, showcases Longfellow's innovation as a cultural critic at the same time as it reveals his artistic self-perception as located between these extremes.

The opening "Dedication" sonnet in *Michael Angelo: A Fragment* (1883) functions as a curatorial note, providing a sense of the mode of artistic collection in Longfellow's drama. Far from Ruskin's hermetic gallery, the collection principle of *Michael Angelo* is open and fluid, equipped with a permeable sense of originality and historical influence. Though this mode is described in terms of the architecture of literature, the ideas translate to later discussions of the visual arts:

> Nothing that is shall perish utterly,
> But perish only to revive again
> In other forms, as clouds restore in rain
> The exhalations of the land and sea.
> Men build their houses from the masonry
> Of ruined tombs; the passion and the pain
> Of hearts, that long have ceased to beat, remain
> To throb in hearts that are, or are to be.
> So from old chronicles, where sleep in dust
> Names that once filled the world with trumpet tones,
> I build this verse; and flowers of song have thrust
> Their roots among the loose disjointed stones,
> Which to this end I fashion as I must.
> Quickened are they that touch the Prophet's bones.[96]

This perspective on artistic creation resonates clearly with Longfellow's other ekphrastic work, both in its lack of emphasis on original conception and its natural analogies. The central trope of building homes (or art-objects) from the pieces of the past underlines the sense of historical continuity that is at the foundation of all of Longfellow's accounts of creation, especially that in "Kéramos." As creation in "Kéramos," *Michael Angelo*'s historical continuity is enabled precisely by breaking apart the forms of the past: "ruined tombs" become "houses," and Longfellow's own poem is constructed alternately of "old chronicles" and "loose disjointed stones," built with little personal volition ("I fashion as I must") or hope for future endurance. As in "Giotto's Tower," the artistic product is also described in terms of natural cycles: clouds that become rain, flowers that vine through the structure.[97] It is fitting, then, that in the 1884 Houghton Mifflin illustrated edition of the poem, this "Dedication" is printed within a full-page engraving of a broken chunk of stone from a building-plaque, with a hazy image of the ruins of the Roman Forum in the background and some trees in the foreground (see figure 9). The artistic space into which the "Dedication" leads us is one of both historic destruction and organic growth. This notion of artistry is at odds with modern notions of high art, inspiration, and artistic will. As Irmscher writes, "There is little here of what Henry James, in one of his prefaces, called 'the muffled majesty of authorship.'"[98] Instead, we find an understanding of artistry that calls attention to the materials of its own production, that shows the gaps between "the loose disjointed stones" in order to emphasize its own fragmented hypermediation.

It is perhaps inevitable given this emphasis that conclusions and inconclusions are a focus both in the "Dedication" and the larger work. Longfellow's ideas about historical influence and continuity prevent the arrival at any conclusion that carries the stamp of personal artistic volition. The phrase "to this end" in the penultimate line of the "Dedication" illustrates this focus, speaking both to a preoccupation with death and with artistic conclusions. In the context of the last lines, the demonstrative "this end" is ambiguous, gesturing both to the literal "end" of the sonnet and to "end" as "purpose" (in this case, the purpose of verse-building). "Quickened are they that touch the prophet's bones" ties up the sonnet, reiterating the ongoing theme of death and rebirth that frame the opening lines ("Nothing that is shall perish utterly"). The drama as a whole is wrapped up in these same questions—how to end itself, how to mark the end of life—but is not nearly as tidily contained as the opening

"Dedication": its existence as "Fragment" is an essential characteristic of its structure, pointing to Longfellow's aesthetic ideal of overflow and influence.

The "Dedication" provides a foretaste of the major forces—craftsmanship and fine art, derivation and originality, history and present—that underlie the drama. But if "Giotto's Tower" functions both structurally and thematically as a defense of incompletion, then *Michael Angelo* offers a much more divided argument. Perhaps the most structurally broken and conceptually derivative of Longfellow's works, its idealized and hypermasculine protagonist nonetheless makes persuasive arguments for unity and aesthetic originality throughout the play. The centering conflict of the work is, I argue, the extent to which fragmentation enters the life narrative of a character aligned with the concept of artistic unity. Neither true protagonist nor antihero, Michelangelo is for Longfellow a figure who tests the boundaries of isolated individuality and iconoclastic genius, and who poses questions about the role of mediation in art. Most strikingly, unlike the dialogue that answers itself in "Giotto's Tower," these questions are honest ones. In this sense, the play supports Longfellow's position as a "middle-class" writer, but relies on elements that go well beyond Fuller's conception of the term, including artistic self-awareness and an interest in formal qualities as a conduit to meaning.

The textual history of *Michael Angelo* confirms the work's investment in open-endedness: the play, which remained unfinished in Longfellow's lifetime, literalizes the argument for the fragment in "Giotto's Tower." The first published edition was based on an interpretation of Longfellow's manuscript, with footnotes and illustrations supplied by the editors. The structurally fragmentary nature of the published document is undeniable: when it was found in Longfellow's desk drawer after his death in 1882, it carried the label "A Fragment" on its first page.[99] Editors have chosen whether or not to emphasize this incomplete state in their own printings. At the poem's first publication in *The Atlantic Monthly* in January 1883 editors dropped the subtitle "A Fragment" in favor of "A Drama" and made no mention of the work's unfinished state. When it was printed in a lavishly illustrated book edition by Houghton Mifflin and Company later that same year, this subtitle became "A Dramatic Poem" and a publisher's note told readers that the work "was written by Mr. Longfellow mainly about ten years before his death, but was kept by him for occasional revision, and printed after his death in *The Atlantic Monthly* from his final copy."[100] It was first anthologized in Longfellow's *Poetical Works* of 1884. Other editions, such as the 1886 Riverside Edition of Longfellow's collected writings,

FIGURE 9. "Dedication" in *Michael Angelo: a Dramatic Poem*, by Henry Wadsworth Longfellow Papers, (Boston: Houghton, Mifflin, 1884). Courtesy, Making of America.

and the 1898 *Complete Poetical Works* reinstate Longfellow's original subtitle and stress the unfinished nature of the work. The comprehensive Riverside Edition also includes an appendix of the scenes that Longfellow excised from his final draft, including a final scene at the artist's deathbed.[101]

The notes to the Riverside edition and the manuscripts on which they are based highlight the difficulty, often elided by editors, of determining

Longfellow's "final copy." This edition includes an appendix documenting the scenes, or expanded versions of scenes, that Longfellow excised from his final draft. None of these scenes appear in any form in the text or editorial apparatus of the *Atlantic Monthly* or the Houghton Mifflin editions. But within the final text of the Riverside edition, the editor places some sections of text in parentheses, indicating that these were passages included in the play only after the first full draft had been written. These passages appear unmarked and integrated into the final copy of the *Atlantic Monthly* and Houghton Mifflin texts. And while the publisher of the latter edition notes simply that the play was printed from Longfellow's final copy, the Riverside publisher stated that it was not possible to say what the final form of Michael Angelo would have been if the author had decided to put it into type versus leaving it in his desk. Critics have followed the earlier editions of the text in glossing over the problematic nature of the "final copy" and the text-as-fragment.

Based on Longfellow's own manuscript drafts, the unfinished nature of the work and its subtitling as "A Fragment" is not an incidental fact of history, but an essential characteristic of the poem's construction. Longfellow's final working draft of the drama, on which the Riverside and other published editions are based, emphasizes process and parts over a stable document. Recorded in a thick, bound book with *Michael Angelo* embossed on the spine, the document is written in pencil and marked by frequent erasures, crossed-out passages, and marginal notes. The draft also includes a section at the end of the work consisting entirely of scenes or passages marked as "rejected" or "omitted," suggesting that Longfellow saw the work as defined more by the process of its creation than its narrative beginning and end.[102]

The play's initial draft emphasizes fragmentation even more dramatically. Unlike many of Longfellow's first drafts, which he wrote in a fairly continuous manner from beginning to end, this draft of *Michael Angelo* is literally written in fragments, recorded on scraps of paper and the back sides of other documents, creating an editorial nightmare of Dickinsonian proportions. These early lines and scenes for the drama were collected in a marble-papered folder now in the Houghton Library, the cover of which is hand-titled "Michael Angelo" (see figure 10). The contents are motley: there are two pencil sketches of Vittoria Colonna, single lines of text on small cards, sections of scenes or exchanges between characters on notebook paper, and outlines of the work as it takes shape. Many of the shorter scraps reflect the drama's preoccupation with death: one card reads simply "Old grave-stones of the past," while another prints the line "Great death, the King of shadows, with a touch / Cured all our evils" on the back of a business card. A monologue labeled "Death" is written out on the back of a list of student absences. Compared to other contemporaneous manuscripts—such as "Kéramos," the first draft of which is a neatly dated clean copy—the thematic focus and the general disorganization of these papers is remarkable.[103] If Longfellow in the final copy of the work emphasizes its construction through parts, the actual state of his manuscript literalizes that emphasis.

That said, the cobbled format of *Michael Angelo*'s drafts was likely due at least in part to the broad timespan over which the play was composed. Though the work takes up less than two-hundred wide-margin, generously illustrated pages in the Houghton Mifflin edition, Longfellow worked on the play for more than thirty years, since 1850, when he composed a scene from the middle of the play in which Michelangelo recounts an apocalyptic dream. He conceived most of the scenes in the early 1870s, but tinkered with the poem until the end of his life in 1882. On April 21, 1872, he wrote to life-long friend George Washington Greene, "I have been writing a poem, which I think will please you. It is not yet finished, but enough is written to make me see my way clear. It is a dramatic poem to be called 'Michael Angelo.' . . . The subject is beautiful, and I shall be disappointed if you do not like it."[104] By May of that year he could write in his journal that "the Poem in its first form is complete."[105] The work then existed in a more or less finished state for the final decade of Longfellow's life, a decade during which he published seven full volumes of new work, one of which, *Kéramos and Other Poems*, included translations of Michelangelo's sonnets originally slated for inclusion in the drama.[106] But Longfellow approached the dramatic work with patience and an emphasis on process over completion. "I want it," he wrote in his journal in March 1872, "for a long and delightful occupation."[107] Longfellow's method of composition, which proceeded scene by scene and scrap by scrap rather than in his more typical linear manner, emphasizes his understanding of the work as a composite of parts rather than a unified whole.

The fragmentary nature of the work infuses even its narrative action and setting, both of which are minimally developed. Longfellow realized this apparent failing in focusing on the artist's late career, writing in his journal when he was first beginning the work: "The subject attracts me; but is difficult to treat dramatically for want of unity of action, and plot in general."[108] Very little happens to Michelangelo in the course of the play, which spans roughly the last twelve years of his life: he stays in Rome, attempting to complete various artworks, interacting with other characters that drift in and out of the scenes and city, and performing long-winded monologues on the merits of various artistic media. The play is divided into three acts, the first two of which have six scenes, the final, eight. Michelangelo is at the center of most of these scenes, though some focus entirely on peripheral action, such as the would-be love affair between Cardinal Ippolito and Julia Gonzago, the friend of Michelangelo's adored Vittoria Colonna. Seventeen characters populate the play at different points, each contributing to the diffusion of any real narrative form. Scenes center alternately on Vittoria's exile and death; Cardinal Ippolito's death; the political conflicts around Michelangelo's *Last Judgment*; the complacency of the painter Fra Sebastiano; the artistic development of the jeweler-turned-sculptor Cellini; the aesthetic discussions of Michelangelo, Titian, and Georgio Vasari; and the musings of an anonymous monk who longs to make a pilgrimage to Rome. The majority of these events are disconnected from one another.

Michael Angelo, then, is a work that willfully defies the ideal of aesthetic unity, and that, like "Giotto's Tower," argues for the artistic value of the unfinished. This argument is complicated by Michelangelo himself, whom the other characters hail throughout the play, much as Emerson did, as an artist embodying unity and the ability to complete artistic undertakings. But Longfellow's Michelangelo, in his words and his actions, resists these characterizations, suggesting that biographical and aesthetic fragmentation can offer the basis for a reevaluation of his artistic career. In Longfellow's writing, the fragmentary nature of Michelangelo's work does not detract from its value, but rather allows viewers a more active engagement with it. Like Giotto's multigenerational tower, the work in Michelangelo's canon invites completion, and its power lies precisely in this invitation. A viewing of the work is necessarily a collaborative act, throwing into question the association of artistic originality with the isolated creator.

LONGFELLOW IN PIECES

Michael Angelo is unique among nineteenth-century depictions of the artist for the radical fragmentation that characterizes all aspects of its construction. The text is broken on many levels: in the diversity of its historical influence,

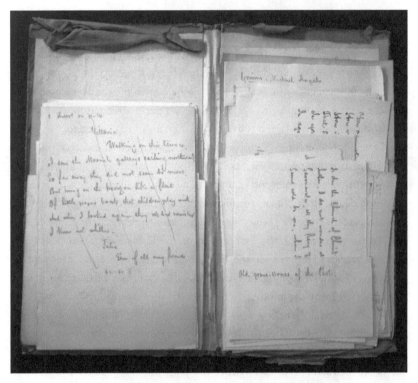

FIGURE 10. *Michael Angelo*. A.MS. Henry Wadsworth Longfellow papers, Houghton Library. Author's photograph. Courtesy, Harvard University.

in its shattered political landscape, and in its dramatically abbreviated conclusion. In these fissures lie Longfellow's contribution to the modern myth of Michelangelo, a myth to which Ruskin, Emerson, Fuller, Lowell, and many others contributed in each their own way. Longfellow's Michelangelo is characterized by instability and constant growth. Against a backdrop of secondary characters who attempt to label him in fixed terms as master and teacher, Michelangelo repeatedly stresses his development as a student and the insecurity of his status as an artist. He sets himself apart from his contemporaries in embracing an aesthetics of flux, but his appreciation for change and movement is also at the root of the play's preoccupation with death, and its ultimate inability to conclude.

Fissures appear in the text through the sheer number of scholarly sources to which Longfellow is indebted. These sources imply what the text later confirms: that Longfellow's Michelangelo is a multifaceted figure, unable to be contained through an argument as polemical or self-contained as Ruskin's or Emerson's. By the time that Longfellow began writing his play in earnest in the early 1870s, many secondary sources on Michelangelo—both recent and historical—existed in English, and many more in Italian. If the nineteenth century was "*the* century when Michelangelo became a text," then Longfellow's *Michael Angelo* is arguably the contemporaneous work that best translates this scholarship.[109] A project in scholarly consolidation, the drama aimed to bring these sometimes erudite, sometimes untranslated documents to a mass audience. Emilio Goggio, in "The Sources of Longfellow's *Michael Angelo*" identifies Longfellow's principle references as biographies and histories written by authors ranging from Michelangelo's to Longfellow's own contemporaries. They include, from earliest to latest, Juan de Valdes's *Alfabeto Christiano* (1546), Giorgio Vasari's *Vite dei pui eccellenti pittori, scultori e architetti* (1550), Asconio Condivi's *Vita di Michelangelo Buonarroti* (1553), Benedetto Varchi's *Storia Florentina* (1721), Benvenuto Cellini's *Vita* (1728), *Rime e Lettere di Veronica Gambara* (1759), Leopold von Ranke's *Die römischen Päpste, ihre kirche und ihr Staat im sechzehnten und siebzehnten Jahrhundert* (1834–1836), Jacopo Nardi's *Istorie della Citta di Firenze* (1858), and Herman Grimm's *Das Leben Michelangelos* (1868).[110] It is likely, though, that the poet consulted even more texts. Longfellow in his journals records reading not just Grimm, Vasari, and Condivi's books, but also more contemporary works, such as John S. Harford's 1857 *The Life of Michel Angelo Buonarroti* and Anna Jameson's 1845 *Memoirs of the Early Italian Painters*.[111] Longfellow's play, then, is a pastiche of the critical perspectives on the Renaissance that by the nineteenth century had infused the literary marketplace in England and America.

Longfellow's faithfulness to his sources—or his remediation of scholarship—has not escaped critical notice. As a reviewer in *Lippincott's Magazine* writes, "the poet seems to have followed Grimm's biography of the great master at every point, and in the interview at the church of San Silvestro, he has given an actual transcription of D'Ollanda's chronicle of the conversation."[112] Goggio also shows Longfellow's borrowings to be extensive, reaching sometimes into actual quotation, and he cites a passage that is "taken almost in its entirety from Juan de Valdés's *Alphabeto Christiano*."[113] In moving through the work, Goggio attributes nearly every scene to a close historical reference. To focus on Longfellow's sources is to see the work as a scholarly museum piece rather that Fuller's ideal of "a new product in which all the old varieties are melted into a fresh form."[114] In this sense, the background texts of *Michel Angelo* gesture toward an understanding of literary creation outside of individual originality, in which pieces of history replace a single consolidated authorial perspective. This resistance to the "melting" of parts according to a writer's creative direction is itself an aesthetic, a means of understanding and broadcasting a particular view of artistry.[115]

But despite being overwhelmingly positive, none of the contemporary reviewers of *Michael Angelo* comments on the stylistic choices or the structure of Longfellow's work. The 1883 reviews in *The Dial* and *The Spectator* focus their comments almost exclusively on the physical appearance of the book, noting the binding, layout, paper-quality, typography, and, of course, illustrations, which they enumerate individually. The beautifully illustrated 1883 book was perhaps in part responsible for guiding this focus. The extensive list of illustrations in the volume credits both illustrators and engravers, creating an enumeration much more detailed than the brief table of contents. The volume also includes editorial endnotes that explicate the various sources for the illustrations, because, as a prefatory note tells readers, "the portraits, which form the chief subject of the notes, could not be referred to except by recourse to a variety of works."[116] In a posthumous volume, these illustrations were an editorial rather than authorial choice, but their reproduction echoes the written text's reliance on appropriation, allusion, and citation.

A close reading of the play reveals the self-consciousness of both *Michael Angelo's* textual and visual remediations. Thematic elements in the play echo the piecemeal qualities of the text's sources, attesting to Longfellow's self-conscious investment in fragmentation as a theme. The play's treatment of its Roman setting and its central monument, the Coliseum, play into this emphasis. *Michael Angelo's* Rome is a city of ghosts and of ruins, broken not only by political discord but also by the simple course of time. This decay suits the spirit of Michelangelo, who, though a Florentine by birth and initially an unwilling exile, embraces Rome in his old age as "a second native land by predilection."[117] Ruin has everything to do with this "predilection": "The very weeds, that grow / Among the broken fragments of her ruins, / Are sweeter to me than the garden flowers / Of other cities."[118] These weeds echo back to the "flowers of song" in the "Dedication" that "thrust their roots among the loose disjointed stones," and like these flowers, the weeds both decorate the stones that they inhabit, and push them further apart, reconfiguring the landscape as they embellish it. Rome, like the "ruined tombs" of the "Dedication" is a living artwork, a historical backdrop in a constant state of development.

Longfellow, Michael Angelo, and the "Middle-Class" Curator   167

This setting is a fitting backdrop to the artwork that has the greatest influence on Michelangelo's work in the course of the play, the Coliseum. Like its setting, the Coliseum is characterized by organic destruction and reconfiguration. It is, as Michelangelo says on a nighttime visit to the ruins, "The marble rose of Rome! Its petals torn / by wind and rain of thrice five hundred years; / Its mossy sheath half rent away, and sold / To ornament our palaces and churches."[119] Yet this destruction and persistence represents a large part of the Coliseum's attraction to the artist. Unlike his companion Cavalieri, Michelangelo does not speak of the fixed moment in its early history "when this rose was perfect" but rather focuses on its present state.[120] Its ruin is less a sign of demise than evidence of a natural evolution, and like Giotto's tower, which "blossom[s]" and "bloom[s]" independently, the Coliseum is described in strikingly organic terms. It remains, as Michelangelo says, a moss-covered rose, "Still opening its fair bosom to the sun," constellations lit up above "like a swarm of bees."[121] As with Giotto's tower, this organic nature represents the object's continual potential: "A thousand wild flowers bloom / From every chink, and the birds build their nests/ Among the ruined arches, and suggest / New thoughts of beauty to the architect."[122] This image of wildflowers blooming from broken pieces of stone resonates again with the image in the "Dedication" of the "flowers of song" that grow "among the loose disjointed stones," positioning Michelangelo's aesthetic in accordance with the same basic principles as Longfellow's text.[123]

In this same scene in the Coliseum, Michelangelo tells Cavalieri about his vision of the world's end.[124] This end depends on the cessation of motion and growth:

> All things must have an end; the world itself
> Must have an end, as in a dream I saw it.
> There came a great hand out of heaven, and touched
> The earth, and stopped it in its course. The seas
> Leaped, a vast cataract, into the abyss;
> The forests and fields slid off, and floated
> Like wooded islands in the air. The dead
> Were hurled forth from the sepulchres: the living
> Were mingled with them, and themselves were dead,—
> All being dead.[125]

The central action of Michelangelo's dream is not an active change, but the simple absence of motion, a divine hand that reaches to the earth and "stopped it." This arrest instantly ends all life: the ocean becomes a waterfall, the forests become wood, and the living become indistinguishable from the dead. All is, as Michelangelo later says, a "wrack of matter." To this striking image of destruction, Cavalieri's only response is, "But the earth does not move," highlighting his own static world-view in contrast to Michelangelo's more progressive perspective. This vision of apocalyptic fragmentation was the first that Longfellow composed, some twenty years before the rest of the scenes were written in the early 1870s.[126] That this dream, connected to the larger unfolding of the play only thematically, is Longfellow's first, suggests the extent to which the theme of movement and stasis is foundational to the play as a whole.

This theme likewise informs Michelangelo's preoccupation with and anticipation of his own death, an "ending" that in fact never occurs in the course of the play. The artist's (at times impatient) anticipation is the central tension that drives the narrative forward. Few scenes end without the death of a character close to Michelangelo or a remark about Michelangelo's own preparation for death. These preoccupations culminate in the final scene of the play, an anti-conclusion that empties out the action of the play without in any way resolving it. The setting is Michelangelo's studio in the late evening, as he is at work on a new project. When Giorgio Vasari drops in after a night of revelry, the artist reveals that he is carving his own tomb, and this last passage follows:

> MICHAEL ANGELO, *letting fall the lamp.*
> Life hath become to me
> An empty theatre,—its lights extinguished,
> The music silent, and the actors gone;
> And I alone sit musing on the scenes
> That once have been. I am so old that Death
> Oft plucks me by the cloak, to come with him;
> And some day, like this lamp, shall I fall down,
> And my last spark of life will be extinguished.
> Ah me! ah me! what darkness of despair!
> So near to death, and yet so far from God![127]

These final lines of the play are anti-climactic, voiding dramatic action in the scene in a way that corresponds to the dominant metaphor of Michelangelo's life as an empty theater. This conceit of life-as-a-theater—unlike the more traditional life-as-play—frustrates any hope for a clear conclusion to the drama's action. The theater, emptied of its light, music and actors, maintains its "life" for as long as it can be identified as a physical structure. The theater-conceit locates Michelangelo in a position of passive spectator to his own (increasingly uneventful) life, a position analogous to that of *Michael Angelo*'s readers, who are by the last scenes witness to a play that has lost any sense of dramatic action.

Longfellow's decision to end the play with this scene allows both Michelangelo's life and the drama to continue according to the model of organic, continuous growth. Earlier drafts of the work reveal this "unfinished" ending to be the product of extensive reworking, the scene between Michelangelo and Vasari taking its place as the play's last only relatively late in the revision process. Longfellow had originally written a much more conclusive final scene to the play—titled definitively "The Last Scene"—documenting Michelangelo's death and final words. In this scene, Michelangelo is surrounded by friends Cavalieri, Volterra, and Asconio, as well as his doctor Donati. The four await Leonardo da Vinci, as Michelangelo passes deliriously in and out of sleep, and dies before this last artist arrives. The scene concludes neatly with Michelangelo's last words ("My soul to God; my body to the earth; / My worldly goods unto my next of kin / My memory—to the keeping—of my friends") and the ringing of the vespers.[128] After writing this scene at the suggestion of George Washington Greene, who had listened to Longfellow's recitation of the poem in 1872, Longfellow later reconsidered its inclusion. In a March 3, 1874 letter to Greene, Longfellow explains his editorial logic: "I have written the new scene, that you suggested for 'Angelo.' I am not dissatisfied with it, and yet do not want to add it. It seems to me better to leave the close a little vague, than to give a tragic ending, though that may be the proper finis of the book."[129] The distinction here between what is "proper" in a general sense, and what Longfellow feels to be "better" in this instance gives insight into his vision for the play as a whole. Leaving the ending "a little vague," is a stylistic echo of Michelangelo's artistic work, which remains, until the end of his life, unfinished.

The only defiance to the self-containment of this alternative final scene is Michelangelo's complaint on his deathbed that he never finished St. Peters: "The saddest thing in dying is to leave / One's work unfinished."[130] In fact, Michelangelo struggles throughout the play with his inability to complete his designs. The last line of the first act records Michelangelo telling Vittoria not to look at the portrait he is painting of her ("Not yet; it is not finished.")

while earlier in that same scene he notes that his work on the Sistine Chapel progresses "But tardily."[131] Michelangelo assumes that even the end of life does not bring a real conclusion to artistic work, and in a conversation with Vasari and Titian in the latter's studio, this inconclusiveness takes on a positive turn that is reminiscent of the collaborative creation in "Giotto's Tower." Speaking of a younger generation of artists with these two older artists, Michelangelo asks, "When you two / Are gone, who is there that remains behind / To seize the pencil falling from your fingers?"[132] Vasari and Titian's responses are both similarly hopeful. Vasari answers that "many hands" are prepared for the task, while Titian responds in terms that echo both the "Dedication" and "Giotto's Tower": "Our ruins / Will serve to build their palaces or tombs. / They will possess the world that we think ours, / And fashion it far otherwise."[133] The reconfiguration of both artwork and the larger world is the task of future generations, a fate that emphasizes the fluidity of both works and worlds.

The emphasis on incompletion and growth in *Michael Angelo* creates an unusually nuanced artist, one that defies the more static characterizations of Emerson and Ruskin. Longfellow implicitly pits his characterization of the artist against these opposing perspectives through the other characters in *Michael Angelo*, all of whom seem to share Emersonian views on Michelangelo as a "unifier." These characters represent the artist alternately as unifying all people, all artistic media, and all artistic compositions. Vittoria Colonna, for instance, when describing Michelangelo to Julia Gonzago in the play's first scene exclaims that "all men" fear him, just as "all men" honor him, and "all" should follow him. So much is he in "all men's thoughts" that when they speak of greatness "his name / Is ever on their lips."[134] This vision of the world as brought together by an identical attitude toward the great man is matched with a vision of Michelangelo as a man who fits the different elements of his own life together cohesively. He is, as Vittoria says, "one who works and prays, / For work is prayer, and consecrates his life / To the sublime ideal of his art, / Till art and life are one."[135] For Vittoria, Michelangelo's magnetic force brings all together in unanimous opinion and integrates the parts of a varied life into a seamlessly functioning whole.

This conception extends to several other characters. When Cardinal Ippolito asks Fra Sebastiano to tell him "of the artists" a few scenes later, the painter replies in a manner that echoes Vittoria's description of Michelangelo. The difference between Vittoria and Sebastiano's characters—the one serious and ascetic, the other jovial and self-indulgent—implicitly illustrates Vittoria's assertion that "all men" are united in their opinion of Michelangelo. As Fra Sebastiano says of contemporary artists:

Naming one
I name them all; for there is only one:
His name is Messer Michael Angelo.
All art and artists of the present day
Centre in him.[136]

On the one hand, this passage reflects on Michelangelo's mastery of "all" three primary visual media—painting, sculpture, and architecture—which set him apart from artists like Fra Sebastiano, who as he himself says is "Only a portrait-painter; one who draws / With greater or less skill, as best he may, / The features of a face."[137] But this distinction also understands Michelangelo as becoming something greater in uniting the parts of his artistry. He is, as Fra Sebastiano says, "a lover / Of all things beautiful" while Fra Sebastiano is, in Cardinal Ippolito's words, a "skilful hand [sic]."[138] Portraiture and other artistic skills are located in parts—the hand, the face—but artistry is located in the whole, in "all things beautiful." In bringing together all of the arts, Michelangelo is more than a skillful artisan: he becomes, as Benvenuto Cellini says later in the play, a "miraculous Master."[139]

This distinction between artistic master and artisan dominates many of the artistic discussions of the text, but it soon becomes apparent that Michelangelo, for all of his monologues on the highest form of art, is ambiguous about his own place in this schema. Michelangelo rails repeatedly against the conflation of craftsmanship and art, both as it relates to himself and to others. In discussing oil painting with Fra Sebastiano, he rants:

When that barbarian Jan Van Eyck discovered
The use of oil in painting, he degraded
His art to a handicraft, and made it
Sign-painting, merely, for a country inn
Or a wayside wine shop. 'Tis an art for women,
Or for such leisurely and idle people
As you, Fra Sebastiano. Nature paints not
In oils, but frescos the great dome of heaven
With sunsets, and the lovely forms of clouds
And flying vapors.[140]

The seemingly slight distinction between the media of oil and fresco is one that implicates the larger distinctions between art and craft, masculine and feminine, natural and commercial. Oil painting is commercial and presumably closely representational, its slow drying properties ideally suited to depicting the detailed and relatively diminutive images of sign-painting. Women, and feminine men like Fra Sebastiano, appreciate these images for their evidence of "handicraft," or what Sebastiano calls "skill" in relation to his own portrait painting (executed, of course, in oil). Fresco painting, on the other hand, imitates not merely the forms of nature but its methods. As nature "frescos" the sky in large sweeping gestures, so too does the artist cover domes of chapel ceilings, as Michelangelo did earlier in the play when struggling to complete the Sistine Chapel paintings. The forms of nature and the artist have no purpose but beauty; "the lovely forms of clouds," unlike the work of sign painting, tell no narrative and elicits no commercial response.

Michelangelo's association of the highest art form with nature is at the root of the contradictions that emerge in his hierarchy of artistry. Michelangelo outlines this schema in lofty discussions about the various merits of the arts of painting, sculpture, and architecture with several other artists in the play including Fra Sebastiano, Titian, Giorgio Vasari, and Benvenuto Cellini. Originality is, within the space of the play, the characteristic that most defines artistry and that prompts Michelangelo's wordy justifications for his preference of architecture over the other visual media. Michelangelo synthesizes this hierarchy in a late conversation with Benvenuto:

> Truly, as you say,
> Sculpture is more than painting. It is greater
> To raise the dead to life than to create
> Phantoms that seem to live. The most majestic
> Of the three sister arts is that which builds;
> The eldest of them all, to whom the others
> Are but the hand-maids and the servitors,
> Being but imitation, not creation.
> Henceforth I dedicate myself to her.[141]

In this passage, painters and sculptors both imitate the appearance of nature, while architects imitate its spirit, creating forms that are wholly original. This formulation closely echoes the distinction between oil painting and fresco painting: in both, the higher form of art imitates nature's creative mode. This artistic hierarchy conforms to Longfellow's nationalist sense that American art should take its starting point in nature. But the problematic built into this understanding of creativity is that the highest forms of artistic originality are also the most craftsmanlike.

If Michelangelo had hoped to escape from "handicraft" such as Jan van Eyck's in his favoring of the more "creative" arts of sculpture and architecture, the drama is clear in showing this effort to be a failure. In working through his designs for St. Peters, for instance, Michelangelo continuously confronts his subservient position toward his patrons. At a meeting with Pope Julius III and a group of discontented cardinals, he defends his plans to the men, who, as he says, "censure what they do not comprehend."[142] When they insist on viewing the architectural designs as he creates them, Michelangelo bristles: "I am not used to have men speak to me / As if I were a mason, hired to build / A garden wall, and paid on Saturdays / So much an hour" (133). He resists viewing this commission, or any of his commissions, as efforts that at all take into consideration the desires of the patrons, saying that their part is merely "to provide the means" while "The designs / Must all be left to me." In spite of this insistence, the artist is clearly in a position of direct accountability to his commissioners.

Furthermore, while Michelangelo repeatedly stresses that what separates true "mastery" from craftsmanship lies in innate knowledge as opposed to learned skill, he himself slips in and out of this categorization. Good craftsmen can be taught—as Fra Sebastiano has gained his "skilful hand" by training—but true artists are chosen, not trained. As Michelangelo tells his color-grinder Urbino, "All men are not born artists, nor will labor / E'er make them artists, but in every block of marble / I see a statue."[143] But Michelangelo's own self-portrayal casts doubt on this category of the "born artist," as when he visits the Coliseum in the guise of "pupil," indicating that he is far from being above artistic influence. His artistic course has likewise been altered by his contemporaries, as he says of Raphael: "He perchance / Caught strength from me, and I some greater sweetness / And tenderness from his more gentle nature."[144] That Raphael is known as much for his oil painting as for his fresco pushes this influence into the border between "handicraft" and art. And Michelangelo's first influence is located even more firmly in the realm of craft. As he explains it to Urbino, his propensity toward sculpture is (at least in part) taught rather than inborn: "I must have learned it early from my nurse / At Setignano, the stone-mason's wife; For the first sounds I heard were of the chisel / Chipping away the stone."[145] This alternate narrative of artistic development calls into question Michelangelo's own monologues on the hierarchy of the arts and the sharp distinctions between "handicraft" and artistry.

Both Longfellow and Michelangelo, then, are "middle-class" and middlebrow because they are self-consciously bound between aesthetic and cultural extremes, between the apparently contradictory worlds of craftsmanship and fine art. Michelangelo's dialogues and monologues reflect on the contradictions of an era that brought the first clearly enunciated distinctions between the fine arts and crafts; Longfellow's great accomplishment in the play lies in reshaping this unlikely artist-figure to become an emblem for his own literary craft in a way that is neither obvious nor self-aggrandizing. While critics, since Longfellow's earliest reviewers, have read *Michael Angelo* biographically or anti-biographically, with a shifting sense of Longfellow's place on the spectrum of craft and fine art, acknowledging that Michelangelo's place on this spectrum is likewise fluid immediately complicates the biographical equation. Michelangelo, rather than residing firmly in the category of fine artist, in Longfellow's account tests the boundaries between craft and art, creating a biographical reference point that is neither simple nor stable.

COLLECTING LONGFELLOW

In collecting authors as in collecting artists, such complication is not always welcome. As we have seen, public collections of Michelangelo as text and image developed rapidly in both England and Italy during the nineteenth century. During the latter part of the century, Longfellow also gained status as a collectible commodity, and as with Michelangelo's work, narratives of meaning developed alongside of these collections. *The Longfellow Collectors' Hand-book: A Bibliography of First Editions* (1885), first published only two years after Longfellow's death, provides a detailed delineation of what is—and what is not—worth holding onto in Longfellow's canon. It was published by William Evarts Benjamin, a dedicated fine books dealer in New York. The preface to the edition notes what this bibliography leaves out: *Poems of Places*, the thirty-one-volume anthology that Longfellow spent much of his last decade editing; any collected editions of Longfellow's work that do not include new writing; illustrated editions that are not strictly first editions; and magazine and journal publications. In other words, any work that is not "original." While these omissions are understandable in light of the bookseller's interests, they also serve the purpose of superimposing degrees of value onto Longfellow's only recently completed canon, a creation of hierarchy that goes against Longfellow's own crow's eye aesthetic. In the case of *Michael Angelo*, for instance, the *Hand-book* makes note only of the illustrated Houghton Mifflin edition, omitting its first magazine-publication as well as its first complete publication (including appendix) in the Riverside edition, which arguably qualifies as "new work."

Longfellow's canon was shaped through works like this *Hand-Book* and the anthologies that followed his death. We have only recently found the means of reshaping it. The *Hand-book*, true to form, mentions only the physical layout of *Michael Angelo*, noting that "The woodcut illustrations are numerous and beautiful." The drama has been only sparsely anthologized since the 1885 Riverside edition. The work's collection in volume one of the 1993 Library of America *American Poetry*, as well as its online availability through Making of America hold the promise of doing to Longfellow's canon what Longfellow attempted to do to Michelangelo's life: to open it up in all its conflicting parts, to allow its contradictions to be visible rather than subsumed within a single narrative. If anyone reads it—which has always been the problem with *Michael Angelo*'s physically beautiful and seemingly shallow text—the drama can help to unhinge notions of Longfellow's one-sided approach to authorship. It shows him to be a writer who, like his drama's protagonist, confronted terms like "originality" and "mastery" without the ultimate goal of overcoming them.

CODA

Ekphrastic Citizenship

Claudia Rankine's American Lyrics

There is perhaps no clearer heir to the nineteenth-century tradition of writing nation through image than Claudia Rankine, who through works like *Citizen* (2014) and *Don't Let Me Be Lonely* (2004)—both subtitled *An American Lyric*—intermeshes text and image in a commentary on the national spectator and subject. These image-texts instruct us retroactively on what ekphrasis has had to contribute to the national and nationalist conversation, and what feminized writers in particular might find in this intermediality.

Rankine's best-known and bestselling *Citizen* (2014) explores national belonging through an often oblique relation between text and image. The text is centered in bodily experience, the performance of African American national belonging staged as a constant corporeal pushing through. A key passage in the text defines citizenship as a continuous action: "Yes, and this is how you are a citizen: Come on. Let it go. Move on."[1] The idea of letting something go, or of moving on, is not a symbolic but a physical act in a text where personal microaggressions as well as the news and histories of physical assaults accumulate on the body in a concretizing residue.

Visuality is fundamental to this problematic. The double-bind of the Black American body as Rankine presents it is that it is both generically hyper-visible, standing out as a generalized threat to suburban front yards, tennis arenas, and college admissions boards, at the same time as it remains stubbornly invisible in the particularities of its humanity, walked past in drug store lines and insistently confused with the other Black employee. *Citizen* records the experience of this visibility and invisibility as it is registered in the body. In one scene in the middle of the book, the text's second-person subject, addressed directly in a way that conflates speaker and reader, comes home after a long day:

> Leaving the day to itself, you close the door behind you and pour a bowl of cereal, then another, and would a third if you didn't interrupt yourself with the statement—you aren't hungry.
>
> Appetite won't attach you to anything no matter how depleted you feel.
>
> It's true.
>
> You lean against the sink, a glass of red wine in your hand and then another, thinking in the morning you will go to the gym having slept and slept beyond the residuals of all yesterdays.
>
> Yes, and you do go to the gym and run in place, an entire hour of running, just you and
>
> your body running off each undesired encounter.[2]

Racialized encounters of visuality—both having one's body called to the fore, and not being seen at all—lodge themselves in this same body as a residue that must be pushed away, covered over, or deadened to get through the daily work of living. This tension of being seen as both too much and too little produces an acute bodily alienation from real, felt appetites that in this scene demands the dual poles of bodily deadening (inebriation) and bodily enlivening (running) to push through.

Haunting the edges of these microaggressions and symbolic bodily assaults is the specter of real violence on a national scale. Assault, the text reiterates, does not have to be directly experienced to be physically felt. Much as Rankine's second-person subject is caught in a crisis of visibility that enacts a concrete physical effect, they experience the pain inflicted on Black American bodies in the national sphere through an assault of images. These images seep into daily life through catalogues of police violence, historical photos of lynching crowds, and even a detail from William Turner's 1840 painting *The Slave Ship*. The question of how to avoid taking in the things that you see is a constant backdrop to *Citizen*, where the body figures as a painfully full receptacle for both personal and national trauma. As such, the book is visually restrained; while the text describes the bodily effect of filtering violence, it reproduces little. In a lynching photograph in the middle of the text, Rankine crops out the body of the victim, focusing the reader's attention instead on the white crowd gathered below the tree, pointing, laughing, and looking in all ways like ordinary citizens.

If citizenship is, as Rankine writes, the ability to move on, to let go of this pain, again and again, what happens when you become lodged in it? The text's implicit answer lies in citizenship's flipside, statelessness. This statelessness is seen in variously charged images of unbelonging: Serena William's anger "against the sharp white background" of the 2009 US Open, the small disappearing leg of a slave into the large ocean of the Turner painting, a list of Black Americans killed by police.[3] But in the light of this default statelessness, the cost of actively choosing belonging and citizenship is high. This choice asks of Black Americans to deny daily feeling ("Let it go. Move on."), in effect to relinquish ownership of and connection to their bodies.

This model of citizenship stands neatly opposed to the eighteenth- and nineteenth-century ideal of liberal selfhood. Rather than extending from an assumption of individuation, agency, and autonomy, the image of Black American citizenship that Rankine paints is one in which a highly permeable self is pummeled by painful outside stimuli and must disconnect from this body in order to exist in the nation. This version of the citizen contrasts in all key points to the classic liberalism that still dominates US government: it is not self-contained but permeable, not individual but generic, and not autonomous but ruled by outside demand. Rankine's citizen, then, is an anti-citizen from the reigning perspective, surrendered to the exigencies of its environment and abandoning any individualized form. The divide between this form of citizenship and statelessness, servitude, or slavery becomes more unclear the closer you look at it. If women writers and writers of color in the long nineteenth century, as Elissa Zellinger argues, used lyric poetry to imagine a selfhood that they could not embody outside of writing, Rankine's text serves to showcase the ways that full citizenship is still an imagination.[4]

In further contrast to the liberal citizen, who is centered in an internalized experience of self, Rankine's racialized citizen is centered on appearances and visuality: on being seen too much, and not seen at all, but also on seeing too much and not having a filter for that sight. In a scene that is central to the text, Rankine chronicles tennis star Serena Williams's bouts of mid-match anger, recalling for each the history of bad umpire calls suffered in silence, and the physical accumulation of historical injustice. As she writes, "Yes, and the body has memory. The physical carriage hauls more than its weight." Williams is for Rankine such a powerful example in large part because of the significance of visuality to her American narrative; not just that she is a highly visible African American in a predominantly white space, but that her being seen, or not seen, is central to her success or failure in this sphere. As Rankine writes, "Every look, every comment every bad call blossoms out of history, through her, onto you. To understand is to see Serena as hemmed in as any other black body thrown against our American background. 'Aren't you the one that screwed me over last time here?' she asks the umpire Asderaki [in the context of a bad call]. 'Yeah, you are. Don't look at me. Really don't even look at me. Don't look my way. Don't look my way,' she repeats, because it is that simple." This quote is cutting because it's of course not that simple: Williams performs under a racialized history of hypervisibility that makes her (apparent) mistakes more pronounced, but also within a profession that depends centrally on spectatorship and image, and that demands that she be seen.[5]

Rankine's version of citizenship—ironic, or at least wry and distorted—is also ekphrastic in the sense that it conforms to ways that she uses imagery. The images that appear in her texts are much less and much more than visual illustrations. The first photograph in *Citizen*, for instance, is a suburban street sign in front of two nearly identical white houses that reads "Jim Crow." The speaker never references the image, but it resonates with exactly the kind of middle- and upper-middle-class microaggressions that dominate the first section of the text: the friend who, early in the friendship calls the text's speaker by the name of her Black maid; the lunchtime acquaintance who considers affirmative action responsible for keeping her son from his college of choice; the neighbor who calls the police on the Black man who is watching the speaker's child. This is a segregation of the suburbs, one that exists even as people work and live alongside one another, because it is a segregation of experience, of perspective, of sight, that feels unbridgeable.

In this approach to visuality, the images that don't appear are as important as those that do. Serena Williams's tennis images—including those of her crashing a racket onto the court—are so ubiquitous in media that it is easy to mentally impose her figure onto Rankine's long description of her on-court anger. But in fact, no photograph of Williams appears in the text. Instead, Rankine reproduces an image of Caroline Wozniacki in which she poses with towels in her bra and shorts, in a controversial exhibition match imitation of Williams. The image, which many derided as racist caricature, stands in stead of Williams's own body, seeming to answer her cry to the umpire: "Don't look at me. Really don't even look at me." Wozniacki's hypersexualized parody forefronts the Black body, and particularly the female Black body, as a site of spectacle, but in refusing to reproduce Williams' actual image, Rankine offers a small gesture of protection that underlines the real power of ekphrasis: to choose the images, from a sea of possibilities, that we turn our attention to.

In *Don't Let Me Be Lonely*, Rankine's earlier collection from 2004, ekphrasis is an even more central aspect of the text's presentation of nation. This book, like *Citizen*, is subtitled *An American Lyric*, and its larger title, like *Citizen*, suggests a longing towards an idea of the collective, national and otherwise. That membership in this collective is one that requires a resignation of the self is an idea that echoes through both texts. Centered more centrally on mass media images, *Don't Let Me Be Lonely* opens with a quotation from Aimé Césaire that prepares readers to take an active stance toward the reproductions that populate the text: "And most of all beware, even in thought, of assuming the sterile attitude of the spectator, for life is not a spectacle."

The book's first image, a television with a staticky screen suggesting the transmission failures of mass media, appears repeatedly, both on the cover, and then in the course of text as a marker of section breaks. Sometimes this television set appears with text or image on its screen, as part of the body of Rankine's narrative. The loneliness of the collection's title has its initial anchor in the feeling of being left behind by death, as the speaker recounts seeing her father after the death of his mother—"he looked to me like someone understanding his aloneness. Loneliness"—or the dialogue the speaker writes in the margin of her notebook: "You'd let me be lonely? I thought I was dead."[6] But this personal loneliness, the ache of a friend dying of cancer, another dying of Alzheimer's, is compounded by the more impersonal and mediated deaths on national or global scale: the lynching of James Byrd Jr. by three white men in Texas, the execution of Oklahoma City bomber Timothy McVeigh, and the deaths of 9/11 in whose wake the book is written.

If *Citizen* attempts to document, on a bodily register, the demands and double-consciousness of being both Black and American, *Don't Let Me Be Lonely* takes on the national experience of living in the world, and in the visual and media culture, of post-9/11 America. The television set is the text's main vehicle for collectivity, a way out of loneliness: a centering object for two friends, a means to sleep for an insomniac speaker, the white background noise of other people and places. But at the same time that television suggests a collective, it also transmits death on a broader societal scale, and consistently disseminates the coercive post-9/11 mantra—"you are either with us or you are against us"—that establishes this kind of collective as dangerous, more centered on exclusions that alliances.[7] *Don't Let Me Be Lonely* is a text that earnestly aspires to human connection as much as it critiques the nationalist narratives that demand strict compliance as its price.

Images and the act of looking play a central role in both real and coerced connections. Television holds the space between friends as much as it functions as a vehicle for policing nationalist boundaries, but media images in the text are isolated and framed in a way that demands that the reader develop a critical stance to the apparent transparency of the medium. As Emma Kimberly writes, Rankine "uses her ekphrastic poems to expose how representations are made, and to reveal gaps and flaws in the representational process by re-creating it. . . . [T]he responsibility of the poem, then, is towards both disconnection and connection, encouraging us to unpick the links of the media narrative and retell it in our own ways as well as to assert our own sense of connection with our fellow human beings in the present."[8]

In spite of the text's sharp critique of nationalism, nation has a place in Rankine's schema of connection, and the subtitle "An American Lyric" is aspirational as much as it is also wry and ironically distanced. At a lunch with her editor, the speaker notes that she is "writing a book about hepatotixity, also known as liver failure," and later, when a cab driver asks her what she does for a living, she answers "I write about the liver." *Don't Let Me Be Lonely* initially introduces the liver as the organ that breaks down drugs and toxins, in relation to the bottle of aspirin that the speaker takes, inducing a coma but ultimately not liver failure, as well as the antidepressants that she and others in the text take. Symbolically, the liver represents an attempt at intellectual and emotional processing, as the speaker considers citing to her editor in the context of their liver conversation, "*man is left, at times thinking, as if trying to weep*," and human resilience, as she reads aloud from a newspaper article, "*it is surprising, given the noxious chemicals that the liver is exposed to, that more drugs do not damage it*."[9]

An illustration of the liver is visually reproduced twice in the text in slightly different sizes, first in the passage where the speaker explains her interest in the liver to her editor, and next, in slightly larger form, after her conversation with the taxi driver. One of only two drawn images in an image-text primarily of photographs, the medical-style image shows an outlined face and torso, with esophagus, liver and stomach filled in in dark ink. The liver is clearly labeled, and in the place where the small and large intestine would be is a map of the United States. In the sense that the liver represents a fine-tuned processing, the intellectual and emotional work of the book, the small and large intestines in this image stand in for a coarser process. Tasked with separating water and nutrients from bodily waste, they align neatly with the book's representation of the American public sphere post-9/11, a place in which the notions of insiders and outsiders dominate as well and the binary sorting logic of "with us or against us."

In this rough schema, it is fitting that the speaker's focus in the text is on the liver, and that she does not mention the intestines, or the striking image of America-as-intestine that the drawings reproduce. This image, like the photograph of the Jim Crow suburbs in *Citizen*, is not the material of the text, but the atmosphere for it, and exists as an undercurrent throughout the discussion of media polarization and American public life. The aspirational work of the text lies in the liver, the finer-tuned filter that allows for a critical working-through of public life, or as Kimberly writes, the goal to "unpick the links of the media narrative and retell it in our own ways as well as to assert our own sense of connection with our fellow human beings in the present."[10]

In this sense, the text's critique of media culture ultimately aspires to a more precise and unmediated connection to the world, even as it repeatedly documents the difficulty of achieving such a connection. In spending time with her sister after the unfathomable tragedy of this sibling's loss of her husband and two children, the speaker struggles to connect with her pain in a way that is specific, felt, and not mediated by outside reports or knowledges. Listening to her sister's experience of having "been asked to assess the value of her dead children's lives" by an insurance adjuster, the speaker reflects, "More than anything I want to tell my sister about [an article that she had read about insurance adjusters], but I don't want to risk generalizing her experience. What I know, I know because of Davidson [the author of the article]; what she knows, she knows because she is being made to perform a life I don't want to live. I ask questions, all the ones Davidson has already answered." In this scenario, lived experience and secondary knowledge results in the same "answers"—but they are clearly answers with a different bodily resonance. The speaker's inability to bridge the gap between knowledge and experience resonates with the text's earlier definition of loneliness as "what we can't do for one another."[11]

Bridging this divide depends at least in part on visual contact, not that of media spectatorship but of individual connection. Eye contact in the text stands in for this connection, as the speaker reflects on her shame at reverting her eyes on the street, a shame that also comes from avoiding other forms of contact and mutual witnessing: "I feel as if I have created a reason to apologize, I feel the guilt of having ignored that thing—the encounter. I could have nodded, I could have smiled without showing my teeth. In some small way I could have wordlessly said, I see you seeing me and I apologize for not knowing why I am alive."[12] Through eye contact and visual acknowledgement, passersby in the text can choose to exist in a space both collective and individually delineated, a space akin to the definition of ekphrasis with which I began this book, the "third thing that is owned by no one, whose meaning is owned by no one, but which subsists between them."[13] I have been arguing throughout this book that the function of ekphrasis is precisely this: to build a form of community that is both sovereign and collective, both individualized and connected. It is the shared glance at something else, and through that process, at each other. It is a form of community, unlike nationalism in its dominant forms, that is not also defined by its exclusions.

Nineteenth-century ekphrastic works also served at least the partial purpose of guiding readers, in an era of rapidly increasing image reproduction, toward a greater visual literary. Such literacy, or "picturacy" as James Heffernan terms it, is also a focus of Rankine's image-texts, though she gravitates toward the cultural image saturation in the twenty-four-hour news cycle and other popular media.[14] In her texts, learning how to see has never been more urgent: what is at stake is nothing less than how we can be together, as a nation and as a world. Such literacy, as I have argued, was equally at stake in the ekphrasis of the nineteenth century, where descriptions of imagery functioned not primarily to stand in for images, but to guide their legibility. As Rankine's nation is formed through the images of mass media, the aspirational nation in the nineteenth century comes together at least in part through a common canon of images, American or otherwise. Ganymede's Eagle, or Michelangelo's sculptures, or Scipio Moorhead's portraiture were reference points for writers on the role that art could perform in a shared national space, and on the ways that readers and writers could come together through an imagined image, to see both alone and together.

Notes

INTRODUCTION

1 Mark Twain, *Life on the Mississippi* (New York and London: Harper and Brothers, 1901), 314.

2 Sophia Hawthorne, *Notes in England and Italy* (New York: G. P. Putnam, 1869), 212. For textual representations, see for instance Percy Bysshe Shelley, *The Cenci: A Tragedy in Five Acts: An Authoritative Text Based on the 1819 Edition*, ed. Cajsa C. Baldini (Kansas City: Valancourt, 2008); Nathaniel Hawthorne, *The Marble Faun*, ed. Susan Manning (Oxford: Oxford University Press, 2009); and Herman Melville, *Pierre: Or, the Ambiguities*, ed. Robert Levine and Cindy Weinstein (New York: Norton, 2017). The portrait was also a popular subject for poetic ekphrases, such as for example Sarah Piatt, "Beatrice Cenci," *Overland Monthly* 7, no. 1 (July 1871): 68.

3 Henry James, *William Wetmore Story and His Friends* (Boston: Houghton Mifflin, 1901), 2, 76.

4 In this case, the instability of the image was compounded by popular misattribution: as Corrado Ricci, Mary E. Finn, and other scholars note, the attribution of the subject as Beatrice Cenci and the painter as Guido Reni began in the eighteenth century and was generally disavowed by the 1920s. Ricci, *Beatrice Cenci*, trans. Morris Bishop and Henry Longan, 2 vols. (New York: Boni and Liveright, 1925); Finn, "The Ethics and Aesthetics of Shelley's *The Cenci*," *Studies in Romanticism* 35, no. 2 (Summer 1996): 177–97.

5 Leo Spitzer, *Essays on English and American Literature* (Princeton, NJ: Princeton University Press, 1962), 72. In critical work on twentieth-century ekphrasis, by contrast, the museum has been the main site of focus; see for example Barbara Fischer, *Museum Meditations: Reframing Ekphrasis in Contemporary American Poetry* (New York: Routledge, 2006); Elizabeth Loizeaux, *Twentieth-Century Poetry and the Visual Arts* (Cambridge: Cambridge University Press, 2008); and Willard Spiegelman, *How Poets See the World: The Art of Description in Contemporary Poetry* (Oxford: Oxford University Press, 2005).

6 The practice of basing ekphrastic works on other ekphrastic works was not unique to the nineteenth century—for instance, John Hollander notes the relative frequency of such responses during the early modern period—but was encouraged by increasing access during this era to textual descriptions of artworks. *The Gazer's Spirit: Poems Speaking to Silent Works of Art* (Chicago and London: University of Chicago Press, 1995), 5.

7 The question of whether images "matter" is an open one in ekphrastic criticism more generally. John Hollander makes the distinction in *The Gazer's Spirit* between ekphrasis between literary works based on known and extant works of art (actual ekphrasis) and writing about fictional works of art (notional ekphrasis) (4). Most other critics do not. As Jean Hagstrum writes, ekphrasis "is a way of seeing and a way of speaking that, in its long history, has created conventions and habits of its own that are sometimes quite unrelated to particular works of art." *The Sister Arts: The Tradition of Literary Pictorialism and English Poetry from Dryden to* Grey (Chicago: University of Chicago Press, 1958), xvi. Or, W. J. T. Mitchell: "Even those forms of ekphrasis that occur in the presence of the described image disclose a tendency to alienate or displace the object, to make it disappear in favor of the textual image being produced by the ekphrasis" *Picture Theory: Essays on Verbal and Visual Representation* (Chicago: University of Chicago Press, 1994), 157, n19. My own failure to make a strong distinction between the "notional" and the "actual" is much more pragmatic: the ekphrasis of the long nineteenth century, which abounds in responses to unnamed, unclear, or inaccurately described works entirely defies such categorizations.

8 Claudia Stokes, *Old Style: Unoriginality and Its Uses in Nineteenth-Century U.S. Literature*, (Philadelphia: University of Pennsylvania Press, 2021), 19.

9 Mitchell, *Picture Theory*, 152.

10 The basic division made famous by Lessing in *Laocoon* (1766) represents the visual arts as spatial and the literary arts as temporal. Each medium also possesses a constellation of associated characteristics, not all of which neatly align. See for instance Gotthold Ephraim Lessing, *An Essay Upon the Limits of Painting and Poetry with Remarks Illustrative of Various Points in the History of Ancient Art*, trans. Ellen Frothingham (Boston: Roberts Brothers, 1887); and Stephen Cheeke, *Writing for Art: The Aesthetics of Ekphrasis* (Manchester: Manchester University Press, 2008). Mitchell, following this tradition, frames the literary mode as a confrontation with "otherness"—particularly sexual and racial difference—and centers his argument in a canon of Romantic and modernist poets including Keats, Shelley, and William Carlos Williams. James Heffernan similarly makes the idea of a "gendered antagonism" central to his study, and mentions a female poet only once in a book that spans from antiquity to the twentieth century. Grant Scott, in his book on Keats, notes that "For Keats, more than for the other Romantic poets, the competitive elements in ekphrasis emerge in terms of the battle of the sexes rather than as any conventional aesthetic battle," a framework indebted in part to this poet's "wariness about contemporary female writers." Murray Krieger, whose 1967 essay on ekphrasis and later book-length study were particularly influential to Mitchell's work, takes on the dynamics of the gendered encounter in his writing, which he calls "an ekphrasis of ekphrasis" and in which he (in a clearly gendered mode) describes encountering ekphrasis as "a maddeningly elusive and endlessly tempting subject." Heffernan, *Museum of Words*, 7; Scott, *The Sculpted Word: Keats, Ekphrasis, and the Visual Arts* (Hanover: University Press of New England, 1994), xiii–xiv; and Krieger, *Ekphrasis: The Illusion of the Natural Sign* (Baltimore: Johns Hopkins University Press, 1992), xiv, 1.

NOTES TO PAGES 5–8 *187*

11 James Edward Ford III, "Notes on Black Ekphrasis," *Early American Literature* 58, no. 3 (2023): 593, qtd. in 594.

12 Mitchell, *Picture Theory*, 181.

13 Louizeaux, *Twentieth-Century Poetry and the Visual Arts*, 173; Plasa, "Ekphrastic Poetry and the Middle Passage: Recent Encounters in the Black Atlantic," *Connotations* 24 no. 2 (2014/2015): 291, 315, 291. For responses to Plasa's article and other treatments of Black Ekphrasis, see for instance Jane Hedley, "Black Ekphrasis?: A Response to Carl Plasa," *Connotations* 26 (2016/2017): 39–46; Vievee Francis, "Beyond Description: Ekphrasis and the Expanding Lens," *Callaloo* 34, no. 3 (Summer 2011): 708–10; and Maria Cristina Fumagalli, *Derek Walcott's Painters: A Life with Pictures* (Edinburgh: Edinburgh University Press, 2023).

14 Loizeaux, *Twentieth Century Poetry*, 9.

15 Jane Hedley, *In the Frame: Women's Ekphrasis from Marianne Moore to Susan Wheeler* (Newark: University of Delaware Press, 2009), 35; Susan Williams *Confounding Images: Photography and Portraiture in Antebellum American Fiction* (Philadelphia: University of Pennsylvania Press, 1997), 33.

16 Lisa Rhody, "Beyond Darwinian Distance: Situating Distant Reading with a Feminist Ut Pictura Poesis Tradition," *PMLA* 132, no. 3 (May 2017): 659–67.

17 Louis Godey of *Godey's Lady's Book* was among the most outspoken, claiming for instance that he "lays every good artist he can catch under contribution" and the magazine's engravings are "superior in effect to any thing ever given in this country or in Europe." See "Visits to the Painters," *Godey's Lady's Book* 20 (December 1844), 277. See also Isabelle Lehuu, *Carnival on the Page: Popular Print Media in Antebellum America* (Chapel Hill: University of North Carolina Press, 2000), 109 for the connection between images and profitability at Godey's.

18 Frederick Hudson, *Journalism in the United States from 1690 to 1872* (New York: Harper & Brothers, 1873), 705.

19 Qtd. in Cynthia Lee Patterson, *Art for the Middle Classes: America's Illustrated Magazines of the 1840s* (Jackson: University Press of Mississippi, 2010), 93. See also Meredith McGill, *American Literature and the Culture of Reprinting, 1834–1853,* (Philadelphia: University of Pennsylvania Press, 2003), 30.

20 Patterson, *Art for the Middle Classes*, 93.

21 See *American Literature* 70, no. 3 (1998), especially Cathy Davidson's preface, "No More Separate Spheres!", 443–63, and the later anthology *No More Separate Spheres: A Next Wave American Studies Reader*, ed. Cathy Davidson and Jessamyn Hatcher (Durham, NC: Duke University Press, 2002).

22 See for instance Jack Halberstam, *Female Masculinity*, (Durham, NC: Duke University Press, 1998), Hannah McCann, *Queering Femininity: Sexuality, Feminism, and the Politics of Presentation*, (New York: Routledge, 2018), and Margaret Fuller, *Woman in the Nineteenth Century* (New York: Greeley & McElrath, 1845).

23 Travis Foster, "Nineteenth-Century Queer Literature," *The Cambridge Companion to American Gay and Lesbian Literature*, ed. Scott Herring, (Cambridge: University of Cambridge Press, 2015), 89.

24 Leo Bersani, *The Culture of Redemption* (Cambridge, MA: Harvard University Press, 1990), 145.

188 NOTES TO PAGES 8–9

25 This focus is indebted to Eliza Richards's groundbreaking study, *Gender and the Poetics of Reception*, which takes on the project of "elucidating the complex gendering of American romantic lyricism in the nineteenth century" through an examination of Poe and several poetesses in his literary circle, arguing that all rely on methods of close allusion and derivation, and "decline to enforce or accept a clear division between original and copy, genius and mimicry, poet and poetess." *Gender and the Poetics of Reception in Poe's Circle*, (Cambridge: Cambridge University Press, 2004), 4, 20.

26 Halberstam, *Female Masculinity*, 1.

27 See, for instance, *Trans Historical: Gender Plurality before the Modern*, ed. Greta Lafleur, Masha Raskolnikov, and Anna Klosowska (Ithaca: Cornell University Press, 2021) for a historically and geographically broad survey of premodern transgender experience and artifacts; Rachel Mesch; Barry Reay, *Trans America: A Counter-History* (Cambridge: Polity, 2020) for a survey from the nineteenth to twenty-first centuries; Jen Manion, *Female Husbands: A Trans History* (Cambridge: Cambridge University Press, 2020) for a US and UK perspective; Jules Gill-Peterson, *Histories of the Transgender Child* (Minneapolis, University of Minnesota Press, 2018) for a twentieth-century US perspective. In the US nineteenth-century literary context specifically, see work such as Eagan Dean, "Androgyny and Desire: Margaret Fuller, Julia Ward Howe, and Fractured Trans Archives," *Legacy: A Journal of American Women Writers* 40, no. 1, (2023): 59–84; the publication of Julia Ward Howe's unfinished manuscript as *The Hermaphrodite*, ed. Gary Williams (Lincoln: University of Nebraska Press, 2009): and the collection *"The Man Who Thought Himself a Woman" and Other Queer Nineteenth-Century Short Stories*, ed. Christopher Looby (Philadelphia: University of Pennsylvania Press, 2017).

28 Glavey, *Wallfower Avant-Garde*, 8, 8–9.

29 Glavey, *Wallfower Avant-Garde*, 5.

30 Margaret Fuller, "American Literature: Its Position in the Present Time, and Prospects for the Future," *Papers on Literature and Art*, (New York: Wiley and Putnam, 1846), 101; Qtd. in Horace Traubel, *With Walt Whitman in Camden, Vol 3*. (New York: Rowman and Littlefield, 1961), 549.

31 Stokes, *Old Style*, 19.

32 From her first volume of poetry in 1815 to her last in 1862, Sigourney wrote at least thirteen poems easily identifiable as ekphrastic, not including the several more that focus on directions to an artist in the composition of an artwork (what John Hollander calls "imperative" ekphrasis), the verse meditations on art-objects interspersed in the travelogue *Pleasant Memories from Pleasant Lands* (1842), or the poems to American monuments. These include: "Pompey's Statue, at whose pedestal Julius Caesar fell, is still preserved in the Palazzo Spadae, in Rome" (1827), "On a Picture of Penitence" (1834), "The Last Supper. A picture by Leonardo da Vinci" (1834), "The Schoolmistress. Adapted to a Picture" (1834), The Consumptive Girl. From a picture" (1834), "Picture of a Sleeping Infant, Watched by a Dog" (1834), "Lady Jane Grey. On seeing a picture representing her engaged in the study of Plato" (1837), "Sabbath Evening in the Country. Suggested by a picture" (1837), "Child Left in a Storm. Adapted to a painting by Sully" (1837), "Statue

of the Spinning Girl, at Chatsworth, the Seat of the Duke of Devonshire" (1841), "The Landing of the Pilgrims. A picture by G. Flagg" (1848), "Powers's Statue of the Greek Slave" (1854), To a Portrait" (1860).

33 Lydia Sigourney, Letter to George Griffin, Box 1, Folder 2, January 12, 1842, Griffin Family and Lydia Sigourney Papers, William Clements Library, University of Michigan.

34 Letter to George Griffin, Box 1, Folder 1, December 16, 1833, Griffin Family and Lydia Sigourney Papers, William Clements Library, University of Michigan.

35 For a more detailed analysis of Sigourney's ekphrastics, see Christa Holm Vogelius, "'To Bind in Admiration All Who Gaze': Lydia Sigourney's Sentimental Ekphrasis" *Amerikastudien/American Studies* 59, no. 3 (2014): 321–33.

36 W. J. T. Mitchell, "Ekphrasis and the Other" in *Picture Theory: Essays on Verbal and Visual Reproduction* (Chicago and London: University of Chicago Press, 1999), 164.

37 John Hollander, *The Gazer's Spirit: Poems Speaking to Silent Works of Art* (Chicago and London: University of Chicago Press, 1990), 4.

38 Wilson, *Specters of Democracy: Blackness and the Aesthetics of Politics in the Antebellum U.S.* (Oxford: Oxford University Press, 2011).

39 Wilson, *Specters of Democracy*, 6.

40 Wilson, *Specters of Democracy*, 7, 8.

41 Seitler, *Reading Sideways: The Queer Politics of Art in Modern American Fiction* (New York: Fordham University Press, 2019), 14.

42 Maggie Nelson, *The Art of Cruelty: A Reckoning* (New York and London: W. W. Norton, 2011), 130.

43 Nelson, *The Art of Cruelty*, 46.

44 Jacques Rancière, *The Emancipated Spectator*, trans. Gregory Elliot (New York and London: Verso, 2011), 15.

45 Mitchell, *Picture Theory*, 164.

46 Benedict Anderson, *Imagined Communities: Reflections on the Origin and Spread of Nationalism*, rev. ed. (London: Verso, 1991), 6–7.

47 In many ways, Perry Miller's 1956 *The Raven and the Whale* still offers the most detailed biographical studies of these literary movements, though critical works have updated understandings of nationalism in the past few decades. For an overview of antebellum nationalism, see Perry Miller, *The Raven and the Whale: The War of Words and Wits in the Era of Poe and Melville* (New York: Harcourt Brace, 1956); and Robert Levine, *Dislocating Race and Nation: Episodes in Nineteenth-Century American Literary Nationalism* (Chapel Hill: University of North Carolina Press, 2008).

48 F. O. Matthiessen, *American Renaissance: Art and Expression in the Age of Emerson and Whitman* (Oxford: Oxford University Press, 1941), vii, ix, vii, ix.

49 Matthiessen, *American Renaissance*, xi. See also Meredith McGill, *American Literature and the Culture of Reprinting, 1834–1853* (Philadelphia: University of Pennsylvania Press, 2003); Van Wyck Brooks, *The Flowering of New England, 1815–1865* (New York, E. P. Dutton, 1836); Richard Poirier, *A World Elsewhere: The Place of Style in American Literature* (Oxford: Oxford University Press, 1966).

50 Levine, *Dislocating Race and Nation*, 10.

51 Levine, *Dislocating*, 1, 7; J. Gerald Kennedy, *Strange Nation: Literary Nationalism and Cultural Conflict in the Age of Poe* (Oxford: Oxford University Press, 2016), 33. See also David Reynolds, *Beneath the American Renaissance: The Subversive Imagination in the Age of Emerson and Melville* (Cambridge, MA: Harvard University Press, 1988).

52 Etienne Balibar and Immanuel Wallerstein, *Race, Nation, Class: Ambiguous Identities* (London: Verso, 1990), 133.

53 Paul Giles, "The Deterritorialization of American Literature," in *Shades of the Planet: American Literature as World Literature*, ed. Wai Chi Dimock and Lawrence Buell (Princeton, NJ: Princeton University Press, 2007), 42.

54 Giles, "Deterritorialization," 41.

55 Leslie, "Regional Nationalism and the Ends of the Literary World," *J19: The Journal of Nineteenth-Century Americanists* 7, no. 2 (Fall 2019): 249.

56 Leslie, "Regional Nationalism," 255.

57 Leslie, "Regional Nationalism," 256.

58 Richards, *Gender and the Poetics of Reception*, 1.

59 See for instance Naomi Sofer, *Making the "America of Art": Cultural Nationalism and 19th-Century Women Writers* (Columbus: University of Ohio Press, 2021), 11–12.

60 Edgar Allan Poe, "The Literati of New York City (Part II)," *The Works of Edgar Allan Poe—Vol. VIII: Literary Criticism III*, ed. E. C. Stedman and G. E. Woodberry (Chicago: Stone & Kimball, 1895), 3.

61 Miller, *The Raven and the Whale*, 155–57.

62 See fx. Joseph Csicsila, *Canons by Consensus: Critical Trends and American Literature Anthologies*, (Tuscaloosa: University of Alabama Press, 2004), xix; John Guillory, "Canon," in *Critical Terms for Literary Study*, ed. Frank Lentricchia and Thomas McLaughlin (Chicago: University of Chicago Press, 1990), 240.

63 Socarides, *In Plain Sight: Nineteenth-Century American Women's Poetry and the Problem of Literary History* (Oxford: Oxford University Press, 2020), 35–70.

64 Evert A. Duyckinck and George L. Duyckinck, eds, *Cyclopedia of American Literature, Vol. 1 and 2* (New York: Charles Scribner, 1855); Rufus Griswold's Americanist anthologies include *The Poets and Poetry of America* (1842), *Gems from American Female Poets* (1942), *Readings in American Poetry for the Use of Schools* (1843), *Prose Writers of America* (1847), *Female Poets of America* (1848), and *Gift Leaves of American Poetry* (1849).

65 Rufus Griswold, *The Cyclopedia of American Literature by Evart [sic] A. Duyckinck and George L. Duyckinck: A Review. From the New York Herald, of Feb. 13, 1856.* (New York: Baker & Godwin, 1856).

66 Qtd. in Miller, *Raven and the Whale*, 330.

67 Duyckinck, *Cyclopedia*, v.

68 Leslie, "Regional Nationalism," 271.

69 Leslie, "Regional Nationalism," 271.

70 Caroline May, ed., *The American Female Poets* (Philadelphia: Lindsay & Blakiston, 1848), v.

71 May, *The American Female Poets*, v–vi.

72 Miller, *Raven and the Whale*, 169.

73 Rufus Griswold, ed., *Female Poets of America* (Philadelphia, Carey and Hart, 1849), 8, 9; Thomas Buchanon Read, *The Female Poets of America* (Philadelphia: E. H. Butler., 1849).

74 Miller, *Raven and the Whale*, 195.

75 Miller, *Raven and the Whale*, 195.

76 Griswold, *Female Poets of America*, 7.

77 Griswold, *Female Poets of America*, 7.

78 Griswold, *Female Poets of America*, 7.

79 Griswold, *The Female Poets of America*, 8.

80 Lara Langer Cohen, *The Fabrication of American Literature: Fraudulence and Antebellum Print Culture* (Philadelphia: University of Pennsylvania Press, 2011), 1, 16.

81 Richards, *Gender and the Poetics of Reception*, 20, 25.

82 William Huntting Howell, *Against Self-Reliance: The Arts of Dependence in the Early United States* (Philadelphia: University of Pennsylvania Press, 2015); Ezra Tawil, *Literature, American Style: The Originality of Imitation in the Early Republic* (Philadelphia: University of Pennsylvania Press, 2018); Stokes, *Old Style: Unoriginality and Its Uses in Nineteenth-Century U.S. Literature* (Philadelphia: University of Pennsylvania Press, 2021).

83 Stokes, *Old Style*, 7.

84 Jessica Forbes Roberts, "A Poetic E Pluribus Unum: Conventions, Imperatives, and the Poetic Call-to-Arms in Frank Moore's Rebellion Record," *ESQ: A Journal of the American Renaissance*, 54, no. 1–4 (2008): 171.

85 See for instance Jessica Forbes Roberts, "'Hear the Bird': Sarah Piatt and the Dramatic Monologue," in *A History of Nineteenth-Century American Women's Poetry*, ed. Jennifer Putzi and Alexandra Socarides, (Cambridge: Cambridge University Press, 2017): 345–58; Alexandra Socarides, *In Plain Sight: Nineteenth-Century American Women's Poetry and the Problem of Literary History* (Oxford: Oxford University Press, 2020); Dorri Beam, *Style, Gender, and Fantasy in Nineteenth-Century American Women's Writing*, (Cambridge: Cambridge University Press, 2010); Jennifer Putzi, *Fair Copy: Relational Poetics and Antebellum American Women's Poetry* (Philadelphia: University of Pennsylvania Press, 2021).

86 Elissa Zellinger, *Lyrical Strains: Liberalism and Women's Poetry in Nineteenth-Century America* (Chapel Hill: University of North Carolina Press, 2020).

87 Stokes, *Old Style*, 15.

88 Theo Davis, *Formalism, Experience, and the Making of American Literature in the Nineteenth Century* (Cambridge: Cambridge University Press, 2007), 40.

89 Davis, *Formalism*, 47.

90 *Imagining Equality in Nineteenth-Century American Literature* (Cambridge: Cambridge University Press, 2008), 77.

91 Davis, *Formalism*, 31; Larson, *Imagining Equality*, 79.

92 Davis, *Formalism*, 35.

93 Archibald Alison, *Essays on the Nature and Principles of Taste*, 5th ed. (Edinburgh: Archibald Constible, 1817), 132.

192   NOTES TO PAGES 24–32

94 Alison, *Essays on the Nature and Principles of Taste.*
95 Qtd. in Charles Capper, *Margaret Fuller: An American Romantic Life, Vol. 2, The Public Years* (New York: Oxford University Press, 2007), 155.
96 Margaret Fuller, "Review of Henry Wadsworth Longfellow, *Poems,*" December 10, 1845, in *Margaret Fuller, Critic: Writings from the New-York Tribune, 1844–1846,* ed. Judith Bean and Joel Myerson (New York: Columbia University Press, 2000), 290.

CHAPTER ONE

1 Paul Gilroy, *The Black Atlantic: Modernity and Double Consciousness* (London and New York: Verso, 1993), 4.
2 Gilroy, *Black Atlantic,* 17.
3 Christina Sharpe, *In the Wake: On Blackness and Being* (Durham, NC: Duke University Press, 2016), 23.
4 Sharpe, *In the Wake: On Blackness and Being,* 23.
5 Sharpe, *In the Wake: On Blackness and Being,* 23.
6 Sharpe, *In the Wake: On Blackness and Being,* 23.
7 Alexis Pauline Gumbs, *Undrowned: Black Feminist Lessons from Marine Mammals* (Chico, CA: AK Press, 2020).
8 For the most comprehensive accounts of Wheatley Peters's life and work, see Vincent Carretta, *Phillis Wheatley: Biography of a Genius in Bondage* (Athens: University of Georgia Press, 2011); and Vincent Carretta, ed., *The Writings of Phillis Wheatley* (Oxford: Oxford University Press, 2019), xv–xlv. See also Rafia Zafar, "1778: The Manumission of Phillis Wheatley," in *A New Literary History of America,* ed. Werner Sollors and Greil Marcus (Cambridge, MA, Harvard University Press, 2009).
9 For a reading of the transit of elegy in Peter's verse as a metaphor for the transit of slavery, see Lucia Hodgson, "Infant Muse: Phillis Wheatley and the Revolutionary Rhetoric of Childhood," *Early American Literature* 49, no. 3 (2014): 666–68.
10 See, for instance, James Edward Ford III, "Notes on Black Ekphrasis," *Early American Literature* 58, no. 3 (2023): 591–618.
11 As Lucia Hodgson argues, Peters's status as child-poet, who wrote her first poem at eleven, published her first poem at fourteen, and published her only book at nineteen, is important to consider in relation to her position in the public and political sphere. Hodgson, drawing on Elizabeth Dillon's classifications of early American white women as "prepolitical" and enslaved African Americans as "apolitical," argues that Peters's youth allowed her the privilege of the latter category, and the implicit imagination that she would one day grow into the political subjecthood. See Hodgson, "Infant Muse," 668. For a discussion of the representation of child characters and nation-building in Peters's work, see Anna Mae Duane, *Suffering Childhood in Early America: Violence, Race, and the Making of the Child Victim* (Athens: University of Georgia Press, 2010), 1444–45; and Caroline Levander, *Cradle of Liberty: Race, the Child, and National Belonging from Thomas Jefferson to W. E. B. DuBois* (Durham, NC: Duke University Press, 2006), 40.

NOTES TO PAGES 32–43   *193*

12 George Light, "Introduction," in *Memoir and Poems of Phillis Wheatley, A Native African and a Slave* (Boston: George Light, 1834), 7

13 "Joining Copies" small copybook, and large copybook, in Phillis Wheatley collection, 1757–1773, Emory University, Stuart A. Rose Manuscript, Archives, and Rare Book Library, Atlanta, GA, http://pid.emory.edu/ark:/25593/901bs.

14 Stokes, *Old Style*, 15.

15 Virginia Jackson, *Before Modernism: Inventing American Lyric* (Princeton, NJ and Oxford: Princeton University Press, 2023), xiii.

16 For a more detailed argument in favor of using Wheatley Peters's married name in criticism, see Zachary Mcleod Hutchins, "'Add New Glory to Her Name': Phillis Wheatley Peters," *Early American literature* 56, no. 3 (2021): 663–68.

17 In the Oxford edition of Peter's poems, Vincent Carretta notes the slight variation between the copybook edition of the poem, and the published version. Maureen Anderson offers an extended reading of the poem's classicism, but does not comment on the variations of the copybook. Carretta, ed., *The Writings of Phillis Wheatley* (Oxford: Oxford University Press, 2019), 192–93. Anderson, "Phillis Wheatley's Dido: An Analysis of "An Hymn to Humanity. To S. P. G. Esq." in *New Essays on Phillis Wheatley*, ed. John C. Shields and Eric D. Lamore (Knoxville: University of Tennessee Press, 2011), 2–18.

18 Amy Wilcockson, "Uncovering the Archive—Phillis Wheatley Collection, 1757–1773, Emory University," Keats-Shelley Association of America, (blog), https://www.k-saa.org/blog/phillis-wheatley-collection.

19 Randall Burkett's statements are cited in Greenwood and Carretta's publications. Julian Mason is quoted in Carretta. Vincent Carretta, *Phillis Wheatley: Biography of a Genius in Bondage*, (Athens and London: University of Georgia Press, 2011), n41, Epub: Emily Greenwood, "The Politics of Classicism in the Poetry of Phillis Wheatley," in *Ancient Slavery and Abolition: From Hobbes to Hollywood*, ed. Richard Alston, Edith Hall, and Justine McConnell, (Oxford: Oxford University Press, 2011), 161–62.

20 See for instance "Against Bribery at Elections," "Their tyrant kings let slaves revere," in the first book, and "The Voice of Freedom" in the second. Phillis Wheatley Copybooks, Stuart Rose Library.

21 Wheatley Copybooks, Rose Library; Carretta, *Biography of a Genius in Bondage*, n41.

22 Griswold, *Female Poets of America*, 9.

23 Griswold, *Female Poets of America*, 8.

24 Griswold, *Female Poets of America*, 9.

25 Griswold, *Female Poets of America*, 9.

26 Griswold, *Female Poets of America*, 30.

27 See for instance Carretta, *Genius in Bondage*, 134–38; Jennifer Thorn, "Phillis Wheatley's Ghosts: The Racial Melancholy of New England Protestants," *The Eighteenth Century* 50, no. 1 (Spring 2009): 86–88.

28 Margaretta Odell, "Memoir," in *Memoir and Poems of Phillis Wheatley, A Native African and a Slave*, ed. George Light (Boston: George Light, 1834), 29.

29 Qtd. in Griswold, *Female Poets*, 31; Rafia Zafar, "Shakespeare's Darker Sister," in

A New Literary History of America, ed. Greil Marcus and Wernor Sollors (Cambridge and London: Harvard University Press, 2009), 95.

30 Griswold, *Female Poets*, 31; Hutchins, "Add New Glory to Her Name," 663–68.

31 Griswold, *Female Poets of America*, 30.

32 Duyckinck, *Cyclopedia*, 368.

33 Duyckinck, *Cyclopedia*, 368.

34 Duyckinck, *Cyclopedia*, 368.

35 Carretta, *Writings*, 193; Jennifer Thorn, "'All Beautiful in Woe: Gender, Nation, and Phillis Wheatley's 'Niobe,'" *Studies in Eighteenth-Century Culture* 37 (2008): 240.

36 Duyckinck, *Cyclopedia*, 368.

37 Thorn, "All Beautiful in Woe," 249. See also Thorn, "Phillis Wheatley's Ghosts," 73–99.

38 Duyckinck, *Cyclopedia*, 369.

39 Socarides, *In Plain Sight*, 2.

40 Odell, "Memoir," in *Memoir and Poems of Phillis Wheatley, A Native African and a Slave*, ed. George Light, (Boston: George Light, 1834), 29.

41 Qtd. in Max Cavitch, "The Poetry of Phillis Wheatley in Slavery's Recollective Economies, 1773 to the Present," in *Race, Ethnicity and Publishing in America*, ed. Cecile Cottenet (London: Palgrave Macmillan, 2014), 218.

42 Cavitch, "The Poetry of Phillis Wheatley," 220.

43 Cavitch, "The Poetry of Phillis Wheatley," 216–19.

44 Cavitch, "The Poetry of Phillis Wheatley," 218.

45 Carretta, *The Writings of Phillis Wheatley*, xxiii.

46 William G. Allen, ed., *Wheatley, Banneker, and Horton: with Selections from the Poetical Works* [of] *Wheatley and Horton, and the Letter of Washington to Wheatley, and of Jefferson to Banneker* (Boston: Daniel Liang, 1849), 7.

47 Jennifer Rene Young, "Marketing a Sable Muse: Phillis Wheatley and the Antebellum Press," in *New Essays on Phillis Wheatley*, ed. J. C. Sheilds and E. D. Lamore (Knoxville: University of Tennessee, 2011), 220.

48 B. B. Thatcher, *Memoir of Phillis Wheatley, a Native African and a Slave* (Boston: G. W. Light, 1834).

49 Cara Glatt, "'To Perpetuate Her Name': Appropriation and Autobiography in Margaretta Matilda Odell's Memoir of Phillis Wheatley," *Early American Literature* 55 no. 1, (2020): 147.

50 Glatt, *Early American Literature*, 147.

51 Light, *Memoir and Poems*, v.

52 Light, *Memoir and Poems*, vi.

53 Light, *Memoir and Poems*, 13.

54 Light, *Memoir and Poems*, 10–11.

55 Light, *Memoir and Poems*, 14, 15.

56 Light, *Memoir and Poems*, 11. For a critical examination of Northern "familial slavery" and Peters's status in the Wheatley family, see Thorn, "Phillis Wheatley's Ghosts," 73–99.

57 Mary Louise Kete, "Phillis Wheatley and the Political Work of Ekphrasis," in *The*

Call of Classical Literature in the Romantic Age ed. K. P. Van Anglen and James Engell (Edinburgh: Edinburgh University Press, 2017), 55.

58 Light, *Memoir and Poems*, 23–24.

59 Light, *Memoir and Poems*, 24.

60 Zafar, "1778."

61 Light, *Memoir and Poems*, 24, 28.

62 Light, *Memoir and Poems*, 26.

63 Light, *Memoir and Poems*, 27.

64 Sharpe, *In the Wake*, 23.

65 Light, *Memoir and Poems*, 11.

66 Light, *Memoir and Poems*, vii.

67 Light, *Memoir and Poems*, 11–12.

68 Light, *Memoir and Poems*, 12.

69 Light, *Memoir and Poems*, 17.

70 Light, *Memoir and Poems*, 18.

71 Light, *Memoir and Poems*, 18–19.

72 Richards, *Gender and the Poetics*, 81; Ellison, "The Politics of Fancy in the Age of Sensibility," in *Re-Visioning Romanticism: British Women Writers, 1776–1837*, ed. Carol Shiner Wilson and Joel Haefner, (Philadelphia: University of Pennsylvania Press, 1994), 228.

73 Richards, *Gender and the Poetics*, 19–20, 81.

74 Griswold, *Female Poets*, 32.

75 Light, *Memoir and Poems*, 2.

76 Henry Louis Gates, Jr., *The Trials of Phillis Wheatley: America's First Black Poet and Her Encounters with the Founding Fathers* (London: Civitas Books, 2003), 29.

77 Joanna Brooks, "Our Phillis, Ourselves," *American Literature* 82, no. 1 (2010): 1–28.

78 Thomas Jefferson, *Notes on the State of Virginia* (Philadelphia: Prichard and Hall, 1848), 150.

79 Jefferson, *Notes on the State of Virginia*, 150.

80 Light, *Memoir and Poems*, 16.

81 Virginia Jackson, *Before Modernism: Inventing American Lyric* (Princeton, NJ: Princeton University Press, 2023), 1.

82 John C. Shields, *Phillis Wheatley and the Romantics* (Knoxville: University of Tennessee Press, 2010), 46–47.

83 Jackson, *Before Modernism*, 118, 119, 119.

84 Jackson, *Before Modernism*, 9.

85 Jackson, *Before Modernism*, 119.

86 Jackson, *Before Modernism*, 120, qtd. in 120.

87 W. J. T. Mitchell, *Picture Theory: Essays on Verbal and Visual Representation* (Chicago: University of Chicago Press, 1994), 164; Jacques Rancière, *The Emancipated Spectator*, trans. Gregory Elliot (New York and London: Verso, 2011), 15.

88 Phillis Wheatley, *The Writings of Phillis Wheatley*, ed. Vincent Carretta, (Oxford: Oxford University Press, 2019): 194; Eric Slauter, "Looking For Scipio Moorhead: An 'African Painter' in Revolutionary North America," in *Slave Portraiture in the*

Atlantic World (Cambridge: Cambridge University Press, 2013): 89–116. Slauter's chapter offers the most extensive analysis of both Moorhead's biographical record and the portrait of Peters. Mary Louise Kete also analyzes the frontispiece in detail in Kete, "Phillis Wheatley and the Political Work of Ekphrasis," in *The Call of Classical Literature in the Romantic Age*, ed. K. P. Van Anglen and James Engell (Edinburgh: Edinburgh University Press, 2017): 53–79.

89 Elizabeth Loizeaux, *Twentieth-Century Poetry and the Visual Arts* (Cambridge: Cambridge University Press, 2008), 174–75.

90 Loizeaux, *Twentieth-Century Poetry*, 175.

91 James Edward Ford III, "Notes on Black Ekphrasis," *Early American Literature* 58, no. 3 (2023): 591, qtd. in 592.

92 Ford, "Notes on Black Ekphrasis," 597.

93 Wheatley, *The Writings of Phillis Wheatley*, 194.

94 *Oxford English Dictionary Online*, s.v., "Pinion," Oxford: Oxford University Press, 2023, https://www.oed.com/search/dictionary/?q=pinion.

95 Wheatley, *The Writings of Phillis Wheatley*, 194.

96 Ford, "Notes on Black Ekphrasis," 606–7, italics in text.

97 June Jordan, "The Difficult Miracle of Black Poetry in America: Something like a Sonnet for Phillis Wheatley," https://www.poetryfoundation.org/articles/68628/the-difficult-miracle-of-black-poetry-in-america; Hodgson, "Infant Muse," 668–69.

CHAPTER TWO

1 Qtd. in Charles Capper, *Margaret Fuller: An American Romantic Life*, vol. 2, *The Public Years* (New York: Oxford University Press, 2007), 155.

2 In particular, Fuller had made plans to accompany John and Eliza Farrar on their trip to Europe beginning in the summer of 1836, which were derailed by financial demands following her father's sudden death in 1835. See Megan Marshall, *Margaret Fuller: A New American Life* (New York: Houghton Mifflin Harcourt), 83–96.

3 Marshall, *Margaret Fuller*, 202.

4 Margaret Fuller, "American Literature, Its Position in the Present Time and Prospects for the Future," in *Papers on Literature and Art* (New York: Wiley and Putnam, 1846), 122.

5 Edward L. Widmer, *Young America: The Flowering of Democracy in New York City* (New York: Oxford University Press, 1999), 107.

6 Colleen Glenney Boggs, *Transnationalism and American Literature, Literary Translation 1773- 1892* (New York: Routledge, 2007), 52. For more on translation influence on *Summer on the Lakes*, see also Christina Zwarg, "Footnoting the Sublime: Margaret Fuller on Black Hawk's Trail," *American Literary History* 5 no. 4 (Winter 1993): 616–42.

7 Christina Zwarg, "Footnoting the Sublime: Margaret Fuller on Black Hawk's Trail," *American Literary History* 5, no. 4 (1993): 616.

8 Fuller, "American Literature," 122, 124.

9 Fuller, "American Literature," 124.

NOTES TO PAGES 68–70   *197*

10 David M. Robinson, "Margaret Fuller, Self-Culture, and Associationism," in *Margaret Fuller and Her Circles*, ed. Brigitte Bailey, Katheryn P. Viens, and Conrad Edick Wright (Durham, NC: University of New Hampshire Press, 2013), 90.

11 Theo Davis, *Formalism, Experience, and the Making of American Literature* (Cambridge: Cambridge University Press, 2007).

12 Kerry Larson, *Imagining Equality in Nineteenth-Century American Literature* (Cambridge: Cambridge University Press), 82.

13 Larson, *Imagining Equality*, 79.

14 J. C. Banerjee, "Associative Reactions" in *Encyclopaedic Dictionary of Psychological Terms* (New Delhi: M. D. Publications, 1994), 24.

15 Margaret Fuller, "Review of Henry Wadsworth Longfellow, *Poems*," December 10, 1845, in *Margaret Fuller, Critic: Writings from the New-York Tribune, 1844–1846*, ed. Judith Bean and Joel Myerson (New York: Columbia University Press, 2000), 290.

16 Fuller, "Review of Longfellow," 288.

17 Stephen Adams, "'That Tidiness We Always Look for in a Woman': Fuller's *Summer on the Lakes* and Romantic Aesthetics," *Studies in the American Renaissance* (1987): 248–49. See also John Matteson, *The Lives of Margaret Fuller: A Biography* (New York: W. W. Norton, 2012), 285 for Fuller's similar critiques of Hawthorne, Emerson, Longfellow, and Lowell.

18 Qtd. in Thomas Wentworth Higginson, *Margaret Fuller Ossoli*, 9th ed. (Boston: Houghton, Mifflin and Company, 1892), 195.

19 Margaret Fuller to Ralph Waldo Emerson, November 12, 1843, in *The Letters of Margaret Fuller*, vol. 3, ed. Robert N. Hudspeth (Ithaca and London: Cornell University Press, 1984), 159.

20 James Freeman Clarke, review of *Summer on the Lakes*, *Christian World*, 2 (July 6, 1844), rpt. in *Critical Essays on Margaret Fuller*, ed. Joel Myerson (Boston: G. K. Hall, 1980), 2.

21 Caleb Stetson, "Notice of Recent Publications," *Christian Examiner* 37 (September 1844): 275.

22 Orestes Brownson, Review of *Summer on the Lakes*, *Brownson's Quarterly Review* 6 (October 1844): 546.

23 Qtd. in Marshall, *Margaret Fuller*, 213–14.

24 See Adams, "That Tidiness," 247–48 for an excellent survey of both contemporary reviews and more recent literary criticism, including critiques of the text's form by Arthur Brown, Lawrence Buell, and Margaret Allen.

25 Adams, "That Tidiness," 248.

26 Adams, "That Tidiness," 250.

27 Bell Gale Chevigny, *The Woman and the Myth: Margaret Fuller's Life and Writings* (Old Westbury, NY: Feminist Press, 1976), 11.

28 Matteson, *The Lives of Margaret Fuller*, 235.

29 Jeffrey Steele, *Transfiguring America: Myth, Ideology, and Mourning in Margaret Fuller's Writing* (Columbia: University of Missouri Press, 2001), 138.

30 Dorri Beam, Style, *Gender, and Fantasy in Nineteenth-Century American Women's Writing* (Cambridge: Cambridge University Press, 2010), 51–52.

198 NOTES TO PAGES 70–74

31 Margaret Fuller, *Summer on the Lakes, in 1843*, with an introduction by Susan Belasco Smith (Urbana and Chicago: University of Illinois Press, 1991), 156.

32 Kathleen Lawrence, "Soul Sisters and the Sister Arts: Margaret Fuller, Caroline Sturgis, and Their Private World of Love and Art," *ESQ: A Journal of the American Renaissance* 57 no. 1–2 (2011): 79.

33 Lawrence, "Soul Sisters," 79.

34 Caroline Sturgis to Ralph Waldo Emerson, Lenox, November 1850, in the Sophia Smith Collection, Smith College, box 1, folder 25. Qtd. in Lawrence, "Soul Sisters," 79.

35 Margaret Fuller to William H. Channing, October 27, 1843, *Letters of Margaret Fuller*, vol. 3, 154.

36 Fuller, *Letters of Margaret Fuller*.

37 It is fitting that it is Channing, the foremost associationist among the transcendentalists, with whom Fuller shares these ideas. See Robinson, "Margaret Fuller, Self-Culture, and Associationism," 93. For more on the influence of Fourierist thought on Fuller's work, particularly *Summer on the Lakes*, see Zwarg, "Margaret Fuller on Black Hawk's Trail," 629–38.

38 Lawrence Buell, "Transcendentalism's Literature of the Portfolio," Paper, Modern Language Association Convention, New Brunswick, NJ, April 3–5, 1986.

39 Cinthia Gannett, *Gender and the Journal: Diaries and Academic Discourse* (Albany: SUNY Press, 1992): 102–3.

40 Stephen Kagle, *Early Nineteenth-Century American Diary Literature* (Boston: Twayne, 1986), 104.

41 Joel Myerson, "Margaret Fuller's 1842 Journal: At Concord with the Emersons," *Harvard Library Bulletin* 21 (1973): 337.

42 Robert Sattelmeyer, "Journals," *The Oxford Handbook of Transcendentalism*, ed. Sandra Harbert Petrulionis, Laura Dassow Walls, and Joel Myerson (Oxford: Oxford University Press, 2010), 298.

43 See Laraine R. Ferguson, "Margaret Fuller as a Teacher in Providence: The School Journal of Ann Brown," *Studies in the American Renaissance* (1991): 59–118; Daniel Shealy, "Margaret Fuller and her 'Maiden': Evelina Metcalf's 1838 School Journal," *Studies in the American Renaissance* (1996): 41–65; Frank Shuffelton, "Margaret Fuller at the Greene Street School: The Journal of Evelina Metcalf," *Studies in the American Renaissance* (1985): 29–46; Paula Kopacz, "The School Journal of Hannah (Anna) Gale," *Studies in the American Renaissance* (1996): 67–113; and Granville Ganter and Hani Sarji, "'May We Put Forth Our Leaves': Rhetoric in the School Journal of Mary Ware Allen, Student of Margaret Fuller, 1837–1838," *Proceedings of the American Antiquarian Society* 177 no. 1 (2007): 61–142.

44 Ganter and Sarji, "Rhetoric in the School Journal of Mary Ware Allen," 61.

45 Ganter and Sarji, "Rhetoric in the School Journal of Mary Ware Allen," 68.

46 Judith Strong Albert, "Margaret Fuller's Row at the Greene Street School: Early Female Education in Providence, 1817–1839," *Rhode Island History* 42 no. 2 (1983): 43–56.

47 Ganter and Sarji, "Rhetoric in the School Journal of Mary Ware Allen," 68.

48 Ganter and Sarji, "Rhetoric in the School Journal of Mary Ware Allen," 63.

49 Mary Ware (Allen) "Johnson, School Journal, 1838 June 20—August 10," Original

NOTES TO PAGES 74–79 *199*

Manuscript, Allen-Johnson Family, Papers, 1759–1992, American Antiquarian Society, 37.

50 Richard Whately, *Elements of Rhetoric* (London, 1828; Boston: Hilliard, Gray, 1833; rpt., Douglas Ehninger, ed. Carbondale: University of Southern Illinois Press, 1963), 209. Qtd. in Ganter and Sarji, "Rhetoric in the School Journal of Mary Ware Allen," 78. In her analysis of Whately's influence on Fuller's feminist manifestos, Annette Kolodny notes that the idea of convincing rather than persuading was central to what Fuller took from the text. See Annette Kolodny, "Inventing a Feminist Discourse: Rhetoric and Resistance in Margaret Fuller's 'Woman in the Nineteenth Century,'" *New Literary History* 25, no. 2 (Spring 1994): 375–79.

51 Ganter and Sarji, "Rhetoric in the School Journal of Mary Ware Allen," 78. See Kenneth Cmiel, *Democratic Eloquence: The Fight Over Popular Speech in Nineteenth-Century America* (New York: William Morrow, 1990) for a discussion of what Cmiel calls this "middling style" in America.

52 Johnson, "School Journal, June 20–August 10 1838," 139.

53 William Huntting Howell, *Against Self-Reliance: The Arts of Dependence in the Early United States*, (Philadelphia: University of Pennsylvania Press, 2015): 118.

54 Howell, *Against Self-Reliance*, 119.

55 Mary Ware (Allen) Johnson, "School Journal, December 19, 1837–April 2, 1838," Original Manuscript, Allen-Johnson Family, Papers, 1759–1992, American Antiquarian Society, 118.

56 Matteson, *The Lives of Margaret Fuller*, 126–7.

57 Elizabeth Palmer Peabody, "Journal of Margaret Fuller's Conversations, November 1839–May 1840," Original Manuscript, Elizabeth Palmer Peabody Papers, American Antiquarian Society.

58 Mary Ware (Allen) Johnson, "School Journal, December 19, 1837–April 2, 1838," Original Manuscript, Allen-Johnson Family, Papers, 1759–1992, American Antiquarian Society, 1.

59 Johnson, "School Journal, December 19, 1837–April 2, 1838," 2.

60 We see evidence of this in both Ware's early and later journals. For instance, in the first journal, on April 2, 1838 she writes: "I generally find Monday morning a good time to make up my journal, which is apt to linger behind. . . . It is not right, I know, but I cannot help it unless I write at noon, which I do not feel inclined to do, for I do not feel in the spirit to write, except in school hours." By the third journal, it is clear that this retroactive record is still the norm for Ware. As she writes on May 25, 1838: "I am so glad to-day, for the first time in this journal, not to be writing a lie. I am sorry to use so strong an expression—but it is the first time that I have written <u>for</u> the day, <u>on</u> the day." This idea, that to write too far after the events recorded is "to write a lie" suggests that though writing from remembrance is an ideal, the reiteration of events needs to occur soon after the original to maintain faithfulness in its variation.

61 Johnson, "School Journal, June 20 1838–August 10 1838,", 10.

62 Qtd. in Joel Myerson, "Margaret Fuller's 1842 Journal," 337.

63 Robert Sattelmeyer, "Journals," 298.

64 Margaret Fuller, "Undated Manuscript Note, Margaret Fuller Papers, 1830–49," Massachusetts Historical Society.

200 NOTES TO PAGES 79–86

65 Margaret Fuller Papers, 1830–1849, Massachusetts Historical Society.

66 Margaret Fuller, "Being Notes of a Journey to the West, by S. M. Fuller, June 1843," Original manuscript journal, Margaret Fuller Papers, Massachusetts Historical Society, 3.

67 Fuller, "Being Notes of a Journey to the West, by S. M. Fuller, June 1843," 6.

68 Fuller, "Being Notes of a Journey to the West, by S. M. Fuller, June 1843," 1.

69 Marshall, *Margaret Fuller*, 127.

70 Qtd. in Margaret Allen, "'This Impassioned Yankee': Margaret Fuller's Writing Revisited" *Southwest Review* 58, no. 2 (1973): 166.

71 Fuller, *Summer on the Lakes*, 42.

72 Margaret Fuller to [?], [Summer] 1844, *Letters of Margaret Fuller*, 202.

73 Lawrence, "Soul Sisters," 79.

74 Marshall, *Margaret Fuller*, 203.

75 Fuller, *Summer on the Lakes*, 34–35; 42–43; 20; 69–70.

76 Fuller, *Summer on the Lakes*, 1.

77 Fuller, *Summer on the Lakes*, 1.

78 Steele, *Transfiguring America*, 141.

79 Fuller, *Summer on the Lakes*, 4.

80 Johnson, "School Journal, December 19, 1837–April 2, 1838," 2.

81 Fuller, *Summer on the Lakes*, 34–35. I use the Danish spelling of Thorvaldsen when not referring to Fuller's title.

82 Caleb Crain, *American Sympathy: Men, Friendship and Literature in the New Nation* (New Haven: Yale University Press, 2001), 208.

83 Margaret Fuller, "The Atheneum [sic] Exhibition of Painting and Sculpture," *The Dial: A Magazine for Literature, Philosophy, and Religion* 1, no. 2 (October 1840): 263.

84 Fuller, "Being Notes of a Journey to the West, by S. M. Fuller, June 1843," 8.

85 Margaret Fuller to James Freeman Clarke, July 9 1843, Margaret Fuller Papers, MHS; Margaret Fuller to Richard Fuller, July 29 1843, *Letters of Margaret Fuller*, 133.

86 Margaret Fuller, "Journal page, July 4 1843," Original manuscript, Margaret Fuller Papers, MHS. A tracing of the full journal is available as Margaret Fuller, "Journal, 17 June–29 October 1844," Perry-Clarke Papers, MHS, and is also reprinted in Martha Berg, Alice de V. Perry, and Margaret Fuller, "'The Impulses of Human Nature': Margaret Fuller's Journal from June through October 1844," *Proceedings of the Massachusetts Historical Society* 102 (1990): 38–126.

87 Marshall, *Margaret Fuller*, 206–8. For more on Fuller's relationship with Sturgis and same-sex desire more generally, see Mary E. Wood, "'With Ready Eye': Margaret Fuller and Lesbianism in Nineteenth-Century American Literature," *American Literature* 65, no. 1 (1993): 1–18; Kathleen Lawrence, "Soul Sisters and the Sister Arts: Margaret Fuller, Caroline Sturgis, and Their Private World of Love and Art," *ESQ: A Journal of the American Renaissance* 57, no. 1–2 (2011): 79–104; and David Greven, "New Girls and Bandit Brides: Female Narcissism and Lesbian Desire in Margaret Fuller's *Summer on the Lakes*," *Legacy: A Journal of American Women Writers* 29, no. 1 (2012): 37–61.

88 Steele, *Transfiguring America*, 149.

89 Martha Berg, Alice de V. Perry, and Margaret Fuller, "'The Impulses of Human Nature': Margaret Fuller's Journal from June through October 1844," *Proceedings of the Massachusetts Historical Society* 102 (1990): 43–51.

90 Steele, *Transfiguring America*, 19.

91 Lauren Berlant, *The Anatomy of National Fantasy: Hawthorne, Utopia, and Everyday Life* (Chicago: University of Chicago Press, 1991), 47.

92 Wai Chi Dimock, *Through Other Continents: American Literature Across Deep Time* (Princeton, NJ: Princeton University Press, 2008), 3.

93 Dimock, *Through Other Continents*, 3.

94 Dimock, *Through Other Continents*, 4.

95 Dimock, *Through Other Continents*, 4.

96 In this vein, Fuller is one of Dimock's central case studies for deep time in "The Planetary Dead: Margaret Fuller, Ancient Egypt, Italian Revolution" in *Through Other Continents*, 52–72.

97 Margaret Fuller to John S. Dwight, May 31 1837, *The Letters of Margaret Fuller*, 280. Fuller's own copies of Goethe's complete works also show an extensive underlining of Goethe's essay on Lessing's *Laocoon*, which discusses the importance of this treatise particularly in terms of the different relationships of time to the arts, with painting as synchronic, or immediately apparent to the spectator, and poetry as diachronic, unfolding through time. Lawrence, "Soul Sisters and the Sister Arts," 94.

98 Fuller, *Summer on the Lakes*, 6.

99 Fuller, *Summer on the Lakes*, 2.

100 Fuller, *Summer on the Lakes*, 6.

101 Steele, *Transfiguring America*, 142.

102 Fuller, *Summer on the Lakes*, 27.

103 For more on the relation of Fuller's writing, and *Summer on the Lakes* in particular, to the contemporary politics of Indian removal, see Zwarg, "Margaret Fuller on Black Hawk's Trail," 616–42; Lucy Maddox, *Removals: Nineteenth-Century American Literature and the Politics of Indian Affairs* (New York: Oxford University Press, 1991), 131–68; and Annette Kolodny, "Margaret Fuller's First Depiction of Indians and the Limits on Social Protest: An Exercise in Women's Studies Pedagogy," *Legacy A Journal of American Women Writers* 18 no. 1, (2001): 1–28. Fuller, *Summer on the Lakes*, 27.

104 Fuller, *Summer on the Lakes*, 31; Fuller, *Summer on the Lakes*, 32.

105 Maddox, *Removals*, 104.

106 Fuller, *Summer on the Lakes*, 32–33.

107 Fuller, *Summer on the Lakes*, 33.

108 See Psalm 104:24. Sometimes translated as "the earth is full of your creatures" or "the earth is full of thy riches."

109 Fuller, *Summer on the Lakes*, 33.

110 Cecile Roudeau, "The Buried Scales of Deep Time: Beneath the Nation, Beyond the Human . . . and Back?" *Transatlantica* 1 (2015): 4.

111 Qtd. in Charles Capper, *Margaret Fuller: An American Romantic Life*, vol. 2, *The Public Years* (New York: Oxford University Press, 2007), 155.

112 Kolodny, "Margaret Fuller's First Depiction of Indians," 14.

113 Fuller, *Summer on the Lakes*, 33.

114 Fuller, *Summer on the Lakes*, 33.

115 This representation of Native stasis conforms to nineteenth-century evolutionary theories of race. As Kyla Schuller writes, "While black and white stood at the poles of the racial hierarchy, Natives and Asian laborers occupied intermediary rungs of evolutionary development /as/ representatives of the past. Indigenous peoples were frequently positioned as the evolutionary origins of the civilized races that could be nudged out of stasis and into the forward movement of time by whites; this idea underwrote the reservation system as well as the century-long off-reservation boarding school movement." Or, as Lora Romero argues, citing Fuller as well as Cooper, "aboriginals represent a *phase* that the human race goes through but which it must inevitably *get over.*" In this light, the reference to Apollo is not likely to be culturally neutral. As Carolyn Sorisio argues, "In the overall context of *Summer*, it is highly probable that Fuller intended her allusion to suggest that the American continent also produced a 'Greek' stage of humankind, similar to the one that Europe claimed as its roots. The emerging race of American will incorporate this sensual, childlike race through the appropriation of their positive values." Kyla Schuller, *The Biopolitics of Feeling: Race, Sex, and Science in the Nineteenth Century* (Durham, NC: Duke University Press, 2017), 55; Lora Romero, "Vanishing Americans: Gender, Empire, and New Historicism," in *Subjects and Citizens: Nation, Race, and Gender from Oroonoko to Anita Hill*, ed. Michael Moon and Cathy N. Davidson, (Durham, NC: Duke University Press, 1995), 93; and Carolyn Sorisio, *Fleshing Out America: Race, Gender, and the Politics of the Body in American Literature, 1833–1879* (Athens and London: University of Georgia Press, 2002), 170.

116 Fuller, *Summer on the Lakes*, 33.

117 Jeffrey Richmond-Moll, "Sculpture and Spectacle: Horatio Greenough's Christ and Lucifer," *Winterthur Portfolio* 50, no. 4 (2016): 210.

118 Henry David Thoreau, *Cape Cod*, ed. Joseph J. Moldenhauer (Princeton, NJ and Oxford: Princeton University Press, 2004), 195.

119 See Annette Kolodny, *In Search of First Contact: The Vikings of Vinland, the Peoples of the Dawnland, and the Anglo-American Anxiety of Discovery* (Durham, NC: Duke University Press, 2012).

120 Daniel Malachuk reads Fuller's "Ganymede" in particular, and *Summer on the Lakes* more generally, as evidence of her status as "quintessential transcendentalist conservationist: she insists that Ganymede's realization of the Divine in the Human—'the full music of the soul'—springs specifically from the 'resplendent' middle landscape." For his structural comparison of Fuller and Goethe's Ganymede poems, see Malachuk, "Green Exultadas: Margaret Fuller, Transcendental Conservationism, and Antebellum Women's Nature Writing," in *Toward a Female Genealogy of Transcendentalism*, ed. Jana Argersinger and Phyllis Cole, (Athens: University of Georgia Press, 2014): 209–10.

121 Fuller, *Summer on the Lakes*, 34.

122 Fuller, *Summer on the Lakes*, 34.

123 Fuller, *Summer on the Lakes*, 36.

124 Crain, *American Sympathy*, 208.

NOTES TO PAGES 93–100   *203*

125 Fuller, *Summer on the Lakes*, 34.
126 Crain, *American Sympathy*, 208.
127 Fuller, *Summer on the Lakes*, 35.
128 Fuller, *Summer on the Lakes*, 36.
129 Fuller, "American Literature," 122.
130 Fuller, *Summer on the Lakes*, 36.
131 Fuller, *Summer on the Lakes*, 39.
132 Fuller, *Summer on the Lakes*, 39.
133 Fuller, *Summer on the Lakes*, 34.
134 Fuller, *Summer on the Lakes*, 27.
135 Fuller, *Summer on the Lakes*, 71.
136 Fuller, *Summer on the Lakes*, 71.
137 Fuller, *Summer on the Lakes*, 39.
138 Fuller, *Summer on the Lakes*, 42.
139 Fuller, "American Literature," 124.
140 Fuller, *Summer on the Lakes*, 37.
141 Fuller, *Summer on the Lakes*, 37.
142 Fuller, *Summer on the Lakes*, 39.
143 Fuller, *Summer on the Lakes*, 102.
144 Dimock, *Through Other Continents*, 4.
145 See for instance Israel Zangwill's 1908 play "The Melting Pot" which popularized the use of this phrase: "Yes, East and West, and North and South, the palm and the pine, pole and the equator, the crescent and the cross—how the great Alchemist melts and fuses them with his purging flame! Here shall the unite to build the Republic of Man and the Kingdom of God." Israel Zangwill, *The Melting Pot: Drama in Four Acts* (New York: Macmillan, 1909), 198–99.
146 J. Hector St. John de Crevecoeur, "Letter III: What is an American?," in *Letters from an American Farmer and Sketches of Eighteenth-Century America*, ed. Albert E. Stone, (New York: Penguin, 1986), 70.
147 Fuller, *Summer on the Lakes*, 24.
148 Randolph Bourne, "Trans-national America," *The Atlantic*, July 1916, https://www.theatlantic.com/magazine/archive/1916/07/trans-national-america/304838/.
149 Fuller, *Summer on the Lakes*, 166.
150 Fuller, *Summer on the Lakes*, 166.
151 Fuller, *Summer on the Lakes*, 166.
152 Matteson, *The Lives of Margaret Fuller*, 246.
153 Fuller, *Summer on the Lakes*, 166.
154 Fuller, *Summer on the Lakes*, 166.
155 Marshall, *Margaret Fuller*, 213.
156 Marshall, *Margaret Fuller*, 213.
157 William Henry Channing, Ralph Waldo Emerson, and James Freeman Clarke, eds., *Memoirs of Margaret Fuller*, Vol. 2 (Boston: Phillips, Sampson, and Company, 1852), 152–53.
158 Marshall, *Margaret Fuller*, 213
159 Matteson, *The Lives of Margaret Fuller*, 250.
160 Marshall, *Margaret Fuller*, 213.

204 NOTES TO PAGES 100–105

161 Richard V. Carpenter, "Margaret Fuller in Northern Illinois," *Journal of the Illinois State Historical Society (1908–1984)* 2, no. 4 (January 1910): 17–18.

CHAPTER THREE

1 For Sophia's exhibition of *Landscape* in 1834, see Marshall, *Peabody Sisters*, 264–70. For Sophia's lessons with Francis Graeter, Thomas Doughty, and Chester Harding in 1829–1830, see 205–11.

2 Claire M. Badaracco, "Pitfalls and Rewards of the Solo Editor: Sophia Peabody Hawthorne," *Resources for American Literary Study* 11, no. 1 (Spring 1981): 96. Italics in text.

3 For a discussion of mimesis and women's writing, see for instance Richards, *Gender and Poe*, 1–28; Cohen, *Fabrication*, 130–61. For the gendering of the copyist in the nineteenth century see Aviva Briefel, *The Deceivers*, 19–53.

4 Eldsen, *Roman Fever*, 74.

5 Noelle Baker, "'Let Me Do Nothing Smale': Mary Moody Emerson and Women's 'Talking' Manuscripts," *ESQ: A Journal of the American Renaissance* 57, no. 1–2 (2011): 24.

6 See for instance Stewart on Sophia's revisions in Hawthorne's *The English Notebooks*. Marta Werner and Nicholas Lawrence present a more sympathetic treatment of Sophia's editing practices in their analysis of her work on the common journal. Randall Stewart, "Editing Hawthorne's Notebooks: Selections from Mrs. Hawthorne's Letters to Mr. and Mrs. Fields," *More Books* 20 (September 1945): ix–xxi; Marta Werner and Nicholas Lawrence, "This Is His—This is My Mystery: The Common Journal of Nathaniel and Sophia Hawthorne, 1842–1843," in *Reinventing the Peabody Sisters*, ed. Monika Elbert, Julie Hall and Katharine Rodier (Iowa City: University of Iowa Press, 2006): 3–22.

7 Sophia Hawthorne, *Notes in England and Italy* (New York: G. P. Putnam & Son, 1869), 544.

8 Hawthorne, *Notes*, 354–55.

9 Hawthorne, *Notes*, 355.

10 This reading follows and expands on Elsden's point at the end of her essay that "the veil itself, rather than what it covers, is the answer. By leaving the veil unlifted, Sophia points toward the representation—the veil in which she envelops her Italian experience in order to share it with readers—rather than the experience." Annamaria Formichella Eldsen, "Watery Angels: Sophia Peabody Hawthorne's Artistic Argument in *Notes in England and Italy*," in *Reinventing the Peabody Sisters*, ed. Monika Elbert, Julie Hall and Katharine Rodier (Iowa City: University of Iowa Press, 2006): 142–43.

11 Richard H. Brodhead, *Cultures of Letters: Scenes of Reading and Writing in Nineteenth-Century America* (Chicago and London: University of Chicago Press, 1993), 51.

12 Brodhead, *Cultures of Letters*, 53.

13 Brodhead, *Cultures of Letters*, 63.

14 See, for instance, Sandra Whipple Spanier, "Two Foursomes in *The Blithedale Romance* and 'Women in Love,'" *Comparative Literary Studies* 16, no. 1 (1979): 59.

NOTES TO PAGES 105–109   *205*

15 Brodhead, *Cultures of Letters*, 55.

16 Marshall, *Peabody Sisters*, 73–74.

17 Marshall, *Peabody Sisters*, 280.

18 Marshall, *Peabody Sisters*, 280–81.

19 Marshall, *Peabody Sisters*, 362.

20 Julie E. Hall, "'Coming to Europe,' Coming to Authorship: Sophia Hawthorne and her *Notes in England and Italy*," *Legacy* 19, no. 2 (2002): 139.

21 Hall, "Coming to Europe," 138.

22 Mary Schriber, *Writing Home: American Women Abroad, 1830–1920* (Charlottesville and London: University Press of Virginia, 1997), 2.

23 Schriber, *Writing Home*, 3.

24 Schriber, *Writing Home*, 4.

25 Schriber sees women's travel writing, through Nina Baym, as a means of breaking down "whatever imaginative and intellectual boundaries their culture may have been trying to maintain between domestic and public worlds" (8) and argues that "from the beginning to the end of the nineteenth century and into the twentieth, writing home from abroad meant writing—and rewriting—'home'" (9). Susan Robertson similarly reads women's travel writing as "a negotiation" struck "between new freedoms and traditional ideas and practices of feminine comportment, between the road and home" (218). Susan L. Robertson, "American Women and Travel Writing," in *The Cambridge Companion to American Travel Writing*, ed. Alfred Bendixen and Judith Hamera (Cambridge: Cambridge University Press, 2009): 214–27.

26 Terry Caesar, *Forgiving the Boundaries: Home as Abroad in American Travel Writing* (Athens: University of Georgia Press, 1995), 58

27 Susan L. Robertson, "American Women and Travel Writing," in *The Cambridge Companion to American Travel Writing*, ed. Alfred Bendixen and Judith Hamera (Cambridge: Cambridge University Press, 2009), 219.

28 Eldsen, *Roman Fever*, 5.

29 Hawthorne, *Notes*, 3.

30 Hall, "Coming to Europe," 138.

31 Hall, "Coming to Europe, 138.

32 Hall, "Coming to Europe, 139.

33 For a discussion of the Hawthornes' financial straights and Sophia's publication, see for instance Mary Schriber, *Writing Home*, 122–23; Thomas Woodson, "Historical Commentary," in *The Centenary Edition of the Works of Nathaniel Hawthorne*, ed. Thomas Woodson and Bill Ellis, (Columbus: Ohio State University, 1997), 733–34. For an extended analysis of Sophia's aesthetic commitment to *Notes*, including an examination of the family's financial situation in the late 1860s, see Hall, "Coming to Europe," 140–41.

34 Sophia Hawthorne, *Journal*, 5 vols., Berg Coll MSS Hawthorne, S. New York Public Library, New York, 1858.

35 Edwin Haviland Miller, "A Calendar of the Letters of Sophia Peabody Hawthorne," *Studies in the American Renaissance* (1986): 202.

36 Hawthorne, *Notes*, 3.

37 See Hall, "Coming to Europe," 137. The extent to which familial associations were

responsible for the success of Sophia's book is of course difficult to track precisely. Sophia's contemporaries, though, were direct about the work's connections. As a review of the second edition in 1870 begins, "That the magic of Hawthorne's name would attract many readers to this volume, and that some passages would acquire especial interest through him, might be expected; but the individual and intrinsic merit of the book will be a real surprise to those who learn, for the first time, of the intellectual companionship he must have found in his wife." "Current Literature," *Overland Monthly and Out West Magazine* 4, no. 3 (1870): 294.

38 Catherine Maria Sedgwick, *Letters from Abroad to Kindred at Home*, vol. 1 (New York: Harper & Brothers, 1841), viii.

39 Alfred Bendixen, "American Travel Books about Europe before the Civil War," *The Cambridge Companion to American Travel Writing*, ed. Alfred Bendixen and Judith Hamera. (Cambridge: Cambridge University Press, 2009), 103–26.

40 W. J. T. Mitchell, *Picture Theory: Essays on Verbal and Visual Representation* (Chicago: University of Chicago Press, 1994). Heffernan.

41 Hawthorne, *Notes*, 524.

42 Hawthorne, *Notes*, 525.

43 Hawthorne, *Notes*, 525.

44 Hawthorne, *Notes*, 232.

45 Hawthorne, *Notes*, 3.

46 Hawthorne, *Notes*, 320.

47 Sophia occasionally comments in *Notes* on botched attempts at artistic preservation, as in this description of a Raphael self-portrait: "It is said that Raphael's eyes in this picture were once blue and the hair fair, and that the cleaners have retouched them and made them dark. . . . Picture cleaners are often the destruction instead of the restorers of works of art" (375). For more on nineteenth-century art restoration and its critics see Briefel, *The Deceivers*, 84–114.

48 Hawthorne, *Notes*, 312.

49 Hawthorne, *Notes*, 312.

50 Hawthorne, *Notes*, 260.

51 Some fail utterly at their task, as one copyist imitating Michelangelo's *Three Fates* "badly," creating a copy that "will deceive somebody" who has not seen the original work. Others Sophia damns with faint praise, as one copyist emulating Guido's *Archangel* in the Church of the Capuchins who "has entirely missed the face and the sway of the attitude, but had succeeded pretty well with the right foot and limb." Hawthorne, *Notes*, 369, 258.

52 Hawthorne, *Notes*, 312.

53 Hawthorne, *Notes*, 309.

54 Hawthorne, *Notes*, 368.

55 Hawthorne, *Notes*, 402.

56 Hawthorne, *Notes*, 508.

57 Marshall, *The Peabody Sisters*, 228.

58 Marshall, *The Peabody Sisters*, 229–31.

59 Marshall, *The Peabody Sisters*, 265.

60 In fact, Sophia at times attempts to maintain this connection between text and image in the published text, which does not reproduce any of her sketches. In a

NOTES TO PAGES 114–117   *207*

March 25, 1858 entry in the first volume of the Roman manuscript journal, she writes of two sculptures: "Marc Anthony has a strong head and face with a great force of will in it—Lepidus is very weak—with small features, a profile tending thus—" After the "thus," on the edge of the sheet is a pen drawing about the size of a nickel, showing a man with curly hair's profile, a triangle superimposed on his profiled features to emphasize his weak chin and forehead. This gesturing "thus," as well as the accompanying image is edited out of the published *Notes*, but later in the same passage, Sophia approximates some of the imagistic properties of her original text. Considering the relation between three sculptures, Sophia writes in the manuscript that Lepidus "stands opposite the powerful Marc Antony—in the transept of the Braccio Nuovo—in the Vatican, and Augustus in the center of the curve—the triumvirate—There they are—perfectly lifelike." Between the final "are" and "perfectly" is a gap of about two inches lengthwise, in which Sophia has drawn a semi-circle with "Lepidus" penned in on the left end, "M. A." on the right, and "Augustus" in the apex. This layout figures in the print publication with a careful spacing of text. Sophia Peabody Hawthorne, *Journal*, Rome, vol. 1, March 25, 1858, Sophia Peabody Hawthorne Collection of Papers, Henry W. and Albert A. Berg Collection of English and American Literature, New York Public Library.

61 Elsden, *Roman Fever*, 87.

62 Hawthorne, *Notes*, 328.

63 Hawthorne, *Notes*, 346–47.

64 Marshall, *The Peabody Sisters*, 125–26.

65 *The Letters of Ralph Waldo Emerson*, vol. 1, ed. Ralph L. Rusk (New York: Columbia University Press, 1939), 449.

66 Marshall, *The Peabody Sisters*, 334–35.

67 Marshall, *The Peabody Sisters*, 396, 425–27.

68 Philip Gura, *American Transcendentalism: A History* (New York: Hill and Wang, 2007), 216.

69 Marshall, *The Peabody Sisters*, 428; Brenda Wineapple, *Hawthorne: A Life* (Knopf: New York, 2003), 333–37.

70 Marshall, *The Peabody Sisters*, 211.

71 Marshall, *The Peabody Sisters*, 544.

72 Ralph Waldo Emerson, ALS to SAPH, December 1, 1836, Sophia Peabody Hawthorne Collection, Berg Collection, New York Public Library.

73 Emerson, ALS to SAPH, January 20, 1838, NYPL.

74 May 18, 1840; Marshall, *The Peabody Sisters*, 408.

75 Anonymous, "Poems," *Southern Quarterly Review* (April 1847): 493.

76 The *Blackwood's* article was a significant coup for Emerson, and was cited in several articles and reviews of his work in the years after its publication. As even an irreverent critic in the *Southern Literary Messenger* acknowledged five years later: "Mr. Emerson has attained to the honour of a laudatory review in *Blackwood's Magazine*, an honour to which very few American writers have attained." Anonymous, "History," *The Southern Literary Messenger* (April 1852): 247.

77 Anonymous, "Emerson," *Blackwood's Edinburgh Magazine* (December 1847): 644.

208 NOTES TO PAGES 117–123

78 Emerson, "The American Scholar," *Emerson's Prose and Poetry*, ed. Joel Porte and Saundra Morris (New York and London: W.W. Norton, 2001), 68.

79 Robert Macfarlane, *Original Copy: Plagiarism and Originality in Nineteenth-Century Literature* (Oxford: Oxford University Press, 2007),11.

80 Hawthorne, *Notes*, 326. The text in the manuscript journal is even slightly more severe: "How could wise and great Mr. Emerson ever say such a stupid thing as that it was just as well not to travel as to travel, and that each man has Europe in him, or something to that effect? Oh no—it would be better if every man could look upon these wonders of genius, and grow thereby. Besides, after Mr. Emerson had been to Europe himself, and seen every thing, how could he tell? Would he willingly have foregone all he saw in Italy? It was a mere transcendental speech, I fancy." Hawthorne, *Journal*, Vol. 2., NYPL.

81 Emerson, *Prose and Poetry*, 133.

82 Hawthorne, *Notes*, 369.

83 As she writes of Michaelangelo's "faithful portrait bust": "I know his face now perfectly well." *Notes*, 403.

84 Hawthorne, *Notes*, 390.

85 Hawthorne, *Notes*, 331–32.

86 Emerson, *Prose and Poetry*, 105.

87 See for instance Marshall, *The Peabody Sisters*, 128–29; 135 for Elizabeth's encouragement of Sophia's Classical education. That the muse of history's name, Clio, stems from the Greek verb "to broadcast" or "to make famous" adds another dimension to this sisterly reference. Elizabeth's tireless promotion of other artists' work made many careers, including Nathaniel's. To send a letter to Elizabeth, Sophia knew from her experience with the "Cuba Journal," was a form of pre-publication.

88 Hawthorne, *Journal*, Vol. 2.

89 Marta Werner and Nicholas Lawrence, *Ordinary Mysteries: The Common Journal of Nathaniel and Sophia Hawthorne, 1842–1843* (Philadelphia: American Philosophical Society, 2006), 317.

90 Sophia Hawthorne, "Preface," in *Passages from the English Notebooks of Nathaniel Hawthorne*, by Nathaniel Hawthorne (London: Strahan & Co., 1870), vii.

91 For instance, in writing to Annie Fields' on Nathaniel's death in May 1864: "In the most retired privacy it was the same as in the presence of men. The sacred veil of his eyelids he scarcely lifted to himself. Such an unviolated sanctuary as was his nature, I his inmost wife never conceived nor knew." Randall Stewart, "Editing Hawthorne's Notebooks: Selections from Mrs. Hawthorne's Letters to Mr. and Mrs. Fields" *More Books* 20 (September 1945): 299.

92 Sophia Peabody Hawthorne, *Diary*, 1859, Sophia Peabody Hawthorne Collection, NYPL.

93 Hawthorne, *Journal*, Vol. 1–5.

94 Stewart, "Editing Hawthorne's Notebooks," 308.

95 Werner and Lawrence, "This is His," 15.

96 The published text's occasional and inconsistent use of footnotes to correct or add statements has a similar effect as ellipses in signaling the existence of an "original"

NOTES TO PAGES 123–131   *209*

manuscript. See for instance Mary Schriber, *Writing Home*, 111–12 for Sophia's use of footnotes and bracketing in *Notes*.

97 The focus, even in the original journals, on art objects, likely made the excision of family circumstances in the published volume relatively simple. Other personal writings were more difficult to adjust. In June 1869, for instance, Sophia reviewed her "Cuba Journal" writings as possible candidates for publication but concluded that it would not be possible: "There is so much about people in them," Hall, "Coming to Europe," 141.

98 Hawthorne, *Notes*, 61.

99 Hawthorne, *Notes*, 126.

100 Hawthorne, *Notes*, 235.

101 Hawthorne, *Notes*, 276.

102 Hawthorne, *Notes*, 185.

103 Hawthorne, *Notes*, 185, 337.

104 Hawthorne, *Journal*, vol. 1.

105 Hawthorne, *Journal*, vol. 1.

106 Hawthorne, *Journal*, vol. 5, 67.

107 See for instance Schriber, *Writing Home*, 108; Hall, "Coming to Europe," 144 for reflections of Sophia's maternity.

108 Hawthorne, *Notes*, 58.

109 Hawthorne, *Notes*, 263.

110 Hawthorne, *Notes*, 184.

111 Hawthorne, *Notes*, 213.

112 Hawthorne, *Notes*, 347.

113 Hawthorne, *Notes*, 203.

114 Hawthorne, *Notes*, 203.

115 Hawthorne, *Notes*, 295.

116 Hawthorne, *Notes*, 295.

CHAPTER FOUR

1 Horace Traubel, *With Walt Whitman in Camden*, vol. 3 (New York: Rowman and Littlefield, 1961), 549.

2 The "Longfellow War" or "little war," was a controversy that raged in periodicals in 1845, initiated by Poe's January review of Longfellow's *The Waif* in the *Evening Mirror*, which implied plagiarism in its detection of a "moral *taint*" in the volume. Responses by Longfellow, Poe, and others followed on both sides of the plagiarism question through a number of different periodicals. Some allege that the media storm was constructed by Poe, then the editor at *Graham's Magazine*, for the sole cause of increasing magazine sales. The "war" continues to be at the center of critical interest in Longfellow with critics including Virginia Jackson, Kent Ljunquist, Meredith McGill, and Burton Pollin weighing in on the issue. This interest—going well beyond the exchanges status as literary scandal—reflects the "war's" broader relevance to issues such as the perception of plagiarism in

print culture, and historical and contemporary lyric reading. Virginia Jackson argues, for instance, that the exchange might be read "not only as a negotiation of the terms of Poe's own authorship, but also as an apprehension of the future of lyric reading," with Longfellow as a stand-in for the academic modes of poetic classification that govern much of contemporary reading practices. Virginia Jackson, "Poe, Longfellow, and the Institution of Poetry," *Poe Studies/ Dark Romanticism* 33, no. 1–2 (2000): 23–28. See also Kent Ljunkvist, "The 'Little War' and Longfellow's Dilemma: New Documents in the Plagiarism Controversy of 1845," *Resources for American Literary Study* 23 (1997): 28–59; Meredith McGill, "Poe, Literary Nationalism, and Authorial Identity," *The American Face of Edgar Allan Poe*, ed. Shawn Rosenheim and Stephen Rachman (Baltimore and London: Johns Hopkins University Press, 1995), 271–305; Burton Pollin, "Poe as Author of the 'Otis' Letter and 'The Bird of the Dream,'" *Poe Studies/ Dark Romanticism* 20, no. 1 (1987): 10–15.

3 Edgar Allan Poe, "Review of *Voices of the Night*," *Burton's Gentleman's Magazine and American Monthly Review* 6, no. 2 (1840): 103.

4 Poe, "Review of *Voices of the Night*," 101.

5 Poe, "Review of *Voices of the Night*," 100.

6 Walt Whitman, *Specimen Days & Collect* (Philadelphia: David McKay, 1883), 194.

7 Edgar Allan Poe, *Essays and Reviews*, ed. G. R. Thompson (New York: The Library of America, 1984), 762.

8 George Santayana, "Genteel American Poetry," *New Republic* 3 no. 30 (May 1915): 73.

9 Van Wyck Brooks, *America's Coming-of-Age*, (New York: Huebsch, 1915), 47, 47, 51.

10 Van Wyck Brooks, *The Flowering of New England: 1815–1865* (New York: World Publishing, 1946), 510.

11 Jackson, "Poe, Longfellow, and the Institution of Poetry," 23–28; Christoph Irmscher, *Longfellow Redux* (Urbana and Chicago: University of Illinois Press, 2006); Mary Louise Kete, *Sentimental Collaborations: Mourning and Middle-Class Identity in Nineteenth-Century America* (Durham, NC and London: Duke University Press, 2000).

12 Lawrence Buell, *New England Literary Culture from Revolution through Renaissance* (Cambridge: Cambridge University Press, 1986), xxv.

13 Eric L. Haralson, "Mars in Petticoats: Longfellow and Sentimental Masculinity," *Nineteenth–Century Literature* 51, no. 3 (1996): 329.

14 One writer went so far, shortly after Longfellow's death, as to consider an influence in artistic matters one of Longfellow's central contributions: "It is not too much to say that he was the most potent individual force for culture in America, and the rapid spread of taste and enthusiasm for art which may be noted in the people near the end of his long and honorable career may be referred more distinctly to his influence than to that of any other American." Anonymous, "Mr. Longfellow and the Artists," *The Atlantic Monthly* 52, no. 314 (1883): 826.

15 Anonymous, "Mr. Longfellow and the Artists," 830.

16 Irmscher, *Longfellow Redux*, 142.

NOTES TO PAGES 134–140   *211*

17 Margaret Fuller, "Poems: By Henry Wadsworth Longfellow," *Papers on Literature and Art* (New York: Wiley and Putnam, 1846), 152.

18 Fuller, "Poems," 158.

19 C. C. Felton, "Simm's *Stories and Reviews*," *North American Review* 62 no. 2 (1846): 377. For a discussion of nature's role in nationalist discussions and Longfellow's work, see also Lloyd Willis, "Henry Wadsworth Longfellow, United States Nationalist Literature, and the Canonical Erasure of Material Nature," *American Transcendental Quarterly* 20 no. 4 (2006): 629–59.

20 Qtd. in Laurence Vail Coleman, *The Museum in America: A Critical Study*, vol. 1 (Baltimore: Waverly Press, 1939), 90.

21 Lawrence Levine, *Highbrow/ Lowbrow: The Emergence of Cultural Hierarchy in America* (Cambridge, MA and London: Harvard University Press, 1988), 149.

22 Levine, *Highbrow/Lowbrow*, 9.

23 Fuller, "Poems," 151, 152.

24 See for example Michael P. Kramer, "A Fine Ambiguity: Longfellow, Language, and Literary History" in *Imagining Language in America: From the Revolution to the Civil War*, ed. Michael P. Kramer (Princeton, NJ: Princeton University Press, 1992), 64–89; and Agnieszka Salska, "From National to Supranational Conception of Literature: the Case of Henry Wadsworth Longfellow," *American Transcendental Quarterly* 20, no. 4 (December 2006): 611–28.

25 For a detailed discussion of Longfellow's relation to the North American environment and nationalism, see Lloyd Willis, "Henry Wadsworth Longfellow, United States National Literature, and the Canonical Erasure of Material Nature," *American Transcendental Quarterly* 20 no. 4 (December 2006): 629–46. Willis argues that Longfellow's "environmental exceptionalism" stands in materialist contrast to Emerson's abstract conception of American nature.

26 Richard Grusin and Jay Bolter, *Remediation: Understanding New Media* (Cambridge: The MIT Press, 2000), 20- 51.

27 Irmscher, *Longfellow Redux*, 3.

28 J. Samaine Lockwood, "Shopping for the Nation: Women's China Collecting in Late-Nineteenth-Century New England," *The New England Quarterly* 81, no. 1 (2008): 64–67.

29 Anonymous, "Mr. Longfellow and the Artists," 826.

30 Coleman, *The Museum in America*, 10–15.

31 For a detailed treatment of Charles Longfellow's travel and collecting practices, see Christine Guth, *Longfellow's Tattoos: Tourism, Collecting and Japan* (Seattle: University of Washington Press, 2004). The "objects" that Longfellow collected included ceramics, furnishings, photographs, and a full-back tattoo of an Asian carp. Prints were made from twenty of Ernest's paintings is *Twenty Poems from Longfellow* (Boston: Houghton Mifflin, 1884).

32 Diana Korzenik, "'That is Best Which Liest Nearest': Longfellow and Family Art, 1804–1924," *The New England Quarterly* 80, no. 3 (2007): 493–95.

33 Irmscher, *Longfellow Redux*, 85.

34 Korzenik, "That is Best," 491–98; Henry Wadsworth Longfellow, *The Seaside and the Fireside* (Boston: Ticknor, Reed, and Fields, 1850), 70.

35 Irmscher, *Longfellow Redux*, 86–93, 143–55.

212 NOTES TO PAGES 140–146

36 Citation from Languages of Art.

37 Ralph Waldo Emerson, *Emerson in His Journals*, ed. Joel Porte (Cambridge, MA: Belknap Press of Harvard University Press, 1982), 447.

38 Irmscher, *Longfellow Redux*, 44.

39 Irmscher, *Longfellow Redux*, 43–44.

40 The Longfellow National Historic Site at the poet's former home in Cambridge, MA houses many of the original prints and negatives of these photographs, and keeps a record and reproductions of images at other institutions.

41 "Henry Wadsworth Longfellow," *Scribner's Monthly* 17, no. 1 (November 1878): 1.

42 Henry Wadsworth Longfellow Papers, Houghton Library, Harvard University. I have not been able to find the source for the article noting Longfellow's "penchant for pipe-collecting" or the ekphrastic poem; as many of the articles in the Craigie House scrapbook, the title and date have been clipped off both. The author of the poem is noted as James Berry Bensel; the Tintoretto portrait has been shown to be inauthentic. It is clear that Longfellow read these newspaper articles carefully, as many include the poet's marginalia and corrections.

43 Virginia Jackson, "Longfellow's Tradition; Or, Picture-Writing a Nation," *Modern Language Quarterly* 59 no. 4 (1998): 471.

44 Irmscher, *Longfellow Redux*, 67.

45 Longfellow's business savvy is well-documented. See for instance Irmscher, *Longfellow Redux*, 53–58; William Charvat, *The Profession of Authorship in the United States: The Papers of William Charvat*, ed. Matthew Bruccoli (Columbus: Ohio State University Press, 1968): 106–67. The division of craft and art in the early nineteenth century depended largely on whether or not one was dependent on such economic "systems of exchange": artisans were, artists were not. After the Civil War, the role of professional (economically dependent) artist gained prestige only as it set itself in opposition to working class "art labor": fabric design, "ornamental terra-cotta brick, ceramics, stained glass, and wrought iron." Korzenik, "That is Best," 497–99.

46 George Putnam, ed., *Homes of American Authors; Comprising Anecdotical, Personal and Descriptive Sketches by Various Writers* (New York: G. P. Putnam, 1852), 266.

47 Putnam, *Homes of American Authors*, 269.

48 Putnam, *Homes of American Authors*, 286.

49 Putnam, *Homes of American Authors*, 278.

50 All citations of this poem are from Henry Wadsworth Longfellow, *The Masque of Pandora and other Poems* (Boston: James R. Osgood, 1875), 151.

51 Irmscher, *Longfellow Redux*, 124–37.

52 All of the citations that follow are from the poem's first publication in book-form, in Henry Wadsworth Longfellow, *Kéramos and Other Poems* (Boston: Houghton, Osgood, & Company, 1878).

53 Longfellow, *Kéramos and Other Poems*, 10.

54 Longfellow, *Kéramos and Other Poems*, 24.

55 Henry Wadsworth Longfellow, *The Letters of Henry Wadsworth Longfellow*, vol. 6, ed. Andrew Hilen (Cambridge: Harvard University Press, 1966), 289.

56 Longfellow, *Kéramos and Other Poems*, 5.

NOTES TO PAGES 146–154   213

57 Longfellow, *Kéramos and Other Poems*, 12.

58 Longfellow, *Kéramos and Other Poems*, 13.

59 Longfellow, *Kéramos and Other Poems*, 14.

60 Longfellow, *Kéramos and Other Poems*, 23.

61 J. Samaine Lockwood, "Shopping for the Nation: Women's China Collecting in Late-Nineteenth Century New England." *The New England Quarterly* 81, no. 1 (2008): 70.

62 Longfellow, *Letters* 6, 298. In spite of Longfellow's broader aesthetic focus, contemporary Anglo-American firms were likely the lens through which many readers understood "Kéramos." A local Boston ceramics dealer, for instance, inspired by the publication of "Kéramos," presented Longfellow with a commemorative pitcher featuring the poet's face on both sides and the titles of his most celebrated works along the spout. The pitcher was created by Wedgewood (Longfellow National Historic Site).

63 Longfellow, *Kéramos and Other Poems*, 25.

64 For a reading of *Kéramos* in the contexts of its periodical publication, see Christa Holm Vogelius, "Kéramos" in *Harper's*: The Contexts of Global Collection," *American Periodicals: A Journal of History & Criticism* 23, no. 2 (2013): 142–55.

65 Citations are from the poem's first collection in *Flower-de-Luce and Other Poems*.

66 Henry Wadsworth Longfellow, *Flower-de-Luce and Other Poems* (Boston: Ticknor and Fields, 1867), 49.

67 Longfellow, *Flower-de-Luce*, 49.

68 Longfellow, *Flower-de-Luce*, 50.

69 Marvin Trachtenberg, *The Campanile of the Florence Cathedral, "Giotto's Tower"* (New York: NYU Press, 1971), 3–5.

70 Lene Østermark-Johansen, *Sweetness and Strength: The Reception of Michelangelo in Late Victorian England* (Cambridge: Ashgate, 1998), 17.

71 Lillian Miller, "'An Influence in the Air': Italian Art and American Taste in the Mid-Nineteenth Century," *The Italian Presence in American Art 1760–1860*, ed. Irma Jaffe (New York: Fordham University Press, 1989), 33.

72 Østermark-Johansen, *Sweetness and Strength*, 22.

73 Østermark-Johansen, *Sweetness and Strength*, 33–50.

74 Østermark-Johansen, *Sweetness and Strength*, 60.

75 Østermark-Johansen, *Sweetness and Strength*, 31.

76 Østermark-Johansen, *Sweetness and Strength*, 60.

77 Østermark-Johansen, *Sweetness and Strength*, 47.

78 Østermark-Johansen, *Sweetness and Strength*, 65.

79 Østermark-Johansen, *Sweetness and Strength*, 75–116.

80 Ralph Waldo Emerson, *The Complete Works of Ralph Waldo Emerson* (Boston and New York: Houghton, Mifflin and Co, 1904), 99.

81 Emerson, *The Complete Works of Ralph Waldo Emerson*, 99.

82 John Ruskin, *The Relation Between Michael Angelo and Tintoret, Seventh of the Course of Lectures on Sculpture Delivered at Oxford, 1870–71* (London: Smith, Elder, & Co., 1872), 3.

83 Ruskin, *The Relation Between Michael Angelo and Tintoret*, 7–8.

84 Ruskin, *The Relation Between Michael Angelo and Tintoret*, 13.

214 NOTES TO PAGES 154–165

85 Ruskin, *The Relation Between Michael Angelo and Tintoret*, 16.

86 Ruskin, *The Relation Between Michael Angelo and Tintoret*, 20, 25.

87 Ruskin, *The Relation Between Michael Angelo and Tintoret*, 44.

88 Ruskin, *The Relation Between Michael Angelo and Tintoret*, 44.

89 Ruskin, *The Relation Between Michael Angelo and Tintoret*, 44–45.

90 Ruskin, *The Relation Between Michael Angelo and Tintoret*, 6.

91 Anonymous, "Current Literature: *Michelangelo; a Dramatic Poem*," *The Spectator*, December 8, 1883, 1587.

92 Anonymous, "Literature of the Day," *Lippincott's Magazine* 33 (1884): 110.

93 Henry Wadsworth Longfellow, *The Complete Poetical Works*, ed. Horace Scudder (Boston and New York: Houghton, Mifflin and Company, 1893), xx.

94 Charles Calhoun, *Longfellow: A Rediscovered Life* (Boston: Beacon Press, 2004), 244.

95 Christoph Irmscher, *Longfellow Redux* (Urbana and Chicago: University of Illinois Press, 2006) 142.

96 Henry Wadsworth Longfellow, *Michael Angelo: A Drama* (Houghton, Mifflin, and Co., 1884), 5.

97 These "flowers of song" refer to the translations of Michelangelo's poetry that Longfellow had initially considered including in the drama, but that he eventually excised and published in *Kéramos and Other Poems* (1878). See Irmscher, *Longfellow Redux*, 218–19.

98 Irmscher, *Longfellow Redux*, 143.

99 Henry Wadsworth Longfellow, *The Writings of Henry Wadsworth Longfellow, with Biographical and Critical Notes*, ed. Horace Scudder, vol. 8 (Cambridge: The Riverside Press, 1886), 46.

100 Henry Longfellow, *The Poetical Works of Henry Wadsworth Longfellow* (Boston: Houghton, Mifflin and Company, 1884).

101 See Longfellow, *The Poetical Works of Henry Wadsworth Longfellow*; Longfellow, *The Writings of HWL*.

102 Henry Wadsworth Longfellow Papers, Houghton Library, Harvard University.

103 Henry Wadsworth Longfellow Papers.

104 Longfellow, *Letters*, vol. 5, 534.

105 Qtd. in Edward L. Tucker, "References in Longfellow's *Journals (1856–1882)* to his Important Literary Works," *Studies in the American Renaissance*, ed. Joel Myerson (Charlottesville: University Press of Virginia, 1994), 343.

106 These volumes are: *Christus: A Mystery* (1872), *Aftermath* (1873), *The Hanging of the Crane* (1875), *The Masque of Pandora and Other Poems* (1875), *Kéramos and Other Poems* (1878), *Ultima Thule* (1880), and *In the Harbor* (1882). Longfellow also published *The Early Poems* (1878) but this volume consists of work from many decades before, most of which had been published in newspapers and magazines.

107 Qtd. in Tucker, "References in Longfellow's *Journals*," 342.

108 Qtd. in Tucker, "References in Longfellow's *Journals*," 342.

109 Østermark-Johansen, *Sweetness and Strength*, 22.

110 Emilio Goggio, "The Sources of Longfellow's *Michael Angelo*," *The Romantic Review* 25 (1934): 314–24.

NOTES TO PAGES 165–169   215

111 Tucker, "References in Longfellow's *Journals*," 342–43.

112 Anonymous, "Literature of the Day," *Lippincott's Magazine* 33 (1884): 110.

113 Goggio, "The Sources of Longfellow's *Michael Angelo*": 319.

114 Fuller, "Poems," 158.

115 The text's illustrations highlight its function as a cobbled museum-piece. Images of Rome, Venice, and Florence intersperse its pages, alongside of portraits of key figures in the play and images of some of Michelangelo's most famous statues. The portraits, as the endnotes specify, are loosely based on historical portraits of well-known figures in the text. Often, individual portraits of characters are merged into compositions adapted to fit the events of the play. In the first scene, for instance, Julia and Vittoria are pictured on a balcony in an engraving composed expressly for the volume; an earlier picture of Julia Gonzago is based on a historical portrait. Other composite portraits feature images of Michelangelo next to his servant, Michelangelo in the Coliseum with Cavalieri, and Michelangelo examining a painting with Titian and Vasari. In all of these compositions, the figure of Michelangelo is closely based on the two reproductions of historical portraits in the frontispiece to the play. Images of Michelangelo's work are treated in a similar manner, as single pieces of sculpture become composite images. Near the end of the book, a three-paneled engraving combines a line drawing of Michelangelo's *Moses*, a more fleshed-out image of Michelangelo working on his *Pietà*, and a line drawing of his *Madonna and Child*. The title page to the second section of the play features an engraving of what appears to be the ornate wall of an exhibition hall. Two of Michelangelo's statues are embedded into wall niches in the left and right of the engraving (*Rebellious Slave* and *Dying Slave*) and the frame in the middle displays Michelangelo's chalk sketch of Vittoria Colonna. That these three works could never have been displayed in this manner is highlighted by their distorted proportions: the sketch of Colonna appears as large as the seven-foot statues. This image is not a reconstruction, but an imaginative recreation of a fictionalized history, much like the individual scenes of the play. The scenes function not to lay out a cohesive factual narrative, but to assemble pieces of different narratives, presenting a collage of historical anecdotes and perspectives in a new, never before-seen form. Longfellow's editors, like Longfellow himself, were tasteful "arrangers."

116 Henry Wadsworth Longfellow, *Michael Angelo, a Dramatic Poem* (Boston: Houghton, Mifflin and Company, 1884), ix.

117 Longfellow, *Michael Angelo*, 148.

118 Longfellow, *Michael Angelo*, 158.

119 Longfellow, *Michael Angelo*, 143.

120 Longfellow, *Michael Angelo*, 143.

121 Longfellow, *Michael Angelo*, 143.

122 Longfellow, *Michael Angelo*, 147.

123 Longfellow, *Michael Angelo*, 5.

124 Longfellow, *Michael Angelo*, 147.

125 Longfellow, *Michael Angelo*, 147.

126 Longfellow, *The Writings of HWL*, 152. This passage is dated September 30, 1850.

127 Longfellow, *Michael Angelo*, 178

128 Longfellow, *The Writings of HWL*, 406.
129 Longfellow, *Letters* 5, 722.
130 Longfellow, *The Writings of HWL*, 405.
131 Longfellow, *Michael Angelo*, 69, 63.
132 Longfellow, *Michael Angelo*, 105.
133 Longfellow, *Michael Angelo*, 106.
134 Longfellow, *Michael Angelo*, 15.
135 Longfellow, *Michael Angelo*, 15.
136 Longfellow, *Michael Angelo*, 35–36.
137 Longfellow, *Michael Angelo*, 36.
138 Longfellow, *Michael Angelo*, 37.
139 Longfellow, *Michael Angelo*, 149.
140 Longfellow, *Michael Angelo*, 97.
141 Longfellow, *Michael Angelo*, 163.
142 Longfellow, *Michael Angelo*, 129.
143 Longfellow, *Michael Angelo*, 166.
144 Longfellow, *Michael Angelo*, 101.
145 Longfellow, *Michael Angelo*, 164.

CODA

1 Claudia Rankine, *Citizen: An American Lyric* (Minneapolis, MN: Graywolf Press, 2014), 151.
2 Rankine, *Citizen*, 79.
3 Rankine, *Citizen*, 29.
4 Elissa Zellinger, *Lyrical Strains: Liberalism and Women's Poetry in Nineteenth-Century America* (Chapel Hill: University of North Carolina Press, 2020), 4.
5 Rankine, *Citizen*, 28, 32.
6 Claudia Rankine, *Don't Let Me Be Lonely: An American Lyric* (Minneapolis, MN: Graywolf Press, 2004), 5, 16.
7 Rankine, *Don't Let Me Be Lonely*, 91.
8 Emma Kimberly, "Politics and Poetics of Fear after 9/11: Claudia Rankine's "Don't Let Me Be Lonely" *Journal of American Studies* 45, no. 4 (November 2011): 782, 789.
9 Rankine, *Don't Let Me Be Lonely*, 53, 89, 55, 54.
10 Kimberly, "Politics and Poetics," 789.
11 Rankine, *Don't Let Me Be Lonely*, 77, 62.
12 Rankine, *Don't Let Me Be Lonely*, 98.
13 Jacques Rancière, *The Emancipated Spectator*, trans. Gregory Elliot (New York and London: Verso, 2011), 15.
14 James Heffernan, *Cultivating Picturacy: Visual Art and Verbal Interventions* (Waco, TX: Baylor University Press, 2006).

Index

abolitionism: and authorship, 56; and citizenship, 47; and freed slaves, 46, 47; and Joseph Lavallée, 46; and *Liberator* (newspaper), 32, 33, 46–47; and literary nationalism, 40, 45; and patriotism, 47; and Phillis Wheatley Peters, 40, 45–47, 57; and race, 49. *See also* Odell, Margaretta

African Americans: and belonging, 176, 178; and Black Ekphrasis, 5–6, 32; and citizenship, 178–179; and *Freedom's Journal*, 46; and identity, 49–50, 178; and national dialogues, 10–11, 32, 33, 47–48, 49; and Phillis Wheatley Peters, 41–42, 46, 47, 49, 50–52, 53, 59; and police violence, 177, 178; and publication, 47, 65; and race, 52, 179, 180; and representation in art, 10–11, 59–60, 180; and slavery, 64, 192n11; and spectatorship, 179; and spirituality, 42; and statelessness, 178. *See also* slavery; Williams, Serena

African diaspora, 31

Alexander, Elizabeth, 6

Alison, Archibald, 23, 24

Allen, Mary Ware, 73–78, 80, 83, 199n60

Allen, William, 47

Allston, Washington, 82, 113, 114, 116

Alphabeto Christiano (de Valdés), 165

American Female Poets, The (May), 18

American Poetry, 175

American Renaissance (Matthiessen), 13, 132

Anderson, Benedict, 12

anthologies, 17–20, 40, 45, 57, 159, 174–75

Art of Cruelty, The (Nelson), 11–12

Ashmolean Museum (Oxford), 152

Asia, 147

associationism, 22–24, 68, 70–71, 79, 84, 198n37

Beam, Dorri, 22, 70

Before Modernism (Jackson), 57

Beloved (Morrison), 58

Beneath the American Renaissance (Reynolds), 14

Bhabha, Homi, 10–11

Black Atlantic culture, 29, 30, 31, 52

Black Atlantic: Modernity and Double Consciousness, The (Gilroy), 29

Black Ekphrasis, 5–6, 22, 32, 33, 60–61, 63–64

Blithedale Romance, The (Hawthorne), 105

Boggs, Colleen, 67, 68

Boston, Massachusetts, 30, 31, 35, 37, 41, 53. *See also* United States

Bowdoin College, 135, 136, 138

Bradstreet, Ann{~?~SN: Check spelling}{~?~BK: It IS Anne, and it needs to be corrected in the main MS file as well. }e, 43

Britain, 31, 34, 42, 50

Brodhead, Richard, 104–105

Brooks, Van Wyck, 132

Brown, Ann Frances, 73

Bryan, Thomas Jefferson, 150

Buell, Lawrence, 132

Burkett, Randall, 37, 39

Butler, Judith, 8

Byron, Lord George, 89

Caesar, Julius, 125

Cape Cod (Thoreau), 93

Caretta, Vincent, 35, 37, 47, 48, 57, 64
Catlin, George, 82, 136
Cenci, Beatrice, 1–2, 26, 127, 129–30, 185n2, 185n4
ceramics, 145–47, 151, 211n30, 212n44, 213n61
Césaire, Aimé, 180
Channing, William Henry, 71, 72
Child, Lydia Maria, 45–46, 47, 69
Citizen (Rankine), 27–28, 176–80, 182
Civil War, 15, 102, 106, 138, 212n44
Clarke, James Freeman, 72, 86
Clarke, Sarah Freeman, 82, 86
Clarke, William, 86
Cohen, Lara Langer, 20
Copley, John Singleton, 59
Craigie House, 141, 142–143, 212n41
Cyclopedia of American Literature (Duyckincks'), 17, 18, 43

Daughters of the American Revolution (DAR), 138
da Vinci, Leonardo, 5, 169
Davis, Theo, 22, 23
della Notte, Gherardo, 111
Democratic Review, The, 16, 18, 26
de Tocqueville, Alexis, 19
Dimoch, Wai Chi, 88, 96
Distant Reading (Moretti), 6
Don't Let Me Be Lonely (Rankine), 27–28, 176, 180–183
Duyckinck, Evert, 13, 15, 16, 17, 18, 25.
    See also Fuller, Margaret; Hawthorne, Nathaniel; nationalism
Duyckinck, George, 17, 43

Eagle's Nest Arts Colony, 100
ekphrasis: and adaptation, 28; and American literary culture, 1–4, 7–11, 26–28, 63; and American monuments, 188n32; and American "originality", 3, 4, 9, 11; and artistic creativity, 4, 10, 11–12, 61; and artwork, 3, 4, 5, 7, 9, 10, 11–12, 24, 28, 82; and art writing, 2, 3, 4, 7, 9–10, 11, 26–27; and audience, 82–83, 109; and "Beatrice Cenci" (Piatt), 185n2; and collectivity,

28, 183; and content, 109, 180; and convention, 9, 23, 24, 28; and copies, 130; and craft, 142, 144; and creativity, 127; definitions of, 1, 5, 12, 183, 186n7; and depiction of Ganymede, 92, 183; and directions to artist, 188n32; and ekphrastic works as base, 185n6; and essays, 3, 5–6; and European ekphrasis, 26; and female writers, 3, 4, 5, 6–10, 24, 26–27, 186n10, 188n32; feminist reconsiderations of, 10; and feminized writers, 176; and fragmentation, 138; and gender, 7, 12, 14, 88, 109; as a genre, 2, 3, 4–5, 7, 8, 10, 14, 27–28, 70; and images, 1–2, 3, 5, 6–7, 9–10, 12, 23–24, 28, 59, 82, 88, 183, 186n7; and imitation, 3–4, 11, 24, 28, 82, 111; and Lake Trasimene, 121; and Longfellow's work, 142, 144, 158; and magazines, 7; and male writers, 5, 6, 10; and Margaret Fuller, 84; and media, 6, 9–10, 23–24, 27, 28; and mediation, 3, 4; and memory, 58–59; and modernism, 5; and museums, 185n5; and nation, 9, 10–11, 12, 14, 24, 27, 176, 183; and national self-consciousness, 16, 183; and "Niobe in Distress for her Children Slain by Apollo" (Peters), 43–44; and novels, 1; and "On a Portrait Owned by H. W. Longfellow and Painted by Tintoretto", 141; and originality, 82, 109; and otherness, 5, 6; and periodical press, 6–7; Peters's practice of, 43–44, 58–61, 63–64; and physical forms, 10; and plays, 1, 3; and poetry, 1, 3, 5–6, 37, 58–61, 63–64, 82, 85, 88, 181, 212n41; and political issues, 3, 10–11; and postcolonial ekphrasis, 6; and public/private space, 102–103, 108–109; and race, 14; and remediation, 25, 28, 80, 82, 136-137, 166; and reproduction, 3, 4, 10; and Romantics, 5, 6; and Sigourney's "Lady Jane Grey", 9; and Sophia Hawthorne, 108, 109, 112, 114–15, 125, 127, 130; and text as masculine, 5, 109; and text to image,

112; and "The Last Supper" (Sigourney), 9, 188n32; and a "third thing", 59, 183; and Titian painting, 127; and travelogues, 1, 3, 4, 9, 102–104, 109; and triangulated structure, 93; as a veil, 104; and visual medium, 137, 183; and Western Ekphrasis, 5; and white male writers, 5; and W. J. T. Mitchell, 59; and women's writing, 4, 7, 10, 16, 24, 26, 102–107; and word-painting, 114; and writers of color, 5–6. *See also* associationism; Black Ekphrasis; Fuller, Margaret; mimesis; Rankine, Claudia

"Ekphrastic Poetry and the Middle Passage" (Plasa), 5–6

Elements of Rhetoric (Whately), 74

Emerson, Ralph Waldo: and American nature, 211n25; and copying, 101, 117, 118, 119; and cultural nationalism, 13; and European muses, 117, 120; and European travel, 208n80; home of, 143; and ideas of history, 119, 120, 121; and intertextuality, 15; and literary nationalism, 117; and Longfellow's art, 140; and Margaret Fuller, 72; and Michelangelo's work, 152–153, 163, 164, 165, 170; and originality, 21, 69, 117; *Poems* of, 117; and Sophia Hawthorne, 103, 115–121; and *Southern Quarterly Review*, 117

Emory University, 35, 65

Euclid, 55

Europe: and America, 84, 94, 97, 165; and England, 113, 120, 122, 127, 147, 151, 152, 165, 174; Florence in, 144, 146, 148, 149; Gaul in, 120; and Great Masters of Art and Architecture, 101, 123; and Hannibal, 119; and Hawthorne family, 101, 116; high-art canon of, 150; Holland in, 147; and Holy Roman Emperor, 144; and human sacrifice, 110; and Italy, 147, 149, 154, 174, 208n80, 215n114; and literature, 67, 107, 117, 144; Longfellow's visit to, 138, 144; and museums, 135, 152–54; and Northern Europe, 147; and

Ponte Vecchio, 144; Rome in, 1, 2, 92, 103–4, 110, 112, 118, 119, 120, 121, 163, 215n114; touring of, 66, 107, 109–10, 135; and travelogues, 107, 135. *See also* Britain; *Michael Angelo: A Fragment* (Longfellow)

Evangeline (Longfellow), 136, 139, 142

Female Poets of America, The (Griswold), 18, 19, 40–41, 54

Female Poets of America, The (Read), 19

femininity: and art objects, 109; and convention, 15–16; and derivation, 4, 8; and domesticity, 8, 107; and "fancy", 54; and gender, 7–8; and Henry Longfellow, 132, 133, 134, 149; and histories of reading, 14; and images, 5, 7; and imitation, 8, 15, 132; and male writers, 8; and nationalism, 15–16; and originality, 15–16; and painting, 172; and private sphere, 102; as signifier, 4, 8; and women writers, 102, 204n3, 205n25

Fern, Fanny, 102

Ford, James Edward, III,{~?~SN: CMS reccomends a comma preceed the roman numerals— Ford, James Edward, III, . . . [15.49]} 5, 6, 61, 64

Fourierism, 22, 68, 71, 198n37

Freeman, William, 95

Freneau, Philip, 12

Fuller, Hiram, 73, 75

Fuller, Margaret: and American literature, 16, 18, 24, 25–27, 66–72, 78–80, 83–85, 88, 94, 95; and "American Literature", 131; and American West, 25–26, 66, 69, 79–80, 81 fig. 5, 86, 88; and artwork, 26, 70–71, 78, 82, 85, 88–89, 99; biography of, 86; and blackberries, 98; and classical European mythologies, 88; and classical figures, 92; and Conversations, 75–78; and creativity, 26, 71, 80, 82, 99; and critique of Longfellow, 131, 132, 133, 165–66; and "deep time", 96; and "Del Sarto's Madonna", 82; and *The Dial*, 72, 85, 99; and the Divine, 202n120;

220 INDEX

Fuller, Margaret (*continued*)
and Duyckinck's network, 24; and
eagle as symbol, 88–89, 90, 93–94;
and ekphrasis, 70–71, 82–83, 84, 85,
88–89, 92; essays of, 67, 91–92, 131;
and European movements, 24, 66;
and Evert Duyckinck, 91, 99; and
feminism, 199n50; and feminized
traditions, 4; and Fourth of July, 86,
96; fragmentary style of, 69–70, 99;
and freedom, 67; and fusion, 67–72,
79, 82, 87, 88, 95, 97; and "Ganymede
to his Eagle" (poem), 85–95, 96,
202n120; and gender binary, 7; and
images, 84, 85, 86, 88, 89, 95; and
imitation, 71, 75, 84–85, 88, 94, 95,
99; and Indigenous life, 91, 94; and
journals, 72–80, 84, 85, 86; and Jove,
93; and knowledge, 26, 71, 75–76;
and Lake Michigan, 99; as literary
editor, 100; and literary nationalism,
131; and Longfellow's work, 9, 69,
70, 131, 134, 135–136, 137, 159; and
Michelangelo, 164; and narratives,
66, 69, 71–72, 76, 79–80, 85, 86, 88,
89, 92, 100; and nation, 77–78, 86–87,
88, 90–91, 96; and Native Americans,
202n115; and nature, 86, 89, 92, 96;
and Niagara{~?~SN: Check spelling}
{~?~BK: OK as is.} Falls, 82, 85, 89,
90; and originality, 69, 70, 77, 82, 84,
94, 99; and *Papers on Literature and
Art*, 67; and pedagogy, 67, 70, 71–78,
83, 85; poetry of, 66, 69, 79–88, 89,
92, 93–97, 98; and the public, 80; and
race, 67–68, 87, 94, 95; and reader's
role, 68, 70–72, 100; relationships
of, 86; and reproduction in writing,
76–77; and self-expression, 25, 70;
and "Silenus, holding in his arms the
infant Pan", 82; and the subterranean,
88, 91; and Temple School, 75; and
translation, 67, 88; and travelogues,
25–26, 66, 69, 79, 82, 85, 86, 88, 89;
and triangulation, 84, 99; and Viking
gods, 85; Western travels of, 24, 66,
82, 86, 87, 88; and women's education,
25, 26, 72–78, 94. *See also* Greene
Street School; *Memoirs of Margaret
Fuller Ossoli* (Fuller)

Gaddi, 144
Gale, Hannah, 73
Ganymede, 86–87, 92, 183, 202n120. *See
also* Fuller, Margaret
"Ganymede with Jupiter's Eagle"
(Thorvaldsen), 87 fig. 6
Garrison, William Lloyd, 46, 47
Gates, Henry Louis, 55, 57
Giles, Paul, 15
Gilroy, Paul, 29, 30, 52
Giotto, 148, 149, 150
"Giotto's Tower"{~?~SN: Check typog-
raphy— italics and quotes?}{~?~BK:
Just quotes (needs to follow usage in
MS)} (Longfellow), 143, 148–50, 158,
159, 163, 170
Godey's Lady's Book (magazine), 16,
187n17
Goethe, Johann von, 88, 93, 99, 201n97,
202n120
Gould, Hannah, 46
Graham's Magazine, 7, 209n2
Greater, Francis, 139
Greeley, Horace, 99–100
Greene Street School, 71, 73, 74–76
Greenough, Horatio, 92, 112
Greenwood, Emily, 37
Gregoire, Abbé, 42, 43
Griswold, Rufus, 17–20, 21, 40–41, 43, 47,
48. *See also* Peters, Phillis Wheatley
Gumbs, Pauline, 30

Hancock, John, 54
Haralson, Eric, 133
Harper's (magazine), 7, 145, 146
Hawthorne, Nathaniel: and American
literature, 13, 18, 101, 103, 105, 106,
129; and *Blackwood's* article, 207n76;
career of, 208n87; characters of,
121, 129; death of, 106, 108, 116,
121, 208n91; and Evert Duyckinck,
26; journals of, 123; and literary
illustration, 7; and *Passages from the*

English Note-books, 121; portrait of, 140; and Sophia Hawthorne, 101, 103, 105–8, 121, 125–26; and trope of veil, 128, 208n91; and Veiled Lady, 105; and women writers, 103, 105, 106

Hawthorne, Sophia: and aestheticization, 125–27; as an artist, 24, 26, 101, 105, 108, 115, 116; children of, 122, 126; and convention, 26, 107; and copies, 26, 101, 102, 109, 110–17, 129; and creativity, 26, 113, 114, 116; "Cuba Journal" of, 105–6, 208n87, 209n97; and descriptions of artwork, 103–4, 108–115, 117–119, 126–127, 129, 208n83; diary of, 122, 124 fig. 7; and ekphrasis, 121, 125, 127–128, 130, 206–207nn60; and England, 127; and feminized traditions, 4, 102; and Great Masters of Art and Architecture, 110, 123; and Hawthorne family, 108–109, 121–122, 126–128, 205–206nn37; and husband's biography, 121; and illustrated journals, 108, 126; and London, 122; and Madonna (by Raphael), 104, 118; and malaria, 110, 122; and mimesis, 122; and mimicry, 26–27; and Nathaniel Hawthorne, 101, 105, 106, 107–108, 121, 125–126; and *Notes in England and Italy*, 79, 101–102, 107–109; and originality, 26–27, 101, 102, 113, 114–117, 122, 127–128; and Pre-Raphaelite painters, 111; and preservation of art, 129, 206n47; and private/public spheres, 104–107, 108, 114–115, 122, 129; and publication, 106, 107–108, 205n33, 208n87, 209n97; and readers, 104, 126, 129; and relationship with Ralph Emerson, 116–20, 208n80; and Rome, 126, 129; sister of, 105–6, 108, 119, 120, 208n87; and spirituality, 111; and translation, 26; and travelogues, 26–27, 101, 102–3, 106, 108–9, 114, 115, 119; and trope of veil, 103, 104–5, 122, 129, 204n10; and use of ellipses, 123, 208–209nn96; and women's writing, 129, 130; and Young America circle, 24. *See also Notes in England and Italy* (Hawthorne)

Heffernan, James, 5, 14, 183, 186n10
Hiawatha (Longfellow), 136, 142
Homes of American Authors (Putnam), 143
Horace, 37
Horton, George Moses, 32, 47
Howell, William Huntting, 21, 74
Hutchinson, Governor Thomas, 54

Interesting Narrative (Equino), 46
In the Wake: On Blackness and Being (Sharpe), 29
Irmsher, Christoph, 132, 133, 140, 156, 158
Irving, Washington, 12, 143

Jackson, Virginia, 57, 58, 61, 132, 141, 209–210nn2
James, Henry, 2, 158
Japan, 146, 147
Jarves, James Jackson, 135, 150, 151
Jeffers, Honorée Fanonne, 6
Jefferson, Thomas, 55, 57
"Joining Copies" (various authors), 35–40, 65
Jordan, June, 65

Kames, Lord, 23
Kavanaugh (Longfellow), 136
Keats, John, 5, 186n10
Kennedy, J. Gerald, 14–15
"*Kéramos and Other Poems*" (Longfellow), 143, 145–48, 158, 162, 213n61, 214n96
Kete, Mary Louise, 50, 60, 132, 196n88
Kirkland, Caroline, 16
Knapp, George, 46
Knapp, Isaac, 47

Laocoon: Or, On the Limits of Painting and Poetry (Lessing), 5, 186n10, 201n97
Larcom, Lucy, 47
Last Judgment (Michaelangelo), 163
Leslie, Alex, 15, 18
Lessing, Gotthold Ephraim, 6, 186n10, 201n97
Letters from New York (Child), 69

Levine, Lawrence, 135
Levine, Robert, 14–15
Liberator, The (newspaper), 32, 33, 46–47
Liberia, 46, 47
Life and Literary Works of Michael Angelo Buonarroti, The (Duppa), 151
Life on the Mississippi (Twain), 1
Light, George, 49, 52
Literary World, The (Duyckinck), 15, 16
Longfellow, Charles, 139
Longfellow, Ernest, 139
Longfellow, Fanny, 139
Longfellow, Henry Wadsworth: and adaptation, 9, 131; aesthetics of, 27, 137–39, 145, 175, 213n61; and American literature, 24–25, 27, 69, 70, 82, 131–32, 147; and art collection, 27, 134, 137, 138, 139, 140–42, 144, 145, 147–48, 157, 211n30; and art objects, 138–141, 143, 148, 158, 211n30, 212n39; and art writing, 133–134, 143; canon of, 174–175; career of, 210n14; and Christians, 149; and craftsmanship, 139, 141–142, 145–146; and creation, 148, 158; and cross gendered sensibility, 133; death of, 143, 159, 162, 174, 210n14; and domestic writing, 132, 139–140, 141; and ekphrasis, 137, 138, 142, 143, 144, 158, 212n41; family of, 139–140, 141; and feminized traditions, 4, 18; and fragmentation, 133, 136, 144, 148, 150, 158–165, 166–167; and imagery, 131–132, 138–140, 146, 158; and imitation, 27, 131, 146–147, 156; and international travel, 140, 145, 146; and intertextuality, 140; and literary nationalism, 136, 147; and "Longfellow Wars", 131, 132, 209–210nn2; and Michelangelo's work and life, 164–174, 214n96; as "middle-class" writer, 27, 134, 135–37, 157, 159, 174; and Mississippi River Valley, 136, 139; and Nature, 69, 145, 158, 167, 171, 172–73, 211n19, 211n25; and originality, 27, 69, 132, 133, 141–42, 145, 156–57, 172–75; as a poet, 27, 131–39, 141–50, 157–60, 162, 214n105; readers of, 132, 141–42,

162; and scholarship, 165–66; and sonnet-form, 149, 157, 158; and world literatures, 136. *See also "Kéramos"* (Longfellow); *Michael Angelo: A Fragment* (Longfellow); *Selected Poems* (Longfellow)
Longfellow Collectors' Hand-book: A Bibliography of First Editions, 174, 175
Lorenzo and Jessica (Allston), 116

Maine Historical Society, 139
masculinity: construction of, 8; and gender, 7–8; and Henry Longfellow, 131, 132, 133, 134, 146; and innovation, 22, 33; and Michelangelo, 133, 159; and originality, 22; and painting, 172; and writers, 9, 133
Massachusetts Historical Society (MHS), 138
Matthews, Cornelius, 136
May, Caroline, 18, 19, 47
Melville, Herman, 13, 26, 67
Memoir (Odell), 57
Memoirs of Margaret Fuller Ossoli (Fuller), 72
Metcalf, Evelina, 73
Michaelangelo: and architectural work, 152, 171, 173; biographies of, 151, 153, 155, 156, 165, 174; and complexity, 150, 165, 174; and copying, 112, 113, 118, 206n51; as craftsman and artist, 27, 153, 154, 155, 156, 157, 171–174; drawings by, 152, 153; English collection of, 152, 153, 154; and fragmentation, 134, 157; frescos of, 152, 172; grandeur of, 133, 151; and Longfellow's work, 144, 156–163, 166–174; and love of Rome, 166; and mastery of art, 171; and Nature, 152; and originality, 133, 156, 157; and painting, 152, 171–173; poetry of, 151–152, 162, 214n96; sculptures of, 152, 171–74, 183, 215n114; and Sistine fresco Judge, 113; translations of, 151–52, 162, 214n96; and unity, 157; and years "1480 to 1520", 154. *See also Michael Angelo: A Fragment* (Longfellow)

Michael Angelo: A Fragment (Longfellow): and architectural work, 172–73; and audience, 143, 153; and beauty, 171, 172; and Coliseum, 166, 167, 173, 215n114; and creator, 148, 158, 159, 162–163, 173; death and rebirth in, 158–59, 161–62, 164, 167–70; and "Dedication" sonnet, 157–59, 160 fig. 9, 166, 167, 170; and *The Dial*, 166; and ekphrasis, 134, 158; "final copy" of, 161–62; and fragmentation, 159–65, 168; and Giotto's tower, 167; God in, 168, 169; and history, 159, 163, 166; illustrations in, 166, 175, 215n114; and individuality, 150; and life of Michelangelo, 27, 133–34, 153, 155, 159, 163, 175; and *Madonna and Child* drawing, 215n114; and nature, 172–173; and originality, 150, 159, 163, 166, 175; photograph of, 164 fig. 10; and plays, 27, 133, 155–56, 159, 161–65, 168–69, 174, 175; and portraits, 215n114; publications of, 175; and remediation, 136–37; Roman setting of, 166–67; and sculpture's merits, 172; and Sistine Chapel, 170, 172; and theme of unfinished work, 169–70; and unity, 159, 162, 163, 170–71; verse of, 155–59; Vittoria Colonna in, 163, 169, 170–71, 215n114

Mill, John Stuart, 68

Milton, John, 31

mimesis, 3, 10, 15, 21, 102, 109. *See also* Hawthorne, Sophia

Mitchell, W. J. T., 4–5, 6, 8, 12, 14, 186n10. *See also* ekphrasis

modernists, 5, 6, 8, 58, 83, 84, 186n10

Moore, Thomas, 144

Moorhead, Scipio, 59, 60, 61, 63, 64, 183

Morrison, Toni, 58, 59

Mowatt, Anna, 16

nationalism: from 1830s to the1880s, 16; and American literary culture, 11–28, 32–33, 66, 67, 94–95, 134; and American travelers, 109; and antebellum nationalism, 14–15, 25, 189n47; and biography, 51; and

Black nationalism, 57; and Christian nationalism, 42; and Common Sense school, 68; and convention, 13, 15–16, 21–23, 33; critique of, 181; and cultural nationalism, 13, 20, 29, 33, 51, 56, 65, 68; and "deep time", 91; and democracy, 13; and dictionaries, 21; and ekphrasis, 13–14, 16; and European models, 13, 15, 67, 85, 147; and Evert Duyckinck, 67; and gender, 14, 16, 17, 19, 40–41, 43; and Henry Longfellow, 136, 147; and imagination, 4, 13, 15; and imitation, 3, 16, 19–21, 22, 33; and immigration, 96; and literary nationalism, 12–28, 32, 40, 67, 68, 85–87, 102, 109, 110, 211n19; and Margaret Fuller, 70, 82, 85–87, 90–91, 93–97, 99; and Nathaniel Hawthorne, 26; and New England, 16, 25, 67; and North American environment, 211n25; and originality, 13, 15, 19–21, 22, 24; and poetry, 20, 37; and political concerns, 15, 22, 110; and race, 22, 32, 42, 43, 93; and regional culture, 15, 16, 19, 21, 24–25; and rural western landscapes, 66; and servitude, 94, 110; and Sophia Hawthorne, 26, 103, 109–10; and transnationalism, 15, 16; and Viking explorers, 92–93; and westward expansion, 13; and white imperialism, 15; and women writers, 4, 13, 15, 16–22, 40–41, 45; and Young American movement, 67, 136. *See also Democratic Review, The*; Emerson, Ralph Waldo

Native Americans: and American identity, 96; and America's landscape, 93; and Black Hawk, 90, 91, 94–95, 100; and burial mounds, 88, 91, 96; and Fuller's aesthetic, 95–96; and longing, 94–95; and Mohawks, 92; and painter George Catlin, 82, 136; and racial hierarchy, 202n115; removal of, 85, 90, 91–92, 94, 95, 201n103; and reservations, 202n115; settlements of, 66; and understanding the US, 85–86

Nature (Emerson), 99

New York: and education, 95; family in, 35; and Knickerbocker camp, 16, 27; and nationalism, 26; and New York Historical Society, 138; and trend of copying, 95; and upstate New York, 66; and William Evarts Benjamin, 174; and Young America circle, 13, 15, 16, 18, 19, 24

New-York Tribune (newspaper), 99–100

Nias, Georgiana, 74

North American Review, The, 134

Notes in England and Italy (Hawthorne): and American literary culture, 26–27, 101–2, 106–9; and artwork, 122; and creativity, 26, 102, 103; and descriptions of Madonnas, 26; and ekphrasis, 127, 130; and gender, 102; and Great Masters of Art and Architecture, 108, 115; and Hawthorne family, 102, 103, 107–8, 115, 123, 125; and illustrated journals, 26; Italian section of, 101, 103–4, 108, 109–14, 118–21; and nationalism, 103, 109; and original/copy distinction, 102–3, 110–15, 118–19, 122–23, 127–28; and originality, 109, 115, 117–18, 120–21, 125, 127–29; and preservation of art, 110–12, 114; public and private life in, 108–9, 114–15, 122–23, 125; publication of, 107–8, 109, 129; and Renaissance paintings, 110–11; and sculpture room, 125; and travelogues, 26–27, 79, 102–3, 106–7, 109–10, 122–23; and trope of veil, 121

Notes on the State of Virginia (Jefferson), 55

Odell, Margaretta: and biography, 33, 42–46, 48–53, 56, 60, 64; and equality, 52; and gender, 53; and imitation, 52; institutionalization of, 48–49, 51; and memory, 52–56; and nation, 49–52; and originality, 52; and race, 49–50, 51, 52–53; and Wheatley family, 48, 49, 50–51

"Ode on a Grecian Urn" (Keats), 5

"Old Bridge at Florence, The" (Longfellow), 143, 144, 148

Osgood, Fanny, 16–17, 102

Ovid, 43–44

Paradise (Tintoretto), 154

Peabody, Elizabeth Palmer, 75, 77, 101, 105–6, 108, 115–16. *See also* Hawthorne, Sophia

Peters, John, 51

Peters, Phillis Wheatley: and abolitionists, 25, 46–47; and "A Farewell to America", 41–42; and African American artists, 25, 34, 35, 60–61, 63; and African American authors, 32–33, 45; and "A Hymn to Humanity", 35, 37–39; and American literary history, 51–53, 54; and Americanness, 64; biography of, 33, 42–43, 45, 46, 48–52, 56, 57, 60, 64; and Boston, 60, 63; and "Celestial" sphere, 63, 64; children of, 44; and citizenship, 52, 65; and collectivity, 39, 60, 61; and convention, 39, 45, 56; and creativity, 33, 34, 39, 54–55, 60–61, 63–64; criticism of, 55, 56–57, 61; death of, 45; and derivation, 25, 57; and dominant tradition, 22, 31, 33, 57; and Duyckinck brothers, 43, 44, 46–47; education of, 37, 39; and ekphrasis, 33, 34, 43–44, 58–61, 63–64; and "Fancy: from a Poem on the Imagination", 54; and freedom, 44, 45, 51, 56, 60, 63–64; husband of, 42–43, 51; and imitation, 32, 37, 39–40, 46, 54, 55, 57; and *Liberator* (newspaper), 33, 46–47; and literary networks, 37–38, 39; and memory, 53–59; name of, 30, 34–35, 43, 51, 65, 193n16; and nation, 24, 25, 32, 33, 34, 37, 41–43, 45, 47, 48, 49, 50–53, 56, 57, 64, 65; and "Niobe in Distress for her Children Slain by Apollo", 43–44; and "On Being Brought to America", 42, 57; and "On Recollection" (poem), 57–59; and originality, 25, 32, 33, 56; poetry of, 25, 30–35, 37–47, 52–65, 193n17; and political poems, 56; and Pope's neoclassicism, 43; portrait of, 59–61, 62 fig.4; and publication, 59,

65, 192n11; and race, 53, 55, 56, 59, 60; readers of, 59; and reference to Damon, 63–64; and religious themes, 38–39, 41–42; and Revolutionary War, 51; and Rufus Griswold, 54; as a slave, 30–32, 34, 39, 41, 50–51, 59, 60; and "The Voice of Freedom", 37, 38 fig. 3; and transit of slavery, 192n9; and transnationalism, 24, 30–32, 34, 64; and Wheatley family, 53. *See also* Odell, Margaretta; "To S. M., a Young African Painter, on Seeing his Works" (Peters)

Poe, Edgar Allen: and American literary culture, 18, 20–21, 209–210nn2; and imitation, 131; and literary nationalism, 16; and Margaret Fuller, 100; and mimicry, 188n25; and original and copy, 188n25; and poetesses, 188n25

Poems of Places (editor Longfellow), 174

Poems on Various Subjects, Religious and Moral (Peters), 25, 31–32, 33

Julius III (pope), 173

"Portrait of Beatrice Cenci" (Reni), 1–2, 2 fig. 1

Putzi. Jennifer, 22

queer theory, 7, 8, 11

Rancière, Jacques, 11, 12, 59

Rankine, Claudia: and belonging, 27–28, 176, 178; and citizenship, 178–79; and collectivity, 180–83; and dominant tradition, 22, 181–82; and ekphrasis, 80, 181, 183; and images, 176–83; and nation, 27–28, 176, 178, 180–83; and popular media, 183; and representation, 11, 181; and spectatorship, 27–28, 176, 180

Raphael: *Belle Jardinière* of, 114; copying of, 112–13; drawings by, 123; grace of, 146; and painting, 104, 173; self-portrait of, 119, 206n47; and years "1480 to 1520", 154

Reading Sideways: The Queer Politics of Art in Modern American Fiction (Seitler), 11

Rembrandt, 123

Reni, Guido, 1, 26, 127, 129–30, 185n4

Richards, Eliza, 15, 20, 21, 54, 188n25

Richmond, M. A., 58

"Rose in Rome/Palazzo Lazarani/Percean Hill" (Hawthorne), 126, 128 fig. 8

Rossetti, Dante Gabriel, 151

Ruskin, John, 152, 153–55, 157, 164, 170

Santayana, George, 132

Sebastiano, Fra, 163, 170–71, 172, 173

Sedgwick, Catharine Maria, 109, 122, , 127, 143

Selected Poems (Longfellow), 132

Senior, Olive, 6

sexuality, 8, 86, 87, 107, 152, 200n87

Shakespeare, William, 37

Shelley, Percy Bysshe, 186n10

Shields, John, 57–58

Showalter, Elaine, 70

Sigourney, Lydia, 9, 10, 46, 47, 188n32, 189n35

slavery: conflict over, 24, 52; and cup-bearer, 90; and domestic slavery, 48, 50–51; and engravings, 215n114; and freedom, 42, 44, 45; and imitation, 22, 33; and Mansfield Act, 42; and narrative, 25, 29–30, 64; and Northern slavery, 44; and Phillis Wheatley Peters, 49, 50, 57, 58, 60, 63, 64; and politics, 37; and relocation of slaves, 45, 46; and Rev. Mr. George Whitefield, 42; and Roman Coliseum, 110; and Scipio Moorhead, 31, 60, 63, 64; and slave ship, 29–30, 34, 178; and slave trade, 5–6, 29–30, 31, 192n9; and Southern slavery, 44; and Wheatley women, 49; and writers, 41, 46, 47, 56, 58, 178. *See also* Peters, Phillis Wheatley

Slave Ship (Turner), 177, 178

Socarides, Alex, 22

Sophia Hawthorne Papers, 122

spectatorship, 11–12, 24, 27–28, 176, 180

Specters of Democracy (Wilson), 10

Spitzer, Leo, 5, 185n5

Stokes, Claudia, 4, 9, 21

Stowe, Harriet Beecher, 105, 107
Sturgis, Cary, 82, 86, 200n87
Summer on the Lakes, in 1843 (Fuller):
and American literary culture, 87–89,
100; and creativity, 70, 84; and cultural blending, 96; and eagle as symbol, 88–91, 93–94; and ekphrasis, 71,
82–83, 92–93; and Evert Duyckinck,
25, 66; and Ganymede, 82, 100; and
images, 68, 71, 84, 88; and journals,
73, 79–80; and linear temporality, 88;
and memory, 90; multi-genre form
of, 69–70; and nationalism, 67, 71–72,
87–91, 97; and poetry, 71, 80–85, 100;
and reader's role, 70–71, 82–83, 97–99;
and travelogues, 66, 69, 71, 72, 78–80,
82, 84, 87, 91

Taft, Lorado, 100
Tawil, Ezra, 21
Terence, 31
Thatcher, B. B., 48
Thompson, Cephas, 118
Thoreau, Henry David, 15, 93
Thorvaldsen, Bertel, 82, 85, 87, 92–93,
99, 107–8
Tintoretto, 153, 154, 155, 212n41
Titian, 154, 163, 170, 172, 215n114
"To S. M., a Young African Painter,
on Seeing his Works" (Peters), 34,
59–61, 63
transcendentalism, 70, 72, 82, 99, 116, 118
transgender studies, 8, 188n27
Treatise on Painting (da Vinci), 5
Trials of Phillis Wheatley, The (Gates), 55
Twain, Mark, 1–2

United States: and Africa, 60, 63;
assimilation in, 97; Boston in, 55,
75, 93, 95, 112, 113, 116, 143; and
Cambridge, 27, 139, 140, 142; Chicago
in, 80, 86; chronology of, 88; class in,
134–35, 147; and colonial Evangelicals,
31; and European immigration, 85,
88, 93, 96–97; European Renaissance
painting in, 150–51; and Fourth of

July, 85; fragmentation of, 67; idea
of, 59, 97; Illinois in, 66, 86, 88, 90;
literary nationalism in, 16–22, 67,
85–87, 96–97; and Maine, 138; and
Manifest Destiny, 91; map of, 182; and
media culture, 182, 183; as a melting
pot, 97, 203n145; Michigan in, 66;
Milwaukee in, 96; and museums, 27,
134–35, 138, 140, 142–43; and national
identity, 151; New England in, 93, 138;
Northern States in, 33; and Oregon,
85; as a patchwork of peoples, 67;
and Phillis Wheatley Peters, 53, 63;
and preservation of antiquities, 138;
Providence in, 71; and relationship
with Europe, 93–94; and Revolutionary War, 31, 32, 50, 52, 141; Salem in,
63; Southern States in, 33; sovereignty
of, 93; unification of, 15; and westward
expansion, 95; and women's travel,
106–7; and women writers, 16–17, 102,
106–7; and Young Americans, 134. *See
also* Boston, Massachusetts; Native
Americans; New York; slavery
utopianism, 22, 68

Venus and Adonis (Titian), 82
Vita (Cellini), 165

*Wallflower Avant-Garde: Modernism,
Sexuality, and Queer Ekphrasis*
(Glavery), 8
Warner, Susan, 105
Washington, George, 44–45, 46, 141, 143
Webster, Noah, 12
West, Benjamin, 92
Wheatley, John, 60
Wheatley, Phillis. *See* Peters, Phillis
Wheatley
Wheatley, Susanna, 30, 42, 49, 50, 53, 54
Whitefield, George, 31
Whitman, Walt, 9, 13, 131, 132
Whittier, John Greenleaf, 46, 47
Williams, William Carlos, 186n10
Williams, Serena, 178–79, 180
Willis, N. P., 16

Wilson, Ivy, 64
Wilson, Richard, 43–44
Woman in the Nineteenth Century
(Fuller), 70

Wordsworth, William, 151
Wozniacki, Caroline, 179–80

Zellinger, Elissa, 22, 178

Christa Holm Vogelius has a PhD in American literature from the University of Michigan and has worked at the University of Alabama, the University of Copenhagen, and the University of Southern Denmark, where she is a New Carlberg Fellow in Art Research. She has published essays on literature and visual culture in *American Periodicals*, *ESQ*, and *Legacy*. She lives in Copenhagen.